W0110065

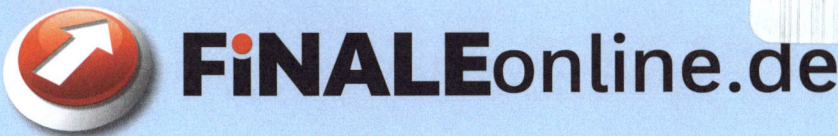

FiNALEonline ist die digitale Ergänzung zu deinem Abiturband. Hier findest du eine Vielzahl an Angeboten, die dich bei deiner Prüfungsvorbereitung zusätzlich unterstützen.

Das Plus für deine Vorbereitung:

➜ Original-Prüfungsaufgaben mit Lösungen (bitte Code von Seite 4 eingeben!)

➜ EXTRA-Training Rechtschreibung
So kannst du einem möglichen Punktabzug bei deinen Abi-Klausuren vorbeugen.

➜ Videos zur mündlichen Prüfung

➜ Tipps zur stressfreien Prüfungsvorbereitung

➜ Abi-Checklisten mit allen prüfungsrelevanten Themen

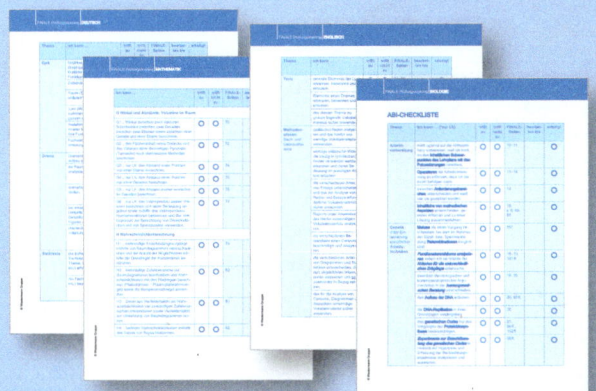

Abi-Checklisten
Sie helfen dir, den Überblick über den Prüfungsstoff zu behalten.

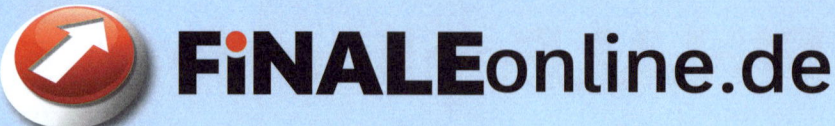

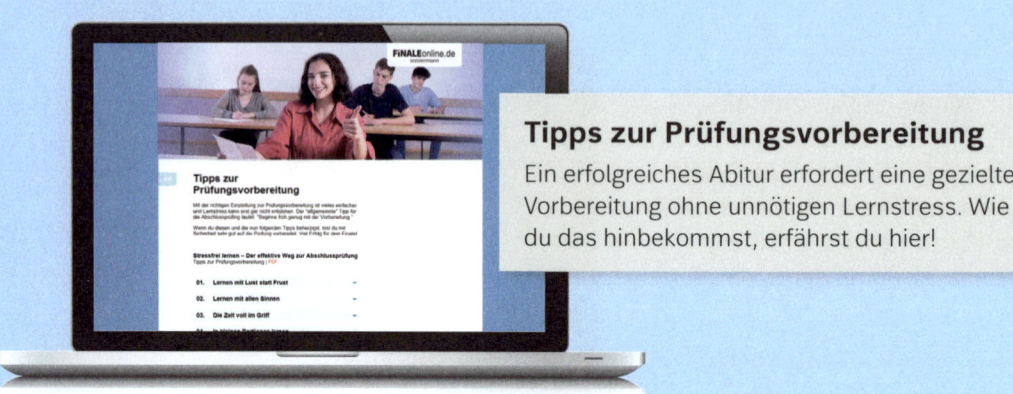

Tipps zur Prüfungsvorbereitung

Ein erfolgreiches Abitur erfordert eine gezielte Vorbereitung ohne unnötigen Lernstress. Wie du das hinbekommst, erfährst du hier!

Videos zur mündlichen Prüfung

Nur wenige Abiturienten wissen genau, wie sie abläuft, die „Mündliche". Die Videos geben dir Einblick in den Ablauf der Prüfung und Tipps für die richtige Vorbereitung.

Die Kombination aus FiNALE-Buch und FiNALEonline bietet dir die optimale Vorbereitung für deine Prüfung und begleitet dich sicher zu einem erfolgreichen Abitur 2024!

www.finaleonline.de

westermann

FiNALE
Prüfungstraining

Baden-Württemberg

Abitur
Englisch

2024

FiNALEonline.de

Liebe Schülerin, lieber Schüler,

sobald die Original-Prüfungsaufgaben zur Veröffentlichung freigegeben sind, können sie unter **www.finaleonline.de** zusammen mit ausführlichen Lösungen kostenlos heruntergeladen werden. Gib dazu einfach diesen Code ein:

EN4Y9B2

Einfach mal reinschauen: www.finaleonline.de

Autor und Autorinnen:
Martina Angele
Sebastian Haber
sowie Lara Jost

© 2023 Westermann Lernwelten GmbH, Georg-Westermann-Allee 66, 38104 Braunschweig
www.westermann.de

Bildnachweis: |Getty Images, München: New York Daily News/Bramhall, Bill 174.1. |MacKinnon, Bruce: 188.1, 189.1. |Peter Wirtz Fotografie, Dormagen: Titel. |Theo Moudakis Cartoons, Toronto: Theo Moudakis „Joe Biden's Big Job", 2021 187.1, 188.2.

Druck A¹/Jahr 2023
Alle Drucke der Serie A sind im Unterricht parallel verwendbar.

Redaktion: lüra – Klemt & Mues GbR; Redaktionsbüro Sabina Piatzer, Hannover
Kontakt: finale@westermanngruppe.de
Layout: LIO Design GmbH, Braunschweig
Umschlaggestaltung: Gingco.Net, Braunschweig
Umschlagfoto: Peter Wirtz, Dormagen
Druck und Bindung: Westermann Druck GmbH, Georg-Westermann-Allee 66, 38104 Braunschweig

ISBN 978-3-07-**172477**-8

Inhaltsverzeichnis

Methoden der Textanalyse

Literarische Texte

Sach- und Gebrauchstexte

Visuelle Materialien

Informationen zur Sprachmittlung

Beispiele für Prüfungsaufgaben

Trainingsaufgaben

Original-Prüfungsaufgaben 2022 und 2023

Arbeiten mit FiNALE

FiNALE Prüfungstraining Englisch bietet Ihnen eine praxisnahe Hilfe zur Vorbereitung auf die Abiturprüfungen. Sie finden in diesem Buch Informationen zu den Qualifikations- und Prüfungsphasen für das Basisfach und das Leistungsfach Englisch, hilfreiche Redemittel für die einzelnen Prüfungsteile sowie Hinweise und Tipps zu Aufbau und Gestaltung Ihrer mündlichen und schriftlichen Beiträge. Des Weiteren bieten wir Ihnen Aufgaben, die passgenau auf die relevanten Inhalte ausgerichtet sind, sowie die kompletten Original-Prüfungsaufgaben 2022, die vom Niveau dem Leistungsfachprofil entsprechen. Zusätzlich finden Sie Aufgaben zu den unterschiedlichen Aufgabentypen auf Prüfungsniveau. Sobald die Aufgaben des Abiturs 2023 zur Veröffentlichung freigegeben sind, können Sie diese unter www.finaleonline.de abrufen.

Das Kapitel „Informationen und Tipps zur Prüfung" dient als Orientierung bezüglich der Rahmenbedingungen und Anforderungen im Basis- und Leistungsfach. Die Erklärungen der gängigen Operatoren und der Bewertungskriterien, nach denen Ihre Lehrerinnen und Lehrer Ihre Arbeiten korrigieren, bieten wertvolle Hilfestellungen.
Auch wenn die thematische Kompetenz äußerst wichtig ist, spielt die sprachliche Leistung in der Fremdsprache immer noch die herausragende Rolle. Ein sicherer Umgang mit den Wörtern und Strukturen der englischen Sprache ist also unabdingbar. Deshalb haben wir diesem Aspekt in *Finale* ein ganzes Kapitel gewidmet.
Das Kapitel „Basiswissen" bietet Ihnen eine kompakte Übersicht über die für das gesamte Abitur in den Kursstufen vorgegebenen Themen, die Ihnen sowohl in den mündlichen Prüfungen als auch in der schriftlichen Prüfung als Wahlmöglichkeit im Teilbereich II (Textproduktion) begegnen können. Das Kapitel hilft Ihnen, das im Unterricht erworbene Wissen zu strukturieren und in seinen Grundzügen abzurufen.
Das darauf folgende Kapitel klärt die Bedeutung des Schwerpunktthemas für das Abitur 2024, „The Ambiguity of Belonging", setzt es in Bezug zu historischen Ereignissen und behandelt den Pflichtkanon, der aus dem Roman *Crooked Letter, Crooked Letter* und dem Film *Gran Torino* besteht. Hintergrundinformationen, wesentliche Aspekte und Interpretationsansätze sowie Verknüpfungen zwischen den Themenbereichen helfen Ihnen, klare Verbindungen herzustellen und Ihr Wissen zu strukturieren und zu vertiefen. Erläuterungen zu verschiedenen Strategien der Arbeit mit Text- und Bildmaterial sowie geeignete sprachliche Mittel dafür liefert Ihnen das Kapitel „Methoden der Textanalyse".

Weitere Übungen zu den unterschiedlichen Aufgabentypen finden Sie im Kapitel „Beispiele für Prüfungsaufgaben", sodass Sie Ihr Wissen individuell selbst überprüfen können.

Wir wünschen Ihnen viel Erfolg!

Informationen und Tipps zur Prüfung

Information zur Abiturprüfung:
https://km-bw.de/,Lde/Startseite/Schule/Abitur+und+Oberstufe

Das Abitur im Basis- und Leistungsfach

Aufbau

Im Folgenden finden Sie die Ihnen bereits bekannte Aufteilung zwischen Basis- und Leistungsfach sowie Informationen zu Inhalten der Qualifikationsphase (in der Sie sich ja bereits befinden) und zur notenrelevanten Leistungsmessung.

Im Basisfach Englisch	Im Leistungsfach Englisch
Inhalte: Das Schwerpunktthema: "The Ambiguity of Belonging" *Crooked Letter, Crooked Letter* *Gran Torino* Mindestens eines der beiden Pflichtwerke ist in angemessenem Umfang auf der Niveaustufe des Basisfachs zu erarbeiten.	**Inhalte:** Das Schwerpunktthema: "The Ambiguity of Belonging" *Crooked Letter, Crooked Letter* *Gran Torino*
Qualifikationsphase: In allen Schulhalbjahren wird mindestens eine Klausur geschrieben. Im Verlauf der vier Kurshalbjahre müssen folgende Aufgabentypen abgedeckt werden: Hörverstehen, Leseverstehen, Analyse, Sprachmittlung sowie Schreiben (persönliche Stellungnahme und gestaltendes Schreiben). Alle drei Anforderungsbereiche müssen abgedeckt werden. Die Anforderungsbereiche I und II sind dabei stärker im Fokus als der Anforderungsbereich III. Im Laufe der vier Schulhalbjahre erbringen Sie einen monologischen (5 Min.) und einen dialogischen (10 Min.) Beitrag (siehe Tipps Seite 17ff.).	**Qualifikationsphase:** In den ersten drei Schulhalbjahren werden mindestens zwei Klausuren und im vierten Schulhalbjahr wird mindestens eine Klausur geschrieben: – Eine Klausur besteht ausschließlich aus einer Sprachmittlungsaufgabe. – Die anderen Klausuren decken die Aufgabentypen der Abiturprüfung ab (siehe Anforderungsbereiche Seite 9 / Operatoren Seite 11ff.). Alle drei Anforderungsbereiche müssen abgedeckt sein. Die Anforderungsbereiche II und III sind dabei stärker im Fokus als der Anforderungsbereich I.

Mündliche Prüfung: siehe Seite 17ff.	Schriftliche Prüfung inklusive Hörver- stehen: siehe Seite 9ff. Mündliche Kommunikationsprüfung: siehe Seite 17ff. (Teil der schriftlichen Prüfung im Leistungsfach)

Die schriftliche Abiturprüfung besteht aus folgenden Teilen:

Teil A: I   Kompetenzbereich Hörverstehen *(Listening)*

        II   Kompetenzbereich Schreiben *(Writing)*

        II.1   Leseverstehen *(Reading)* → aspektbezogene Zusammenfassung

        II.2   Analyse *(Analysis)*

        II.3   persönliche Stellungnahme bzw. gestaltende Textaufgabe
            (Composition)

Teil B: Mündliche Prüfung: Kommunikationsprüfung

Am Tag des schriftlichen Abiturs findet nach dem Hörverstehensteil eine 15-minütige Pause statt. Danach beginnt der Teil A II der Prüfung (Kompetenzbereich Schreiben). Sie bekommen zwei Aufgabensätze und müssen einen zur Bearbeitung auswählen. Beide Aufgabensätze bestehen aus jeweils einem Text mit einer Aufgabe zur aspektbezogenen Zusammenfassung, einer Analyseaufgabe und gestaltenden Textaufgaben. Einer der Aufgabensätze behandelt das Schwerpunktthema.

Die Anforderungsbereiche der Prüfung (schriftliche Klausuren)

Auf der Grundlage des Gemeinsamen Europäischen Referenzrahmens bestehen die schriftlichen Leistungsmessungen aus drei Anforderungsbereichen:

Im Basisfach wird der **Anforderungsbereich I** (Reproduktion) in Form von Lese- und Hörverstehen während der vier Halbjahre in schriftlichen Klausuren geprüft. Dieser Anforderungsbereich ist auch ein Teil der mündlichen Abiturprüfung (siehe Seite 17).

Im Leistungsfach wird der Anforderungsbereich I durch das Hörverstehen im schriftlichen Abitur abgeprüft (Teil A I). Dabei werden verschiedene Aufgabentypen verwendet. Typisch sind hier Multiple-choice-Aufgaben, bei denen Sie die korrekte Aussage markieren müssen, Zuordnungsaufgaben, bei denen Sie beispielsweise Überschriften verschiedenen kurzen Radioausschnitten zuordnen müssen, und halboffene Aufgaben, bei denen Sie unter anderem Kurzantworten geben müssen.

Beispiele: *While you are listening to the interview, tick the correct answer. There is only one correct answer.*

oder *While listening, match the headings a–h to the speakers 1–7. There is one more heading than you need.*

oder *While listening, fill in the missing information. You do not have to write complete sentences. Name only one aspect.*

Der **Anforderungsbereich II** (Reorganisation) betrifft die Analyse sowie die Reorganisation von Texten. Sowohl im Basis- als auch im Leistungsfach schreiben Sie eine ca. 60-minütige Sprachmittlungsklausur. (Dies ist möglicherweise bereits erfolgt.) Bei der Sprachmittlung sollen Sie gemäß der jeweiligen Aufgabenstellung bestimmte Information aus einem deutschen Text in englischer Sprache in einen vorgegebenen Kontext einbetten. Dabei sind Sprachregister, Adressat, Kontext und Inhalt zu beachten (siehe auch Kapitel „Informationen zur Sprachmittlung", Seite 148).

Beispiel: *During his stay in Germany, your American exchange partner was surprised to find that some of the ideas he had about Germans, such as constantly drinking beer and eating "schnitzels", did not align with reality. He has returned home and has asked you for help because he is preparing a presentation about German stereotypes. You have found the following article. Write to your friend, summarizing the most important points of the article.*

Der Anforderungsbereich II wird im Leistungsfach auch durch den Teil A II.1 *(Reading)* des schriftlichen Abiturs abgeprüft. Hier müssen Sie im Gegensatz zu den Abiturprüfungen der letzten Jahre eine sogenannte aspektbezogene Zusammenfassung des gegebenen Textes schreiben. Darin müssen Sie nur einen bestimmten Aspekt bzw. mehrere Aspekte des Textes wiedergeben. Es wird also von Ihnen gefordert, dass Sie diese Aspekte zuerst im Text identifizieren und sie dann zusammenfassen.

Beispiel: *Summarize the reasons the author mentions to underline her point of view regarding the current role of the British monarchy.*

Der Anforderungsbereich II wird außerdem durch die Analyse im Teil II.2 des schriftlichen Abiturs abgedeckt. Dabei geht es um die vertiefte Auseinandersetzung mit einem Thema auf der Grundlage des vorgelegten Textes. Im Zentrum steht die Analyse der dargestellten Inhalte bzw. der Textabsicht. Bei der Analyse der Textabsicht ist es wichtig, die Argumentationsweisen und Intentionen des Textes oder des Autors bzw. der Autorin zu erklären und zu belegen. Dazu gehört beispielsweise eine Analyse der verwendeten rhetorischen Stilmittel und Erzähltechniken sowie des Textaufbaus.

Beispiel: *Analyse the strategies that the author employs in the article to persuade the readers of his point of view.*

Der **Teil** *Composition* betrifft den **Anforderungsbereich III** (Werten und Gestalten). Die Aufgabenstellung verlangt eine persönliche argumentative Stellungnahme oder eine gestaltende Textproduktion. Dabei müssen Sie anhand Ihrer Methodenkompetenz strukturiert komplexe Sachverhalte und Materialien verarbeiten. Hierzu gehören eigene Deutungen, Begründungen und Wertungen. Wieder dienen Ihnen die im Unterricht erworbenen themenspezifischen Kenntnisse, Methoden und Arbeitstechniken als Grundlage. Sie werden die Möglichkeit haben, aus zwei Aufgabenstellungen zu wählen.

Beispiele: *Compare the challenges described by the contemporary witness in the given text with Walt's experiences and his overall attitude.*

oder *Based on the interpretation of the following cartoon, outline the social challenges globalization creates and the various ways in which developing and developed countries deal with them.*

Operatoren für die Anforderungsbereiche

Operatoren sind Arbeitsanweisungen. Im Folgenden sind die Operatoren nach Anforderungsbereichen sortiert.

TIPP zum Punktesammeln

Machen Sie sich mit der Bedeutung der auf den folgenden Seiten aufgeführten Operatoren gut vertraut, um die entsprechenden Anforderungen der Aufgaben erfüllen zu können. Bedenken Sie stets, dass jeder Text, den Sie verfassen (Sprachmittlung, Analyse und *composition*), immer aus Einleitung (Hinführung zum Thema), Hauptteil und Schluss bestehen muss.

Anforderungsbereich I: Textverständnis und Reproduktion

Operator	Definition	Beispiel
complete	vervollständigen	*Complete the sentences with information from the text.*
match	zusammenfügen	*Match the headings with the paragraphs.*
tick	abhaken	*Tick the correct answer.*
paraphrase	einen Satz, eine Aussage oder eine Passage eines Textes mit anderen Worten sinngemäß wiedergeben	*Paraphrase the following statements.*
fill in/fill in the gaps	ausfüllen, die Lücken füllen	*Fill in the gaps using suitable information.*
prove	beweisen	*Prove your chosen answer with a quote from the text.*

Anforderungsbereich II: Reorganisation und Analyse

Operator	Definition	Beispiel
analyse	die wesentlichen Textelemente (Form und/oder Inhalt) erkennen, sachgerecht erläutern, wie diese für den vorliegenden Text wirksam sind, abschließend die Ergebnisse in einer schlüssigen Gesamtaussage bündeln	*Analyse the relationship between the two protagonists in the given excerpt.*
characterize	den Charakter einer Person beschreiben und dem Text/den Texten passende Beispiele entnehmen	*Characterize the main protagonist in "Crooked Letter, Crooked Letter".*
compare/ contrast	Kategorien oder Vergleichsmomente je nach Aufgabenstellung selbst erarbeiten oder der Aufgabe entnehmen, Gemeinsamkeiten oder Unterschiede klar und abstrahierend benennen und mit entsprechenden Textbeispielen belegen	*Contrast the different concepts of the American Dream as explained in the text and shown in the cartoon.*
contrast/ juxtapose	Unterschiede/Gegensätze beschreiben und analysieren	*Contrast the protagonist's belief with the main message of the President's speech.*
delineate	Argumente oder Geschehnisse sinnvoll sortieren und ordnen	*Delineate the development of events that lead to Walt's death in "Gran Torino".*
examine	untersuchen: bestimmte Aspekte eines Textes/Sachverhalts detailliert beschreiben und erklären	*Examine the use of stylistic devices in the given excerpts.*
explain	erklären: detailliert beschreiben und klar begründen	*Explain Larry's struggle to belong in contrast to Silas' struggle to belong.*
illustrate/show	etwas anhand von Beispielen erklären/ verdeutlichen	*Illustrate the character's real intentions.*
outline	umreißen: die grundsätzlichen Aspekte zusammenfassend darstellen (d. h. ohne unwesentliche Details)	*Outline the protagonist's attitude towards the traditions of his/her culture.*
put into context	eine Handlung, einen Sachverhalt oder eine Aussage mit relevanten historischen oder themenbezogenen Aspekten verbinden	*Put the character's inner development into the context of racial profiling.*

| relate | in Beziehung setzen: einen oder mehrere Aspekte eines Textes herausfiltern und eine sinnvolle Beziehung zu Aspekten eines anderen Textes oder eines Bild-impulses herstellen oder aufzeigen | *Relate the photograph and its meaning to the behaviour of the gangs in "Gran Torino".* |
| sum up/ summarize | zusammenfassen | *Summarize the events.* |

TIPP

Die Operatoren *sum up, summarize* und *outline* werden in Aufgabenstellungen zur aspektbezogenen Zusammenfassung synonym verwendet. In allen Fällen wird eine Zusammenfassung der relevanten Aspekte erwartet.

Anforderungsbereich III: Werten und Gestalten

Operator	Definition	Beispiel
assess/ evaluate	allgemein gültige und der Aufgabenstel-lung entsprechend relevante Kriterien nennen, daraus argumentativ ableitend eine differenzierte Bewertung vorneh-men, aus dieser Bewertung eine schlüssi-ge Gesamteinschätzung ableiten	*Evaluate the chances of the protagonist's plan.*
comment on/ state	ähnlich einer linearen Erörterung im Fach Deutsch klar und differenziert Stellung nehmen und dies mit aussagekräftigen Argumenten und Beispielen untermauern	*Comment on the immi-gration policy of the US.*
contrast	die Unterschiede/Gegensätze zwischen zwei oder mehr Sachverhalten/Aussa-gen/Positionen erläutern	*Contrast the protagonist's ideas of freedom with your own theories and ideas.*
discuss	die wesentlichen Aspekte des Themas untersuchen, diese in pro und kontra gliedern; anhand der genannten Argu-mente und deren Abwägung gegeneinan-der eine Schlussfolgerung auf sachlicher oder persönlicher Ebene ziehen	*Discuss advantages and disadvantages of gene-tic engineering.*

interpret	die Bedeutung eines Textes/eines Zitats/ einer Aussage/einer Kampagne/einer Position/eines Bildimpulses anhand einer Analyse klären (siehe Seite 10), in den soziokulturellen Kontext stellen und zu einer schlüssigen Gesamtaussage gelangen, wobei eine kurze persönliche Bewertung am Ende möglich ist	*Interpret the author's use of language.*
justify	Behauptungen/Aussagen anhand von adäquaten Beispielen begründen	*Justify the protagonist's point of view.*
write a + *text type*	einen kreativen Text im vorgegebenen Stil schreiben	*Write a letter/diary entry/inner (= interior) monologue/…*

Prüfungsdauer der schriftlichen Abiturprüfung und erlaubte Hilfsmittel

Die Prüfung dauert **255 Minuten auf erhöhtem Anforderungsniveau** (30 Minuten für das Hörverstehen und 225 Minuten für den Kompetenzbereich Schreiben) und **225 Minuten auf grundlegendem Anforderungsniveau** (30 Minuten für das Hörverstehen und 195 Minuten für den Kompetenzbereich Schreiben).

Erlaubt sind ein in der Kursstufe eingeführtes einsprachiges Wörterbuch (Englisch) und ein in der Kursstufe eingeführtes zweisprachiges Wörterbuch Englisch – Deutsch/ Deutsch – Englisch sowie ein Nachschlagewerk zur deutschen Rechtschreibung und Zeichensetzung. Sie erhalten alle benötigten Lösungsbögen und ausreichend Konzeptpapier direkt vor der Prüfung im Prüfungsraum. Bringen Sie Ihre Schreibutensilien (Füller, Tinte, Kugelschreiber, Bleistift usw.) mit.

> Beachten Sie: Mobiltelefone und Smartphones sind in der Prüfung nicht erlaubt (auch nicht als „Uhr")!

Prüfungsaufgabe und Prüfungsthemen

Sie werden zwei Aufgabensätze zum Kompetenzbereich Schreiben vorgelegt bekommen. Einer davon wird zum Schwerpunktthema sein. Sie müssen einen Aufgabensatz auswählen und komplett bearbeiten.

Das Schwerpunktthema für die schriftliche Abiturprüfung lautet *The Ambiguity of Belonging.* Es umfasst den folgenden Pflichtkanon:
1. *Crooked Letter, Crooked Letter* von Tom Franklin (2010)
2. *Gran Torino* (Film USA 2008, Regie Clint Eastwood)

Die Themen sind nicht strikt voneinander getrennt zu sehen, sondern greifen ineinander:

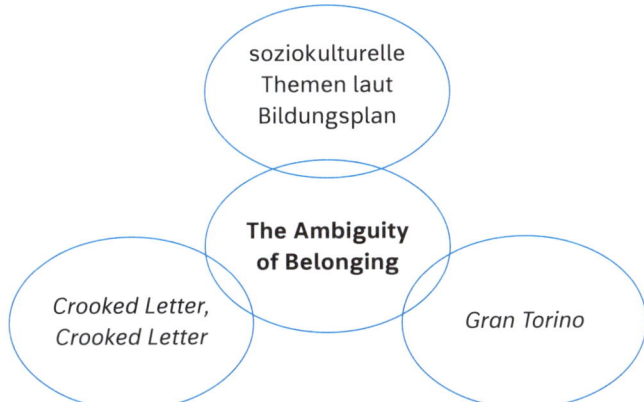

TIPP zum Punktesammeln

Bedenken Sie, dass Hintergrundwissen über die politischen und kulturellen Entwicklungen in den USA für das Verständnis des Literaturthemas und des Films unabdingbar ist.

Die **thematischen Aspekte**, die Sie in den Kursstufen behandelt haben und die Ihnen als Wahlmöglichkeit im Teilbereich II.3 oder in der Kommunikationsprüfung begegnen werden, sind durch den Bildungsplan vorgegeben und umfassen unter anderem:

- zentrale Elemente des nationalen Selbstverständnisses Großbritanniens und der USA
- das heutige Großbritannien vor dem Hintergrund seiner Geschichte als Weltmacht: *European Union, Brexit, Commonwealth, Empire, constitutional monarchy*
- wichtige Erscheinungsformen des zeitgenössischen Lebens und der politischen Kultur in Großbritannien und den USA
- politische, kulturelle und gesellschaftliche Entwicklungen in den USA: *American myths and American Dream, immigration, multicultural society, human rights (Declaration of Independence, constitution, civil rights), global role*
- die jeweilige Bedeutung der Beziehungen zwischen Deutschland und Großbritannien bzw. den USA
- die Beziehung zwischen Individuum und Staat (Balance zwischen staatlicher Fürsorge/Aufsicht und Selbstverantwortung, Freiheitsverständnis, politische Teilhabe) in den Zielkulturen Großbritannien und USA
- die Frage der nationalen und individuellen Identität in multikulturellen Gesellschaften *(national myths, Britishness, politics of immigration, melting pot versus salad bowl, language and identity, struggle for racial equality)* in Bezug auf die Zielkulturen Großbritannien und USA
- die aktuellen Lebensbedingungen und politischen Verhältnisse in Großbritannien und den USA, auch in ihrer historischen Bedingtheit
- Chancen und Probleme durch sozialen Wandel vor dem Hintergrund der Globalisierung sowie Spannungsfelder zwischen Wissenschaft und Ethik

- Globalisierung als Chance und Herausforderung (Arbeitswelt, *gap between rich and poor,* Menschenrechte, internationale Konflikte und Friedensbildung/*peacekeeping*)
- ausgewählte Aspekte eines weiteren, über Großbritannien und die USA hinausgehenden Teils der englischsprachigen Welt (z. B. Kanada, Australien, Neuseeland, Indien, karibische Länder)
- mindestens zwei umfangreichere Werke der englischsprachigen Literatur und Beispieltexte verschiedener literarischer Gattungen
- die Bedeutung des Englischen als *lingua franca* und die Probleme des sogenannten Sprachimperialismus.

Die Vorgaben des Ministeriums können auf dem Bildungsserver des Landes Baden-Württemberg nachgelesen werden: http://www.kultusportal-bw.de, Stichwort Bildungspläne)

Bewertung und Punkteverteilung der schriftlichen Prüfung

Eine inhaltlich sehr gute Arbeit weist zum Beispiel folgende Merkmale auf:
- Die Aufgabe ist umfassend und korrekt erfüllt.
- Der verfasste Text ist klar strukturiert, in hohem Maße schlüssig, durchgängig kohärent und ohne Wiederholungen oder für die Aufgabenstellung überflüssige Informationen.
- Der Text ist durchgängig plausibel, präzise, differenziert und mit treffenden Beispielen oder Textbelegen versehen.

Eine sehr gute sprachliche Leistung zeichnet sich unter anderem aus durch:
- sehr gute Verständlichkeit und nahezu korrekten Sprachgebrauch
- sehr präzise, korrekte und variable Wortwahl mit typischen Redewendungen
- sehr variablen Satzbau und durchgängig funktionalen Einsatz von grammatischen Strukturen
- sehr gute funktionale Verwendung textstrukturierender Mittel
- in hohem Maße umgesetzte Textsortenmerkmale sowie situations- und adressatengerechte Verwendung der Sprache.

TIPP zum Punktesammeln

Bei der Bewertung Ihrer Arbeit werden die Punkte für Inhalt und Sprache gesondert gegeben. Es ist also sinnvoll, sowohl inhaltlich als auch methodisch – und natürlich sprachlich – gut vorbereitet zu sein. Ebenso spielt die optische Gestaltung der Texte eine Rolle. Die Übersichtlichkeit sollte durch eine gute Gliederung und einen sinnvollen Aufbau gegeben sein.

Die mündliche Prüfung

1. Die mündliche Prüfung im Basisfach

Grundlagen

Die Prüfung im Basisfach wird als Einzelprüfung durchgeführt. Sie erhalten einen Prüfungstext von etwa 200 bis 300 Wörtern Umfang aus den Bereichen Literatur und soziokulturelles Orientierungswissen/Themen des Bildungsplans und dazu eine oder höchstens zwei Aufgabenstellungen, die alle drei Anforderungsbereiche (Reproduktion, Reorganisation, Stellungnahme) abdecken. Anhand dieser Aufgaben sollen Sie einen zusammenhängenden 10-minütigen Vortrag entwickeln. Der Schwerpunkt liegt dabei in den Anforderungsbereichen I und II.

Ablauf

Sie erhalten Ihren Text und haben eine 20-minütige Vorbereitungszeit unter Aufsicht, in der Sie ein einsprachiges und ein zweisprachiges Wörterbuch verwenden dürfen, um Ihre Aufzeichnungen zu machen.

Durchführung

Sie halten Ihren 10-minütigen Vortrag vor der Prüfungskommission. Im anschließenden Prüfungsgespräch wird das Thema erweitert und vertieft und es wird eventuell auch in einen weiteren Themenbereich übergeleitet. Hierdurch werden Ihre Flexibilität des Denkens und Ihre Fähigkeit zur Vernetzung der verschiedenen Kompetenzen geprüft.

2. Die mündliche Kommunikationsprüfung im Leistungsfach

Die mündliche Kommunikationsprüfung im Leistungsfach ist ein Teilbereich der schriftlichen Abiturprüfung und zählt 25% der Gesamtnotenpunktzahl.
Sie besteht aus zwei Teilen: Im ersten Teil halten Sie einen Vortrag anhand von Material, das Ihnen zuvor ausgehändigt wurde. Danach folgt ein Prüfungsgespräch zwischen Ihnen und einer Lehrkraft mit dem Schwerpunkt auf den Anforderungsbereichen I und II. Sie haben 15 Minuten Vorbereitungszeit allein, während der Ihnen ein einsprachiges Wörterbuch und ein zweisprachiges Wörterbuch (Englisch – Deutsch, Deutsch – Englisch) als Hilfsmittel zur Verfügung stehen. Bei einer Tandemprüfung diskutieren Sie mit Ihrem Partner/Ihrer Partnerin im zweiten Teil meist über ein Thema und sollen zu einer Entscheidung oder einem Kompromiss gelangen. Hier geht es vor allem um Ihr Vermögen, auf andere einzugehen (Diskursfähigkeit).

Beispiel: **Monolog:** *Interpret the cartoon and explain the negative aspects of globalization.*

Dialog: *Comment on the arguments presented by your partner and discuss whether the circumstances illustrated in the visuals should be opposed or supported.*

Vorgehen in den mündlichen Prüfungen (Basis- und Leistungsfach)

Im Folgenden finden Sie eine *Step-by-step*-Anleitung, die Ihnen ein mögliches Vorgehen in der mündlichen Prüfung aufzeigt.

Schritt 1: Vorbereitungszeit (im Vorbereitungsraum)

Im Basisfach Englisch	Im Leistungsfach Englisch
20 Minuten	**15 Minuten**
Bereiten Sie sich vor, indem Sie die Aufgabenstellung auf Ihrem Material (authentischer Text im Umfang von 200 bis 300 Wörtern) bearbeiten.	Bereiten Sie sich vor, indem Sie die Aufgabenstellung auf Ihrem Material (kurzer Text, Foto, Cartoon, Diagramm) bearbeiten.
– Entwerfen Sie einen Monolog zu Ihrem Thema gemäß der Aufgabenstellung, d. h., notieren Sie die inhaltlich relevanten Punkte in sinnvoller Reihenfolge.	– Entwerfen Sie einen Monolog zu Ihrem Thema gemäß der Aufgabenstellung, d. h., notieren Sie die inhaltlich relevanten Punkte in sinnvoller Reihenfolge.
– Untermauern Sie Ihre Argumente durch Fakten und Beispiele (aktuelle Anlässe, historische Fakten, Zitate, eigene Erfahrungen).	– Untermauern Sie Ihre Argumente durch Fakten und Beispiele (aktuelle Anlässe, historische Fakten, Zitate, eigene Erfahrungen).
– Fertigen Sie Mindmaps oder Stichpunkte an, die Sie in Ihrem Vortrag stützen.	– Fertigen Sie Mindmaps oder Stichpunkte an, die Sie in Ihrem Vortrag stützen.
– Überlegen Sie sich, welche Themen mit dem Ihnen vorliegenden Thema verknüpft sein können – so sind Sie auf weiterführende Fragen und eventuelle Themenwechsel vorbereitet.	– Vorbereitung für den Dialog: Überlegen Sie sich, welche Argumente Ihr Tandempartner oder Ihre Partnerin anführen könnte und wie Sie darauf reagieren können.

Schritt 2: Ihr Vortrag (Monolog)

Im Basisfach Englisch	Im Leistungsfach Englisch
10 Minuten	**mindestens 5 Minuten**
Halten Sie Ihr Referat. Sie sollten eine überzeugte Haltung zeigen, ohne dabei in Übereifer zu verfallen.	Halten Sie Ihr Referat. Sie sollten eine überzeugte Haltung zeigen, ohne dabei in Übereifer zu verfallen.
– Geben Sie zu Beginn eine kurze Übersicht über die inhaltliche Vorgehensweise und die Reihenfolge.	– Geben Sie zu Beginn eine kurze Übersicht über die inhaltliche Vorgehensweise und die Reihenfolge.
– Tragen Sie Ihre Hauptpunkte vor und achten Sie auch auf Ihre Körpersprache und auf Blickkontakt zu den Lehrkräften.	– Tragen Sie Ihre Hauptpunkte vor und achten Sie auch auf Ihre Körpersprache und auf Blickkontakt zu den Lehrkräften.

– Fassen Sie das Wesentliche noch einmal zusammen und runden Sie Ihr Referat mit einer persönlichen Stellungnahme ab.

– Fassen Sie das Wesentliche noch einmal zusammen und runden Sie Ihr Referat mit einer persönlichen Stellungnahme ab.
– Sollten Sie wider Erwarten vor Ablauf der fünf Minuten noch Zeit haben, dann sprechen Sie über Ihre persönlichen Erfahrungen mit dem Thema.

Schritt 3: Prüfungsgespräch

Im Basisfach Englisch	Im Leistungsfach Englisch
Ihr Lehrer oder Ihre Lehrerin wird Sie mit Fragen, Aussagen und Argumenten konfrontieren. – Hören Sie Ihrem Lehrer oder Ihrer Lehrerin aufmerksam zu. – Machen Sie Notizen zu seinen/ihren Aussagen und vergleichen Sie diese mit Ihrer Vorbereitung. – Versuchen Sie, eine Basis für eine gemeinsame Schlussfolgerung zu finden. – Auch hier sind Blickkontakt und ab und zu ein Lächeln durchaus angebracht.	**In einer Einzelprüfung:** Ihr Lehrer oder Ihre Lehrerin wird Sie mit Fragen, Aussagen und Argumenten konfrontieren. – Hören Sie Ihrem Lehrer oder Ihrer Lehrerin aufmerksam zu. – Machen Sie Notizen zu seinen/ihren Aussagen und vergleichen Sie diese mit Ihrer Vorbereitung. – Versuchen Sie, eine Basis für eine gemeinsame Schlussfolgerung zu finden. – Auch hier sind Blickkontakt und ab und zu ein Lächeln durchaus angebracht. **In einer Tandemprüfung:** Während Ihr Partner/Ihre Partnerin seinen/ihren Vortrag hält: – Hören Sie ihm/ihr aufmerksam zu. – Machen Sie sich Notizen zu seinen/ihren Aussagen und vergleichen Sie diese mit Ihrer Vorbereitung. – Versuchen Sie, eine Basis für eine gemeinsame Schlussfolgerung zu finden. – Führen Sie kein Schauspiel auf, bei dem Sie einstudierte Argumente wiedergeben und diese durch übertriebene Sprache untermauern.
Versuchen Sie, gelassen und sicher aufzutreten. Auch hier helfen Körpersprache und Blickkontakt zu den Lehrkräften. Ein Lächeln an der richtigen Stelle entspannt Sie und das Gespräch ebenfalls!	Versuchen Sie, gelassen und sicher aufzutreten. Auch hier helfen Körpersprache und Blickkontakt zu den Lehrkräften und/oder Ihrem Partner/Ihrer Partnerin. Ein Lächeln an der richtigen Stelle entspannt Sie und das Gespräch ebenfalls!

– Ergänzen Sie die gehörten Argumente oder zeigen Sie deren Schwachstellen auf. Widerlegen Sie sie nötigenfalls anhand von Fakten und Beispielen.
– Stärken und verteidigen Sie Ihre Argumente durch Beispiele und Details.
– Wichtig ist, dass Sie Ihre Schlussfolgerungen auf Fakten aufbauen und somit auch erklären können.
– Für beide Teile (Monolog und Gespräch) gilt: Sprechen Sie authentisch und ohne Ihre Stimme künstlich zu verändern.

– Ergänzen Sie die gehörten Argumente oder zeigen Sie deren Schwachstellen auf. Widerlegen Sie sie nötigenfalls anhand von Fakten und Beispielen. Stellen Sie gezielte und produktive Fragen.
– Stärken und verteidigen Sie Ihre Argumente durch Beispiele und Details.
– Versuchen Sie, eine Einigung zu erzielen, wobei Sie durchaus Kompromisse eingehen können. Wichtig ist, dass Sie Ihre Schlussfolgerungen auf Fakten aufbauen und somit auch erklären können.
– Für beide Teile (Monolog und Gespräch) gilt: Sprechen Sie authentisch und ohne Ihre Stimme künstlich zu verändern.

Hilfreiche Redewendungen

Monolog (Ihr Referat)

Einleitung	
– Begrüßung, Vorstellung – Was ist Ihr Thema? Worüber werden Sie sprechen? – In welcher Reihenfolge werden Sie welche Aspekte behandeln?	– Good morning … – I would like to speak about … – My topic is … – First I will … and then …, followed by … – To start with, I'll …. Next … – Firstly, … Secondly, … Thirdly, … Finally, …
Hauptteil	
– Ihre Aspekte – Überleitungen von einem Aspekt zum nächsten	– The first point I would like to look at is … – First, we should ask ourselves … – To begin with, … – First and foremost, … – The next point to be considered is … – We must also take into account that … – We should also consider the fact that … – Another argument is … – In the second place, …

Schluss	
– Womit schließen Sie? – Was ist Ihre persönliche Schlussfolgerung? – Wo positionieren Sie sich?	– In conclusion … – So, all things considered, I would like … – Well, let me just sum up my main points … – So, to wrap things up, …

Dialog (das Prüfungsgespräch)

Rückfragen klären um Erklärung bitten um Beurteilung bitten	– Do you mean to say that …? – Have I understood you correctly …? – Could you please specify …? – Would you be kind enough to elaborate on this? – Could you please explain that in a bit more detail? – What do you mean by …? – What is your main point? – What do you think of …? – What is your opinion on …? – What do you make of …?
zustimmen Zweifel ausdrücken widersprechen/Einwände erheben etwas billigen/einräumen	– I'm right behind you on the point of … – I agree entirely with you about the fact that … – I endorse the fact that … – … is exactly how I see it. – I have my doubts as to whether … – Whether … is more than doubtful. – I'm not quite sure about your argument that … – I'm afraid I have to contradict you. – Considering …, I see this matter rather differently … – I can't help feeling … – Your assertion is only partly correct. – You haven't explained the facts correctly/ fully. – You may well be right, but consider … too. – I don't think we can draw that conclusion. – That is not acceptable. – There can be no objection to that. – Your objection is justified/legitimate. – You are right, I didn't consider that.

zusammenfassen und sich einigen	– The crucial points can be summarized as follows: ... – Summarizing, we have been able to agree on the following points: ... – We can assume then ... – So it is perfectly conceivable that ... – I am with you on that. – Maybe it would be a compromise to say that ... – Whether or not ... is a matter of speculation/is impossible to say/... – It would be safe to say ...

Hilfreiche Redemittel zum Formulieren der eigenen Meinung

Stellung nehmen	– As for/With regard to/As to the question of ..., it should be pointed out that ... – In contrast/opposition to this ... – With regard to this/the author's statement ..., I would like to point out ... – I'd like to emphasize the fact ...
Gründe angeben	– The main reason for this is ... – A point to consider is ... – Not only ... (+ inversion) but (...) also ... – This inevitably leads to ... – This is caused by ...
Ähnlichkeiten, Analogien aufzeigen	likewise/similarly/in the same way
Gedanken hinzufügen	in addition/furthermore/besides/in the same way
Gedanken abschließen	in brief/in conclusion/on the whole
Gegenteil/Kontrast ausdrücken	however/on the other hand/on the contrary/in contrast to/in spite of/although
Schlussfolgerung ausdrücken	consequently/hence/thus/accordingly/therefore/it follows that ...
Beispiel anführen	for instance/for example/such as/as can be seen
zeitliche Verknüpfung herstellen	now/while/as soon as/after/as long as/initially/previously/recently/finally/eventually/meanwhile/at the same time/at last/from now on/time and again/off and on

Idiomatische Redewendungen

Idiomatic expressions verleihen Ihrem Vortrag und auch dem anschließenden Gespräch Lebendigkeit und Authentizität. Sie sollten im Umgang mit englischen Redewendungen sicher sein und sie durch Intonation, Mimik und Gestik unterstreichen. Suchen Sie sich einige Redewendungen aus, die zu Ihrem persönlichen Stil passen und verwenden Sie diese in sinnvollen Zusammenhängen.

Die sprachliche Leistung im Abitur

Im Abitur spielt die sprachliche Leistung eine herausragende Rolle. Die Entwicklung der Sprachkompetenz entwickelt sich über viele Jahre hinweg als Prozess. In diesem Kapitel werden Ihnen die für das Abitur wesentlichen Aspekte erläutert. Listen mit hilfreichen Redemitteln runden Ihre Auseinandersetzung mit den Anforderungen an die sprachliche Leistung für das Abitur 2024 ab.

Kommunikative Textgestaltung

Kohärenz, Adressatenorientierung und Leserleitung

Kohärenz

TIPP zum Punktesammeln

Bemühen Sie sich, Ihren Text kohärent, also inhaltlich und sprachlich zusammenhängend zu gestalten. Schaffen Sie sinnvolle Verknüpfungen zwischen Satzteilen, Sätzen und Sinnabschnitten. Verwenden Sie dazu sogenannte **Konnektoren,** die als Verbindungsglieder zum besseren Textverständnis beitragen.

Hier ist eine Liste der wichtigsten Konnektoren, geordnet nach ihrer Funktion im Satz.

Reihung von Argumenten

and	und
First(ly), … Second(ly), … Third(ly), …	erstens, zweitens, drittens
Furthermore, …	außerdem, darüber hinaus
in addition to …	zusätzlich zu
Moreover, …	ferner, überdies
not only … (+ inversion) but also …	nicht nur … , sondern auch
as well as	sowie
Finally, …	schließlich

Gegensatz

but	aber, sondern
although	obwohl
However, …	jedoch
despite the fact that	trotz der Tatsache, dass
in spite of	trotz

Nevertheless, …/Nonetheless, …	nichtsdestotrotz
Even so, …	selbst dann
On the contrary, …	im Gegensatz dazu
on the one hand, … on the other hand, …	einerseits …, andererseits …
unlike	anders als
whereas	während/wogegen
while/whilst	während (dagegen)
yet	dennoch

Bedingung

if	falls, wenn
unless	wenn nicht
otherwise	ansonsten

Grund und Folge

because	weil
since	da
due to	wegen, aufgrund
that is why	deshalb
so	daher
consequently	folglich
as a result	demzufolge
therefore	daher, deshalb

Vergleich

like	wie
in comparison with	im Vergleich zu
similarly	ähnlich
equally	gleichermaßen

Adressatenorientierung

Schneiden Sie Ihren Text genau auf den Adressaten zu und drücken Sie sich präzise aus. Je nach Aufgabenstellung müssen Sie in der Abiturklausur unterschiedliche Sprachebenen verwenden. So kann es bei einem Brief an einen Freund aus den USA durchaus angebracht sein, *contracted forms (I'm, they're …)* oder andere Elemente des informellen Sprachgebrauchs zu verwenden, während zum Beispiel bei einer Stilmittelanalyse im Teil A II.2 eine formale oder zumindest neutrale Sprachebene zu wählen ist.

Leserleitung: *Writing a comment/Discussing a topic*

Die Art und Weise, wie Lesende durch einen Text geleitet werden können, wird im Folgenden am Beispiel des *comment* und der *discussion* gezeigt.

In beiden Textsorten muss die eigene Meinung zu einem Thema begründet werden. Während jedoch in einem *comment* nur der eigene Standpunkt dargelegt wird, wägt man in einer *discussion* Pro- und Kontra-Argumente ab.

Tipp: Überlegen Sie gut, in welcher Reihenfolge Sie Ihre Argumente anordnen wollen. Die Einleitung in das jeweilige Thema des *comment* oder der *discussion* weckt das Interesse der Lesenden und legt die zentrale These, die Ausgangsfrage, das Ausgangsargument oder das gestellte Problem dar.

Comment	Discussion
– Sie beleuchten ein Problem oder eine Fragestellung ausschließlich aus Ihrer spezifischen Perspektive, d. h., Sie brauchen keine Aspekte zu berücksichtigen, die nicht Ihrer Meinung entsprechen. – Die Basis Ihres Textes sollte eine sogenannte *thesis* sein, die Sie beweisen möchten. Nennen Sie diese nach der *introduction*. – Führen Sie plausible Argumente, Fakten, Beispiele und Schlussfolgerungen an. – Fassen Sie die wichtigsten Punkte in der *conclusion* zusammen. – Bringen Sie Ihre Meinung entweder in der introduction oder in der conclusion klar zum Ausdruck.	– Legen Sie zunächst den Standpunkt dar, der NICHT Ihrer Meinung entspricht. Schreiben Sie etwa drei Absätze zu der genannten These und führen Sie geeignete Argumente, Fakten, Beispiele und Schlussfolgerungen an. – Erläutern Sie dann die Position, die Sie selbst vertreten. Gehen Sie auch hierbei so vor, dass Sie Argumente, Fakten, Beispiele und Schlussfolgerungen anführen. – Fassen Sie die wichtigsten Punkte in der *conclusion* zusammen. Ihre eigene Meinung muss klar zum Ausdruck kommen.

TIPP zum Punktesammeln

Jeder Absatz, den Sie im Hauptteil eines *comment* oder einer *discussion* schreiben, sollte klar strukturiert sein. Nennen Sie im ersten Satz eines Absatzes Ihr Argument, sodass die Lesenden sofort wissen, worum es geht *(topic sentence)*. Vertiefen Sie anschließend das Argument, indem Sie es erläutern und Beispiele anführen.

Eine Sicherheit ausdrücken

It is a (well-known) fact that …	Es ist eine (bekannte) Tatsache, dass …
It cannot be denied that …	Man kann nicht leugnen, dass …
It goes without saying that …	Selbstredend …

Undoubtedly, ...	Zweifellos ...
I am convinced that ...	Ich bin überzeugt davon, dass ...
It is indisputable/obvious that .../ There is no doubt that ...	Es ist unbestreitbar/offensichtlich, dass .../Es besteht kein Zweifel, dass ...

Eine Vermutung ausdrücken

Apparently, ...	Anscheinend ...
They will probably ...	Sie werden wahrscheinlich ...
It seems highly (un)likely that ...	Es scheint äußerst (un)wahrscheinlich, dass ...
It may be the case that ...	Es kann sein, dass ...

Einen Zweifel ausdrücken

It is doubtful whether ...	Es ist zweifelhaft, ob ...
I wonder whether ...	Ich frage mich, ob ...
There is no proof/evidence that ...	Es gibt keine Beweise, dass ...

Einen Sachverhalt betonen

In order to stress that ...	Um hervorzuheben, dass ...
to emphasize	betonen
I would like to make it clear that ...	Ich möchte klarstellen, dass ...

Eine Meinung ausdrücken

In my opinion/To my mind/In my view ...	Meiner Meinung nach ...
My thoughts on the subject are ...	Meine Meinung zu diesem Thema ist ...
Personally, I think that .../My personal view is that ...	Ich persönlich denke, dass ...
As far as I am concerned, ...	Was mich betrifft, ...
From my point of view, ...	Aus meiner Sicht ...
I assume ...	Ich vermute ...
I am (not) convinced that ...	Ich bin (nicht) überzeugt davon, dass ...
I can't help thinking that ...	Ich kann nicht umhin zu denken, dass ...
I am afraid that ...	Ich fürchte, dass ... (abschwächend)
Honestly, .../To be honest, ...	Ehrlich gesagt ...
I can't judge ...	Ich kann ... nicht beurteilen.
I am in no position to say ...	Es steht mir nicht zu, mich zu ... zu äußern.

Einen Widerspruch einräumen

in contrast to	im Gegensatz zu
On the contrary, …	Ganz im Gegenteil … (am Satzanfang)
whereas	während (dagegen)
I strongly object to …	Ich spreche mich deutlich gegen … aus.
One could argue that …, but …	Man könnte argumentieren, dass …, aber …
Although it is true that …, it would be wrong to claim that …	Obwohl es wahr ist, dass …, wäre es falsch zu behaupten, dass …

Zustimmung ausdrücken

Fortunately, …	Glücklicherweise …
I entirely agree with …/I share the opinion that …	Ich stimme vollkommen mit … überein.
I support his view.	Ich unterstütze seine Meinung.
I share her views.	Ich teile ihre Meinung.
I am of the same opinion (as) …	Ich bin der gleichen Meinung (wie) …
I approve of his/her opinion.	Ich bin mit seiner/ihrer Meinung einverstanden.
I take your point about …	Ich akzeptiere Ihre Meinung über …
I am in favour of …	Ich bin für …
He rightly mentions that …	Zu Recht betont er, dass …
I won't object to …	Ich widerspreche … nicht.
It cannot be justified that …	Es gibt keine Rechtfertigung für …
Nobody would disagree with this statement.	Niemand würde dieser Behauptung widersprechen.
This statement is very convincing.	Diese Aussage ist sehr überzeugend.
I have to admit that the author …	Ich muss zugeben, dass der Autor/die Autorin …

Ablehnung ausdrücken

It is only partly true that …	Es entspricht nur teilweise der Wahrheit, dass …
I disagree completely with …	Ich bin ganz anderer Meinung als …
I see things differently.	Ich sehe den Sachverhalt anders.
I must/have to disagree on this matter.	Ich bin in dieser Angelegenheit anderer Meinung.
One cannot possibly accept that …	Man kann unmöglich akzeptieren, dass …

I must object to …	Ich muss … widersprechen.
I have to criticize strongly that …	Ich muss scharf kritisieren, dass …
I doubt whether …	Ich bezweifle, dass …
This statement contradicts …	Diese Behauptung widerspricht …
However, …	Jedoch …
It is not as simple as it seems.	Es ist nicht so einfach, wie es scheint.
Unlike the author, I think …	Abweichend vom Autor/der Autorin glaube ich …
I cannot share the author's view on …	Ich kann die Meinung des Autors/der Autorin über … nicht teilen.

Einen Grund angeben

As/Since …	Da/Weil …
In view of the fact that …	Angesichts der Tatsache, dass …
The reason for this problem lies in …	Der Grund für dieses Problem liegt bei …
This causes confusion.	Das sorgt für Verwirrung.
That is why …	Aus diesem Grund …
Given that …	In Anbetracht der Tatsache, dass …
therefore	deshalb
That was caused by …	Das wurde verursacht durch …
For this reason …	Aus diesem Grund …

Eine Folge darstellen

Consequently, … /As a consequence, …	Folglich (am Satzanfang)
In view of this statement, …	In Anbetracht dieser Behauptung …
in order to	um zu
as a result of	als Folge von

Vergleiche anstellen

to be comparable	vergleichbar sein
compared to/in comparison with	im Vergleich zu
to be different from	sich unterscheiden von
to distinguish between (A and B)	(A von B) unterscheiden
to be considerably better than	wesentlich besser sein als
to get more and more difficult	immer schwieriger werden
Nowadays, it is less and less common …	Heutzutage ist es immer weniger üblich …

superior/inferior to	überlegen/unterlegen
the former; the latter	der/die erstere, Ersteres; der/die letztere, Letzteres
They have little in common.	Sie haben wenig gemeinsam.
The countries are roughly equal in size.	Die Länder sind ungefähr gleich groß.

Beispiele anführen

For example/For instance	Zum Beispiel
Let me give an example.	Lassen Sie mich ein Beispiel anführen.
such as	wie (zum Beispiel)
Look at …	Sehen wir uns einmal … an.

Conclusion

To sum up, …	Zusammenfassend kann man sagen …
I come to the conclusion that …	Ich komme zu dem Schluss, dass …
In short, …	kurz gesagt
To put it in a nutshell, …	Um es auf einen Nenner zu bringen, …
I can support the author's view on …	Ich kann die Ansicht des Autors/der Autorin zu … unterstützen.
To summarize, …	Um das zusammenzufassen, …
All in all, I believe that …	Insgesamt glaube ich, dass …

Autorenintention

Es kann sein, dass Sie Ihre Aussagen in der Abiturklausur in Beziehung zu einer Autorenmeinung setzen müssen. Dafür sind beispielsweise folgende Ausdrücken nützlich:

He/She points out/argues that …	Er/Sie weist darauf hin/argumentiert, dass …
He/She implies/claims/states that …	Er/Sie behauptet, dass …
He/She believes/suggests …	Er/Sie glaubt/schlägt vor …
He/She emphasises …	Er/Sie betont …
He/She writes with the intention to …	Er/Sie schreibt mit der Absicht …
His/Her aim is to …	Sein/Ihr Ziel ist es, …
His/Her attitude towards …	Seine/Ihre Einstellung gegenüber …
When he/she says/writes …, he/she means that …	Wenn er/sie sagt/schreibt …, meint er/sie, dass …
According to the author, …	Dem Autor/Der Autorin zufolge …

Verweise und Zitate

Um Ihre Aussagen zu belegen, fügen Sie geeignete Zitate aus dem Originaltext in Ihre Antworten ein. Setzen Sie diese in englische Anführungszeichen – diese beginnen oben und enden oben. Da der Abiturklausur ein relativ kurzer Ausgangstext zugrunde liegt, genügt als Quellenangabe die Zeilennummer in Klammern direkt hinter dem Zitat.

Beispiel: *In his New Hampshire Primary Speech, Barack Obama said: "Yes we can, to justice and equality. Yes we can, to opportunity and prosperity. Yes we can heal this nation. Yes we can repair this world. Yes we can." (ll. 68–71)*

Wenn Sie nicht das ganze Zitat verwenden, können Sie die ausgelassenen Passagen mit drei Punkten in eckigen Klammern kennzeichnen.

Beispiel: *"This year, in considering the status of women, […] we must also consider the status of democracy."*

Genauso können Sie ein Bezugswort in eckigen Klammern einfügen, wenn dies aufgrund der Satzkonstruktion notwendig ist.

Beispiel: *The opposition leader said that "the time for radical change [had] come."*

Die wörtliche Übernahme von Formulierungen aus dem Ausgangstext bzw. einem anderen Text ohne entsprechende Kennzeichnung ist nicht zulässig und wird negativ bewertet.

Zitate stehen normalerweise nach einer Behauptung, da sie diese belegen oder bekräftigen. Von daher sollten Sie die Aussage eines Zitats zunächst mit eigenen Worten paraphrasieren. Nehmen Sie bei Bedarf Ihr einsprachiges Wörterbuch zu Hilfe, um passende Synonyme zu finden.

Textstruktur und Absätze

Formalia

Zunächst eine generelle Bemerkung: Die Leserinnen und Leser Ihrer Englischprüfung werden Ihnen grundsätzlich wohlgesonnen sein und werden Ihre Leistung gerecht bewerten wollen. Dazu ist es natürlich gerade in einer Fremdsprache eine wichtige Voraussetzung, dass Ihre Handschrift gut lesbar ist und die Buchstaben und die Wortgrenzen klar erkennbar sind. Reduzieren Sie nachträgliche Ergänzungen auf ein Minimum. Lassen sich diese nicht vermeiden, nummerieren Sie sie fortlaufend und deutlich und listen Sie den eingefügten Text entweder jeweils am Seitenende oder nach Abschluss des Textes in chronologischer Reihenfolge auf.

Rücken Sie die erste Zeile zur besseren Lesbarkeit 2 bis 3 Zentimeter ein, wenn Sie einen neuen Absatz beginnen.

TIPP zum Punktesammeln

Vermeiden Sie formale Nachlässigkeiten. Es ist unnötig, auf solche Weise Punkte zu verschenken.

Ausdrucksvermögen/Verfügbarkeit sprachlicher Mittel

Klarheit und Präzision

Die Formulierung der Abituraufgaben folgt klar definierten Regeln. So werden als Arbeitsanweisungen nur bestimmte Verben verwendet, die sogenannten **Operatoren** (siehe Seite 11ff.).

Beantworten Sie die Fragestellung mithilfe der Operatoren klar und präzise. Achten Sie beim Verfassen Ihrer Antwort auf Fehler, die leicht vermieden werden können. Im Folgenden werden einige typische Fehlerquellen genannt und erläutert.

Textökonomie

– Schreiben Sie nach dem Grundsatz der Textökonomie: „Jeder Satz ein Statement".
– Vermeiden Sie Wiederholungen im Wortschatz und umständliche inhaltliche „Schleifen".
– Vermeiden Sie die Formulierung von Allgemeinplätzen.
  (Beispiel: *It is well known that Europe is suffering from many problems these days.*)
– Stellen Sie sicher, dass die sprachlichen Bezüge korrekt sind. Verwenden Sie passende Pronomen und Possessivbegleiter.
– Achten Sie auf die korrekte Verwendung der Zeiten.

Vermeiden Sie Fehler, indem Sie sich *false friends* einprägen.
Hier ist eine Liste der häufig verwechselten Wörter:

deutsch	englisch	*false friend*
bekommen	to get	*become* – werden
Kritik	criticism	*critic* – der Kritiker
Politik	politics	*policy* – persönliche Strategie; außer in Begriffen wie „foreign policy" = Außenpolitik
sensibel	sensitive	*sensible* – vernünftig
meinen	to think	*mean* – bedeuten (oder Adj. = gemein)
aktuell	current	*actual* – eigentlich, tatsächlich, konkret
also	so	*also* – auch
brav	honest, good	*brave* – mutig, tapfer
Chef	boss	*chef* – der Koch, die Köchin
engagiert	committed	*engaged* – verlobt; beschäftigt, besetzt
eventuell	possibly	*eventual* – etwaig, möglich; schließlich
Handy	mobile phone (AE: cellphone)	*handy* – praktisch, nützlich, handlich
Konfession	denomination	*confession* – die Beichte
Konkurrenz	competition	*concurrence* – Übereinstimmung

konsequent	consistent	*consequent* – daraus folgend
mobben	to bully	*to mob* – umringen, umlagern
Mörder	murderer	*murder* – der Mord
prägnant	concise	*pregnant* – schwanger
prinzipiell	fundamentally, basically, in/on principle	*principally* – hauptsächlich
Prospekt	brochure, leaflet	*prospect* – Aussicht, Wahrscheinlichkeit
Publikum	audience	*public* – Öffentlichkeit
rentabel	profitable	*rentable* – zu mieten
Rückseite	back	*backside* – Hinterteil, Hintern
spenden	to donate	*to spend* – ausgeben

Wortschatz

Der in Ihren Texten verwendete Wortschatz sollte sachlich und stilistisch angemessen sein. Demonstrieren Sie, dass Sie über einen differenzierten allgemeinen Wortschatz verfügen, und variieren Sie in Ihrem Ausdruck.

Ausdrucksmöglichkeiten im Wortfeld „sagen"
to say, to tell, to relate, to describe, to let somebody know, to state, to speak, to talk, to answer, to respond, to reply, to inform, to advise, to recommend, to brief, to update somebody, to promise, to lie, to whisper, to shout, to scream, to yell, to report, to repeat, to argue, to converse, to allude to something, to articulate, to suggest, to demand, to insist, to urge, to ask, to question

Um Ihren Wortschatz zu erweitern, können Sie mithilfe von einsprachigen Wörterbüchern oder Synonymlisten auch Ersatzformulierungen für „think", „this means that" und viele weitere Standardausdrücke sammeln. Achten Sie darauf, dass die gewählte Ersatzformulierung inhaltlich passend ist. Die folgenden Beispiele bieten eine kleine Auswahl:

Formulierung	Ersatzformulierungen
because	accordingly, for this reason, hence, otherwise, since, thus, as a result, for this purpose, therefore, subsequently, alternatively
but	instead, however, regardless, in contrast to, admittedly, though, nevertheless, still, even though, although, nonetheless, on the one hand – on the other hand
for example	especially, for instance, such as, similarly, in this case, in particular, including, as an illustration, using the example of ...

Achten Sie in der Abiturvorbereitung bei jedem Übungstext auf die Verwendung der richtigen Präpositionen nach Verben und Adjektiven und den korrekten Gebrauch von Kollokationen sowie von thematisch angemessenem und fachspezifischem Wortschatz (siehe Glossare der themenrelevanten Kapitel in diesem Buch sowie das Kapitel „Methoden der Textanalyse", Seite 117).

Differenzierte Satzgestaltung

Neben der Gewandtheit im Wortschatz wird natürlich auch Ihr Können im Bereich Syntax bewertet. Wechseln Sie je nach Kontext zwischen Parataxen und Hypotaxen, d.h. zwischen Reihungen von Hauptsätzen und komplexen Satzgefügen mit Nebensätzen. Verbinden Sie Sätze mit Konnektoren (siehe Liste Seite 24f.) und stellen Sie temporale, kausale, konzessive, konditionale und resultative Bezüge her.

Übersicht über die möglichen Konjunktionen

temporal	when, while, before, after, until, since
kausal	because, since, as, for
konzessiv	although, though, while/whilst, whereas
konditional	if, unless
resultativ	so (that)

Integrieren Sie Partizipial-, Gerundial- und Infinitivkonstruktionen sowie Passivkonstruktionen. Sorgen Sie zusätzlich durch Inversion und gelegentliche Verwendung von (rhetorischen) Fragen für Abwechslung im Satzbau.

Beispiele: Partizipialkonstruktion: *Bernard is one of the main characters in the novel "Brave New World", written by Aldous Huxley in 1932.*

Gerundialkonstruktion: *Making the reader feel sympathy with the tragic hero is one of the main aims of the author.*

Inversion: *Not only does the author of the article present his personal opinion but he also backs it with numerous relevant examples and explanations.*

Eigenständigkeit

In der Abiturklausur werden Ihr Textverständnis und Ihre Ausdrucksfähigkeit bewertet. Ihr Ziel muss es deshalb sein, ein umfassendes Bild von Ihrer Ausdrucksfähigkeit zu geben. Wenn Sie häufig auf längere Textpassagen des Originaltexts zurückgreifen, kann die Eigenständigkeit der Leistung nicht ausreichend bewertet werden. Denken Sie also daran, Zitate nur zum Belegen Ihrer eigenen Thesen zu verwenden.

Sprachliche Richtigkeit (Fehlerschwerpunkte vermeiden)

Orthografie und Grammatik

Orthografie

Rechtschreibfehler passieren leicht aus Flüchtigkeit. Um sie zu vermeiden, sollten Sie sich eine Zeitplanung für Prüfungen aneignen, die Ihnen genug Spielraum lässt, Ihren Text nach Abschluss der produktiven Phase noch einmal durchzulesen und bei Bedarf Korrekturen vorzunehmen. Achten Sie dabei auch auf Interferenzen aus dem Deutschen.

Grammatik

Wie bereits zu Eingang des Kapitels erwähnt, kann in diesem Rahmen keine umfassende Grammatikwiederholung stattfinden. Gehen Sie also Ihre individuellen Problempunkte selbst an.

Dennoch seien an dieser Stelle einige gängige Fehlerquellen genannt, auf die Sie besonders achten sollten:

Verben

Sehen Sie sich vor der Prüfung noch einmal die Liste der unregelmäßigen Verben an und prägen Sie sich die Formen ein, die keinem gängigen Schema folgen, z. B. *lie – lay – lain, lay – laid – laid, catch – caught – caught.* Denken Sie darüber hinaus auch an *phrasal verbs,* deren Bedeutung zum Teil nicht aus den Bedeutungen der Einzelwörter erschließbar ist, z. B. *turn down* (etwas ablehnen).

Adverbien

Adverbien können im englischen Satz an verschiedenen Stellen stehen, die oft nicht mit dem Deutschen übereinstimmen: am Satzanfang; vor dem Verb, das sie näher bestimmen (bei zusammengesetzten Verbformen nach dem Hilfsverb); am Satzende.

Beispiele:

Unfortunately, the turnout for the country's first free election was very low.
Nevertheless, the bad news weighed heavily on them.
I often wonder what became of him.
We must also consider the opposite case.
They had counted the votes carefully.

TIPP zur Fehlervermeidung

Es kann sinnvoll sein, sich anhand der Fehler in den Klausuren der Qualifikationsphase einen Überblick über die eigenen Fehlerschwerpunkte in den Bereichen Orthografie und Grammatik zu verschaffen. Durch gezieltes Nachlesen in einer Grammatik und entsprechende Übungen können Sie sich verbessern. Achten Sie in der Abiturprüfung beim Korrekturlesen besonders auf die Vermeidung der betreffenden Fehlerschwerpunkte.

Basiswissen

Great Britain

Great Britain: Tradition and Change

Great Britain comprises England, Scotland and Wales, three countries in which traditions still play an important role. The head of state and head of the Church of England (the national Christian church since the 16th century) is the monarch. Two of Europe's oldest universities, Oxford and Cambridge, are located in Britain. London, one of Europe's biggest cities, is also one of the world's most important financial centres. Modern Britain is characterized by a mixture of tradition and modernity.

From 1952 until her death in September 2022, Queen Elizabeth II was monarch of the United Kingdom of Great Britain and Northern Ireland, also known as the UK. King Charles III acceded to the throne directly after his mother's death. Politically, the UK is a constitutional monarchy and a parliamentary democracy. The British parliament is the legislative power of the UK; it makes the laws. The government, which enforces the laws, is the executive power. As for the judiciary, the Supreme Court and some tribunals have a UK-wide jurisdiction, but England, Scotland and Wales also have separate judiciaries.

The role of the monarch

- The British monarchy has ceremonial duties, but the monarch holds no political power.
- The monarch represents the country on a national and an international level.
- The monarch officially opens Parliament each year after the summer recess.
- The monarch signs all bills before they become law. If he or she refuses to do so, the passing of a law could be prevented, but this is very unlikely to happen.
- The prime minister is officially appointed by the monarch after a general election.
- The monarch holds weekly meetings with the prime minister to discuss current issues.

The role of Parliament

Parliament consists of the House of Commons and the House of Lords:

House of Commons	House of Lords
Elected Members of Parliament (MPs) meet to discuss policies and current issues and to make laws.	Members are not elected. Most of them are life peers appointed by successive prime ministers. The life peers' seats are non-hereditary. There are also some aristocrats with hereditary seats and a group of Lords Spiritual, who belong to the Church of England.

The Lords have only limited powers, e.g. they can suggest amendments to legislation or delay the passing of a new law for twelve months.

Monarchy and modern democracy

Despite being a monarchy, the United Kingdom has a long history of parliamentary structures. (Early attempts to limit the power of the monarch and give rights to the people date back to the Magna Carta of 1215 and the Bill of Rights of 1689.) The British constitution is not codified and it is only partly written. British legislature is based on laws passed by Parliament, the European Convention on Human Rights, and decisions by courts of law. Parliamentary sovereignty is the leading norm. Parliament constitutionally consists of the monarch, the House of Lords and the House of Commons. All political power rests with the prime minister and his/her cabinet and the monarch has to act on their advice.

Devolution

Much of the country's legislative power has undergone **devolution** from the UK parliament to the **Scottish Parliament**, the **Welsh Parliament (Senedd)**, and the **Northern Ireland Assembly**. **England** did not get its own parliament, but is still governed by the **national parliament**. In 2014 a referendum on full independence was held in Scotland. There was a narrow majority for the country to remain in the UK. After Brexit some Scottish politicians and parts of the Scottish public advocated a second referendum on independence. However, in November 2022 the Supreme Court ruled that it could not take place without the consent of the British government.

Republicanism vs. Monarchy

In the UK, **republicanism** is a movement which works for the **abolition of the monarchy** and its replacement by a president, elected either by the people or by parliament. However, opinion polls show that the monarchy is still supported by the majority of the British population.

Arguments for the monarchy	Arguments against the monarchy
– A head of state can be a safeguard against Britain becoming a dictatorship. – The monarch boosts national unity as well as British traditions and values. – A monarch ideally remains in power for a long time and thus grants stability and can act as a political intermediary. – The monarch is not involved in party politics and can therefore act as an impartial representative of the country. – The members of the Royal Family have important functions in charities; they help them to continue their good work. – The monarchy attracts huge numbers of visitors to the UK.	– An elected head of state is accountable to an elected parliament whereas the royal prerogative can be misused to bypass parliament. – A monarchy is inappropriate if a society wants to be classless. – As the British monarchy is hereditary, the successor to the throne takes the crown regardless of his or her suitability. – In a democracy the people should be able to elect their head of state and choose instruments to check him/her. – A monarch is much more expensive than an elected head of state. He/She costs the UK over £100 million a year.

Britishness

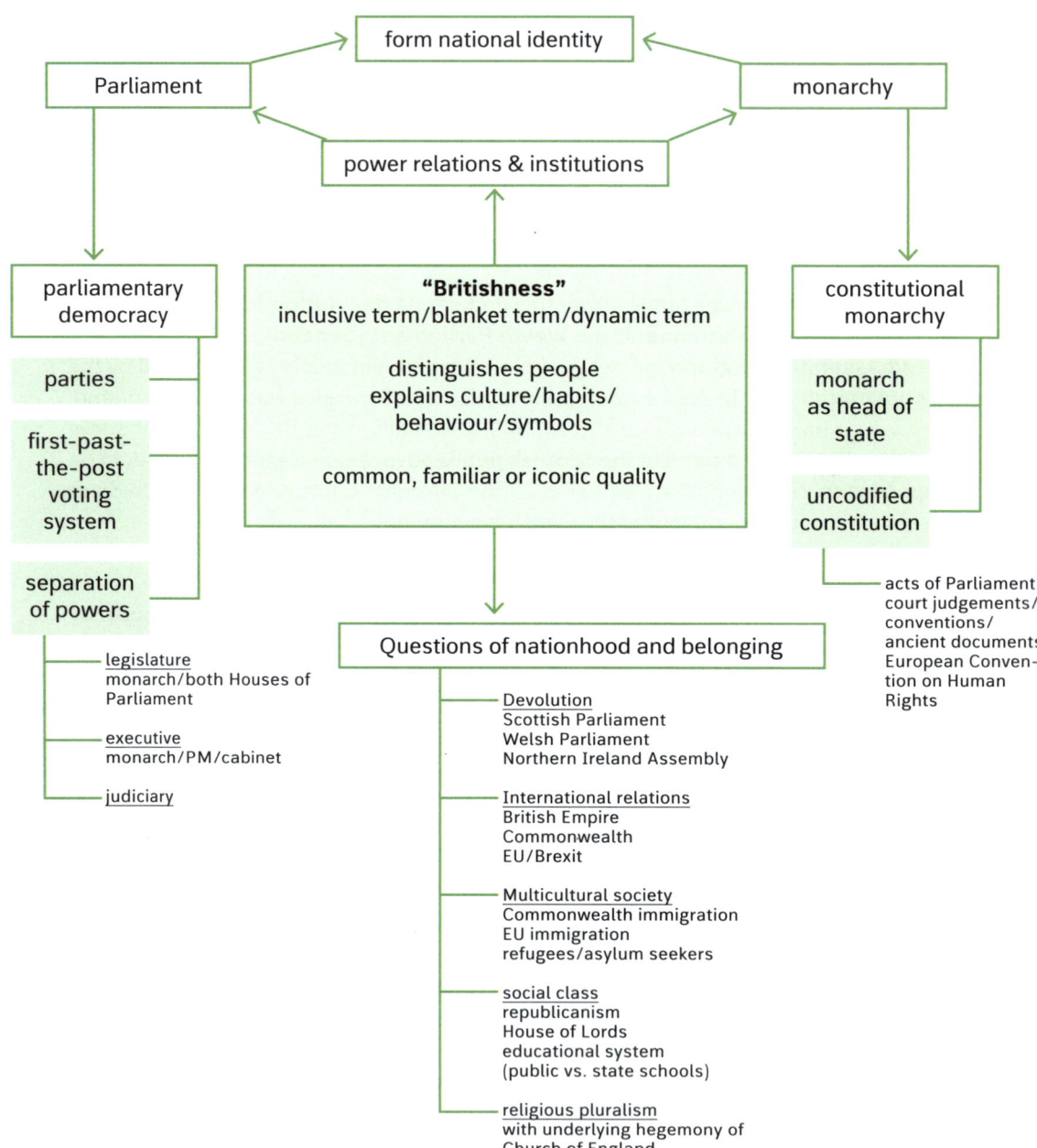

form national identity

Parliament

monarchy

power relations & institutions

parliamentary democracy

"Britishness"
inclusive term/blanket term/dynamic term

distinguishes people
explains culture/habits/
behaviour/symbols

common, familiar or iconic quality

constitutional monarchy

parties

first-past-the-post voting system

separation of powers

monarch as head of state

uncodified constitution

legislature
monarch/both Houses of Parliament

executive
monarch/PM/cabinet

judiciary

Questions of nationhood and belonging

acts of Parliament/
court judgements/
conventions/
ancient documents/
European Conven-
tion on Human
Rights

Devolution
Scottish Parliament
Welsh Parliament
Northern Ireland Assembly

International relations
British Empire
Commonwealth
EU/Brexit

Multicultural society
Commonwealth immigration
EU immigration
refugees/asylum seekers

social class
republicanism
House of Lords
educational system
(public vs. state schools)

religious pluralism
with underlying hegemony of
Church of England

Britain and Europe

On January 31, 2020 the United Kingdom left the European Union (EU). It had long been torn between its alliances and did not join the European Community (an association that came before the EU) until 1975. Scepticism towards Europe continued to prevail in certain political and public circles, and the loss of Britain's former grandeur as a colonial empire influenced the country's attitude towards EU politics. This eventually led to a referendum on Brexit ("British exit") in 2016. 51.9% voted to leave the EU. A phase of negotiations followed in order to finalize the terms of a new trade deal by 31 December 2020. It was a difficult and complex process, but an agreement was eventually reached a week before the deadline.

Timeline: British-European relations since the end of World War II

1946	Prime Minister Winston Churchill proposes "a kind of United States of Europe". However, his vision is not widely accepted in Britain.
1951	The European Coal and Steel Community is forged, but Britain does not join it.
1957	Britain declines the invitation to take part in the founding of the European Economic Community (EEC).
1961	As France and Germany are recovering from the war and forming a strong alliance, Britain changes its mind and applies to join the EEC, but French President Charles de Gaulle vetoes its entry.
1975	Britain eventually joins the EEC. In a referendum more than 67% of the population vote for membership.
1980s	The relations between Britain and the EU become tense as the European Community is aiming to create a more federal Europe and a single currency. Prime Minister Margaret Thatcher demands money back from the EEC and rejects "a European super-state exercising a new dominance from Brussels".
1985	The Schengen Agreement is signed by five member states of the EEC. Border checks are largely abolished between the member states. More Schengen treaties will follow and Schengen will become a core part of EU law by the end of the 20th century. Britain does not join the Schengen Area, but British citizens have the right to freedom of movement within the EU.
1992	7 February: the Maastricht Treaty creates the European Union (EU). The UK secures an opt-out from the planned common currency and the Social Chapter. The treaty involves huge transfers of power to the EU. British critics of the treaty say that it undermines the sovereignty of Parliament.
2008	The eurozone crisis begins and British Euroscepticim becomes even stronger.

2013	As support for the anti-EU UK Independence Party (UKIP) becomes stronger, conservative Prime Minister David Cameron promises that, in case of a re-election, he will renegotiate Britain's terms of membership in a "reformed EU".
2015	The Conservatives win the majority in the UK election.
2016	23 June: in a referendum the British vote to leave the EU. Cameron resigns.
2020	31 January: Britain officially leaves the EU and enters a transition period. 31 December: the UK leaves the EU single market and customs union.

Consequences of Brexit

Trade	– Before Brexit, British companies could trade goods across EU borders without paying taxes or having restrictions as to quantity and diversity. – The UK and the EU had to agree on some shared rules and standards regarding workers' rights. – They also had to agree on rules and standards for many social and environmental issues. – The UK can now design its own trade policy and negotiate deals with other countries. – The UK would seem to have performed worse than comparable EU economies under the impact of the COVID-19 pandemic.
Life and work	– UK citizens no longer have the right to live and work in the EU. – UK citizens need a visa if they want to stay in the Schengen area for more than 90 days during a 180-day period. – Northern Ireland decided to follow many EU rules in order to avoid conflicts at its border with the Republic of Ireland.
International relations	– The UK has established strong connections with the US in foreign policies (which partly results from the two countries' alliance during World War II and the formation of NATO). – Britain regards the UN as an important framework for promoting foreign policy. – Britain is a permanent member of the UN Security Council.

The debate about leaving the EU went on for years in the UK. Britain is still coming to terms with the results of Brexit. The arguments for or against membership in the EU are still being debated.

Arguments against the EU	Arguments for the EU
– loss of national identity and sovereignty – an imbalance between the cost of what had to be put into the EU and the share that came back – interference in British domestic affairs by Brussels through EU laws – EU citizens have the right to live in other EU countries, so Britain had to accept an increasing number of immigrants.	– economic support by the EU – free trade within the EU – EU subsidies from which Britain profited – freedom for British citizens to work and live in other EU countries

From Empire to Commonwealth

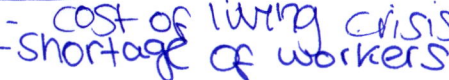

– cost of living crisis
– shortage of workers (BSP NK)

The British Empire existed from the late 16th century until the mid-20th century. At its height in the early 1900s it was the largest and most powerful empire in human history. Known as "the empire on which the sun never sets" – for there would always be daylight in some part of it – it comprised over 20% of the world's land area and about 458 million people. By the later 19th century it controlled some two-thirds of world trade.

Post-colonialism and migration

During the 20th century the vast British Empire started to crumble. Its break-up was a slow but unstoppable process.

Main reasons for the Empire's break-up:
– Demand for the right to self-government (Australia, New Zealand, Canada).
– Demand for independence and growing sense of nationalism in some states.
– Great Rebellion or Indian Mutiny[1] (1857–1859), also known as India's First War of Independence; later passive resistance under Gandhi, starting in 1920.
– Rejection of measures such as the conscription of citizens of British colonies or dependencies to fight for Britain during World War I (and to a lesser extent World War II).

Independence, however, brought new challenges in its wake. After decades of being treated as inferior, many people in the former colonies felt utterly displaced and rootless. Having partly assimilated to the British way of life, they had to find their own identity as a nation and recreate their own values and traditions when the British rulers were gone.

After World War II Britain welcomed immigrants from its former colonies, as workers were needed in many industries and services (e.g. London Transport), but gradually (partly due to the economic crisis in the 1970s) attitudes toward immigration changed.

---

[1] The "Great Rebellion" in India started as a mutiny of Sepoys – Indian soldiers recruited by the Mogul Empire, the British East India Company and the British Indian Army – but was soon followed by other mutinies and civilian uprisings, thus causing a major threat to British rule.

The British Commonwealth

Today the Commonwealth of Nations is a free association of 56 (as of May 2023) independent states that support each other. Membership is voluntary, and some of its largest members include Canada, Australia and India. With the exception of Mozambique, Rwanda, Gabon and Togo, all the countries were once part of the British Empire. The Commonwealth was founded in 1926 and is headed by the British monarch, whose position is symbolic. English remains the common language within the Commonwealth, which runs many institutes, societies and professional as well as university exchange programmes. The Commonwealth is committed to some important principles, such as the Singapore Declaration of 1971, which emphasizes a commitment to peace, equality, the fight against racism, and economic and social development. The Harare Declaration of 1991 places an emphasis on democracy, human rights and social justice. If these commitments are violated, punishments, such as economic sanctions, expulsion (as was the case with of South Africa under apartheid from 1961 to 1994) or suspension (as was the case with Zimbabwe in 2002, leading to its departure from the Commonwealth in 2003) may be expected.

Modern British multicultural society

> **Keyword:**
> **British Nationality and Status of Aliens Act (1914):** Inhabitants of the dominions were given British citizenship.

- Between the 1960s and 1980s many Indians, Pakistanis and Bangladeshis immigrated to Britain, and they now form the largest immigrant communities.
- Many of them settled in the Midlands or in towns in Lancashire, Yorkshire, and Strathclyde, where they used to work in the manufacturing, textile, and service sectors.

Britain today

- **Ethnic diversity** enriches Britain, not only in terms of music, fashion and food, but also in other ways. Many people embrace the opportunities and advantages it entails.
- However, others fear that "Britishness" will be lost. They interpret multiculturalism as meaning that various cultures coexist peacefully but without sharing values.
- **Second-generation immigrants,** i.e. children born to parents who immigrated to Britain prior to (or shortly after) their birth, face a variety of challenges:
  - > They often experience a clash of cultures. Outside their parents' home, they adopt a western lifestyle similar to that of their friends and classmates from British families. At home, however, they live according to values, beliefs and traditions typical of their parents' home countries, which many of these children and teenagers have never visited. Quite often, they do not speak their parents' language. For some, the tension between two different lifestyles is not easy.
  - > They sometimes have difficulties when it comes to living up to the expectations of their parents, friends, teachers, etc.
  - > They often face discrimination.

Glossary – Great Britain

administration	Verwaltung (im AE auch: Regierung)
Act (of Parliament)	(verabschiedetes) Gesetz
adapt to sth.	sich an etw. anpassen
asylum seeker	Asylsuchende/-r
be oppressed by s.o.	von jemandem unterdrückt werden
bill	Gesetzesvorlage
chamber	Kammer (z. B. House of Commons)
checks and balances	gegenseitige Kontrolle der einzelnen Verfassungsorgane
receive/be granted citizenship	die Staatsbürgerschaft erhalten
clash of two cultures	Aufeinanderprallen zweier Kulturen
colonialism; colonizer; colonized	Kolonialismus; Kolonisator/-in; kolonisiert
constituency; constituent	Wahlkreis; Wähler/-in
discriminate against s.o.	jdn. benachteiligen, diskriminieren
domestic/foreign policy	Innen-/Außenpolitik
election; electorate	Wahl; Wählerschaft
empire	Imperium, Weltreich
ethnicity; ethnic minority	Volkszugehörigkeit; ethnische Minderheit
excluded (from sth.)	(von etw.) ausgeschlossen
Foreign/Home Secretary	Außen-/Innenminister/-in
have a racist attitude	eine rassistische Einstellung haben
hereditary vs. non-hereditary	erblich vs. nicht erblich
hostile	feindlich, feindselig, ablehnend
imperialism; imperialistic	Imperialismus; imperialistisch
indigenous	einheimisch
loss of identity	Identitätsverlust
MP (Member of Parliament)	Abgeordnete/-r
mutual understanding and respect	gegenseitiges Verständnis und Respekt
to hold office; to take office	amtieren; ein Amt antreten
life peer	(lebenslanges) Mitglied des Oberhauses
permanent residence permit	unbefristete Aufenthaltserlaubnis
pluralistic society	pluralistische Gesellschaft
representative	Volksvertreter/-in
the Speaker	Vorsitzende/-r des Unterhauses
to stand down	zurücktreten
universal suffrage	allgemeines Wahlrecht

Globalization

What is Globalization?

> **Keyword:**
> **Globalization** (also spelled "globalisation" in BE) is a worldwide movement that involves the integration of financial, economic, and communications systems. It is often seen as an unstoppable process which affects people worldwide, regardless of whether they live in industrialized or developing countries, big cities or rural villages. While it makes the transfer of goods, capital, services, and communication easier, smaller economies may suffer from the development.
> The world is said to be getting smaller, and it has become a "global village". This term was coined by Marshall McLuhan, a Canadian philosopher and key thinker of media theory.

Globalization in the past

Sometimes we tend to forget that globalization is not a modern phenomenon, but that throughout history, people have been exploring new regions, trading with each other, and bringing their culture to other parts of the world. Here are some examples:

- The ancient Greeks and Romans spread their culture within the areas they conquered, which covered large parts of the known world. Trade was an important pillar of their societies.
- The Silk Road was a network of ancient trade routes that connected East and Southeast Asia, the Indian subcontinent, Central Asia, the Middle East, East Africa, and Europe.
- During the Islamic Golden Age (approx. 750–1258) Islamic civilization spread throughout North Africa, the Arabian States, Spain, northern India and Central Asia, and western China. During that time studies in mathematics, different sciences, art, philosophy, architecture, and technology were cultivated, and the results influenced European culture too.
- In the late 15th century, European explorers set out to discover unknown parts of the world and travelled thousands of miles to establish new trade routes. Different kinds of food (e.g. potatoes from South America), plants (e.g. tobacco from North America) and animals (e.g. grey squirrels from North America) were taken back on these voyages, thus introduced far from their original countries.
- The slave trade was one of the worst effects of European expansion.
- Europeans also spread diseases in the territories they discovered, causing many indigenous people to die.
- One might say that modern globalization started with the Industrial Revolution, which began in Britain during the late 18th century and made mass production of goods possible. The development of new technologies, such as steam power and the telegraph, made it easier to communicate and transport goods, facilitating the growth of global trade.

Globalization today

Everyone can experience the results of globalization, e. g.,
- when travelling,
- when keeping in touch with friends or business partners in distant countries with the help of modern means of communication,
- when buying goods produced in faraway places.

Globalization is not always regarded as a positive process for different reasons:
- Some people fear that individual cultures will finally blend into a single global culture, thereby losing all their characteristic features.
- Thousands of people in developing countries have not profited from globalization, but still suffer from malnutrition or die of curable diseases.
- Others suffer from cruel working conditions, producing goods which will be shipped to industrialized countries and sold there at a low price.
- The financial crisis which began in the USA in 2008 showed that such crises will ultimately affect other countries as well, as global trade is the rule and businesses are interconnected.
- Due to globalized trade and travel, diseases like H1N1 ("Swine Flu") or COVID-19 can easily spread all around the globe, developing into a pandemic. Because of the COVID-19 pandemic, the world faced an unprecedented burden on the global economy, healthcare, and globalization processes. There were difficulties in the supply chain, major challenges in education and academia, and huge problems in the healthcare systems. Millions of people lost their jobs or their businesses. Events and travels had to be cancelled for a long time.
- Terrorism has become an ongoing global threat which has led to a growing feeling of insecurity in many societies. In some countries (e. g. Israel) terrorist attacks have virtually been a permanent feature of life for several decades. In most Western as well as Middle Eastern countries, what we know as Islamist terrorism (Al-Qaeda, the Islamic State) began to escalate with the attacks on the World Trade Center in New York and the Pentagon in Washington on September 11, 2001 ("9/11"). This led to military reactions from the USA and its allies. Since then, the world has seen a large number of terrorist attacks connected with Islamist ideology (e. g., in France, England, Nigeria, and Berlin).
- The ideology of white supremacy also challenges liberal societies, as terrorist attacks in Christchurch, New Zealand and Utøya, Norway have shown.

Aspects of Globalization

Progress

- The development of planes, fast ships, and trains made fast transportation of goods from one country to another possible.
- New means of communication, especially the Internet, facilitate collaboration between business partners.
- Multinational companies have branches all over the world, and cost-effectiveness is a decisive factor when new production sites are set up.

Global conflicts

- Due to the economic interdependence caused by globalization, conflicts have a significant impact on individual economies, as demonstrated by the war between Russia and Ukraine. For instance, many countries experienced shortages of wheat and sunflower oil when Russia blocked Ukraine's Black Sea ports.
- Global conflicts have highlighted the need for reshoring, which involves bringing back industries such as manufacturing to domestic markets. Moreover, developing renewable energy sources appears to be the most sensible way to achieve greater energy security. The ongoing debate about which countries are acceptable providers of other energy sources like gas and oil concerns aspects such as democracy and human rights (e.g. in Qatar or Saudi Arabia).
- At present, most wars occur within a particular country or its neighbouring countries. However, many of these conflicts are proxy wars, which involve groups or smaller countries representing the interests of larger powers fighting for dominance and receiving support from them (e.g., the factions in the civil war in Yemen are supported by Iran and Saudi Arabia, which are enemies).

Economic challenges

Today's customers wish to buy products with the best cost–performance ratio, making the global market highly **competitive,** and leading to the following (and related) consequences:

- While global players prioritize efficiency, speed, flexibility, and profits, employees increasingly struggle to defend their rights.
- More and more jobs are being outsourced or off-shored to reduce production costs, severely impacting local labour markets.
- Workers in low-wage countries often toil in **sweatshops** for long hours, earning minimum wages and working in inhumane conditions.
- Multinational companies are often accused of exploiting the poor and indirectly supporting child labour by prioritizing their own profits.
- Workers often assemble products they cannot afford themselves or do not know how to use, such as computers.
- People in developing countries often live in poor conditions without access to education or new means of communication, which hinders them from reaping the benefits of globalization.
- Advocates of sweatshops argue that these factories allow the poor to provide for their families, and that critics overlook the actual situation of people in developing countries when opposing them.
- Fair trade is becoming increasingly important to reduce the number of sweatshops. Its aim is to ensure that workers and small-scale producers in poor countries are paid a fair price for their work and products.
- Despite efforts to address these issues, there is growing concern that the gap between the rich and the poor is widening.
- The refugee crisis in Europe can be partly attributed to globalization. People from all over the world seek to partake in the growing economic wealth. Many from poor

countries hope to find a better future and leave their homes, much like emigration to America in the last two centuries. Civil wars and other conflicts also force people to emigrate. As more countries close their borders, problems, such as desolate conditions in large refugee camps, increase and thousands of people die during dangerous journeys each year.

Ecological challenges and the role of customers

Environmental pollution is rapidly expanding, and several factors contribute to global problems:

- Factories emit **exhaust fumes** that are among the most dangerous air pollutants.
- Over the last few decades the number of **vehicles** with combustion engines has steadily increased, even in developing countries. This means that a higher amount of exhaust gases such as carbon dioxide, carbon monoxide, and mono-nitrogen oxides pollute the air worldwide.
- More and more people travel by **plane** because tickets have become affordable. However, several governments, organizations, and companies have imposed restrictions and even prohibitions on **short-haul flights** in recent years because they want travellers to use more environmentally friendly means of transportation for shorter distances, especially trains.
- Until a few decades ago, most people bought locally grown and seasonal produce, but now many want certain products all year round. As a consequence, more goods are air-freighted, increasing the rate of **food miles**. Environmentally conscious consumers consider whether it is better to buy local products than food (even fair trade products) transported between continents.
- Every individual leaves a **carbon footprint**, either directly and indirectly. A person can control their direct emissions to have an influence on the environment. Indirect emissions are related to the individual, such as the carbon produced by the country the person lives in.
- **Greenhouse gases** damage the atmosphere, such as by creating the ozone hole, and cause global warming.

Global warming and its consequences

- Greenhouse gases accumulate in the Earth's atmosphere, allowing the sun's light to pass through, but trapping the heat that reflects back from the Earth's surface. This results in a temperature rise on Earth, known as global warming.
- Climate change has numerous consequences, including flooding in coastal areas, heavy rainfall in some regions and drought in others, and the melting of polar ice caps.
- Biodiversity is threatened, with many plants, flowers, and animals dying out. Desertification is an increasingly frequent phenomenon today (see page 48).

INFO

Die gängige deutsche Bezeichnung für *carbon footprint* ist „CO_2-Bilanz".

Environmental sustainability

- Due to overgrazing of land by too much cattle, over-extraction of groundwater, unwise use of water resources, e. g., by diverting rivers for industrial or private use, deforestation (slash-and-burn agriculture), vast areas of land in relatively dry areas deteriorate (e. g., because of rising soil salinity) and become useless (desertification).
- Environmental sustainability is on the agenda of many governments and has been an important topic at various summits to date.

Attempts to reduce global warming

- The **Kyoto Protocol** from 2005 aimed to reduce the emission of greenhouse gases by 5.2% below 1990 levels between the years 2008 and 2012. China and the United States did not sign the treaty, so critics questioned how effective it would be. Another issue was the fact that the agreement did not require developing countries to reduce their emissions.
- At the **Paris UN Climate Change Conference** in **2015**, a global agreement on the reduction of climate change was reached and adopted by 195 countries. The **Paris Agreement** replaced the Kyoto Protocol. It reaffirmed the goal of limiting the global average temperature to well below 2°C above pre-industrial levels, while pursuing efforts to limit the temperature increase to 1.5°C above pre-industrial levels. In November 2020, during the Trump administration, the US withdrew from the Paris Agreement. However, on January 20, 2021, the first day of his term, President Joe Biden reentered it on behalf of the United States.
- In **2022**, the **UN Climate Conference in Sharm El Sheikh** established a loss and damage fund to help countries that suffer harm caused by human-generated climate change.

Fridays for Future

- In August 2018, Greta Thunberg, a 16-year-old Swedish climate change activist, started protesting outside the Swedish parliament in Stockholm to raise awareness of the dangers of climate change. She sat there every day for three weeks during school hours, holding a sign that read "School strikes for climate". Photos of the first day went viral, and from the second day, Thunberg was joined by other activists.
- According to Thunberg, governments were not taking enough action against climate change and were thus putting our planet's future at risk.
- In March 2019, only a few months after Thunberg's first protest, about 2,200 school strikes were organized in 125 countries. More than one million young people took part.
- By now, millions of teenagers and young adults worldwide have been going on school strike on Fridays and calling for enforced measures to stop the climate crisis. The movement is known as Fridays for Future. During the COVID-19 pandemic, it was impossible to demonstrate, but the protesters tried to use other ways of spreading their message.
- The speedy action of governments in response to the COVID crisis and the immense sums of money they provided seem to prove Fridays for Future's point that immediate

action is possible, but governments all over the world do not regard an effective fight against global warming as a top priority.

Conflict between economic and ecological aspects of globalization

- Companies face global competition: cost-effectiveness and profits seem more important than ecological issues.
- Some governments refrain from passing strict laws to protect the environment because this might drive away multinational companies that offer employment.
- As environmental pollution does not stop at borders, international cooperation to raise ecological standards is crucial – and will become even more so in the future.
- The question of green energy has become central, as using nuclear power and purchasing gas from Russia and other autocratic countries lead to further global problems.

The UN and the EU
The UN

- October 24, 1945: a group of 51 countries founded the United Nations (UN) as a successor to the League of Nations.
- The UN headquarters are located in New York City, and the current secretary-general is António Guterres.
- The UN has 193 member states (as of 2023).
- It defends human rights and fundamental freedoms.

The UN has **six main bodies**. Five of them (the General Assembly, the Security Council, the Economic and Social Council, the Trusteeship Council, and the UN Secretariat) are located in New York City, while the International Court of Justice is in The Hague in the Netherlands. The Security Council consists of five permanent members: the United States, the United Kingdom, France, Russia, and China.

Various **programmes**, **funds, and specialized agencies** are affiliated with the UN, such as UNICEF (United Nations Children's Fund), WFP (World Food Programme), and WHO (World Health Organization). UNHCR (United Nations High Commissioner for Refugees) is another important body. It protects refugees and helps displaced persons to return home or to be resettled.

Aims of the UN
- To maintain international peace and security
- To promote friendly relations among nations
- To support international cooperation with regard to economic, social, cultural and humanitarian issues

- Apart from **peacekeeping** and **peacemaking** operations, **peace-building** has become more and more important.
- The UN and its affiliated organizations work to equip national groups with skills in conflict management and to ensure that lasting peace can be established.

- **Humanitarian aid** is also of major importance, such as providing relief for people affected by either man-made or natural disasters, and helping refugees and displaced persons in many countries.
- Another main concern of the UN is the advancement of the rule of **law and development** at the national and international levels, such as by establishing internationally agreed-upon standards which support sustainable development.

The EU

- Currently, the European Union (EU) has 27 member states.
- After World War II, there was a desire for a united Europe in order to prevent extreme forms of nationalism. The European Coal and Steel Community, the European Economic Community (EEC), and the European Atomic Energy Community (Euratom) were merged into the European Communities (EC) in 1967.
- The EU, as we know it, came into existence in 1993 when the Maastricht Treaty was ratified. The individual member states came to be regarded as a single global player.
- At present, the EU faces the challenge of maintaining its unity as the member countries have very different attitudes towards solving the refugee problem.
- On January 1, 2020, the United Kingdom left the EU ("Brexit", cf. pp. 39–41).

Aims of the EU
The EU's goals are laid out in the Lisbon Treaty from 2007. Some of the aims of the EU within its borders are:
- To promote peace, its values, and the well-being of its citizens.
- To offer freedom, security, and justice without internal borders.
- To establish an internal market.
- To achieve sustainable development.
- To protect and improve the quality of the environment.
- To fight social exclusion and discrimination.
- To enhance solidarity among its member states.
- To respect its cultural and linguistic diversity.

In defence matters, the individual member countries are sovereign. However, there is military cooperation in peacekeeping missions.

The seven decision-making bodies of the EU are:
- The European Parliament (located in Strasbourg, France): the Members of the EU Parliament, which is one of the law-making bodies of the EU, are elected every five years by EU voters. Currently, there are 705 members (as of May 2023).
- The Council of the European Union (located in Brussels) is the second legislative body. Ministers of the governments of EU member states meet in different configurations to amend, approve or veto laws. They also discuss policies.
- The European Commission (located in Brussels) is part of the executive branch of the EU. It is also called European Government. There are 27 members headed by a president (currently Ursula von der Leyen).

- The European Council (located in Brussels) is the other part of the executive. It is composed of the heads of state or government of the member countries, the President of the European Council (currently Charles Michel), and the President of the European Commission. It defines EU policies.
- The other three institutions are the Court of Justice of the European Union (located in Luxembourg), the European Central Bank (located in Frankfurt), and the European Court of Auditors (located in Luxembourg).

TIPP zur Wissensvertiefung

For more information on the EU and its institutions visit:
https://european-union.europa.eu/institutions-law-budget/institutions-and-bodies_en

International peacekeeping

International peacekeeping is one of the aims of the UN.
- United Nations peacekeeping operations are, in principle, deployed to support the implementation of a cease-fire or a peace agreement, but they often have to play an active role in peacemaking efforts, and they may also be involved in early peace-building activities while a conflict is still ongoing.
- The UN Security Council authorizes a peacekeeping mission by adopting a resolution. After that, the Secretary-General appoints a Head of Mission to direct the operation.
- As there is no UN army or police force, member states are asked to send military and police personnel for the mission. These peacekeepers act under the control of the UN but still belong to their national armed forces. They wear their country's uniform and can be identified as peacekeepers only by a UN blue helmet or beret and a badge.
- The peacekeepers oversee the peace process, e. g. by upholding the security of elections, providing reconstruction aid, and supervising the withdrawal of combatants.
- The Secretary-General provides regular reports to the Security Council on the mission. The Security Council reviews them and renews and adjusts the mission mandate until the operation is completed.
- Regional organizations (e. g. NATO) can be authorized by the UN to lead peacekeeping missions. They can also deploy peacekeeping missions of their own.
- The role of the US within the UN has a rather controversial and dynamic history, ranging from unquestioning support to massive criticism. The US is the largest financial contributor to the UN, paying 22 percent of the budget (2020: $ 820 million). Germany has been a member of the UN since 1973. It is the organization's fourth-largest contributor, paying some six percent of its annual budget (2023: over $ 178 million).
- In addition, member states pay compulsory contributions to finance peacekeeping operations, and they also make voluntary contributions, e. g. to UNICEF, UNHCR and WFP.

Migration – a global challenge

- Migration has been a worldwide phenomenon since the beginning of human history.
- People have had a number of reasons for leaving their places of origin. It is important to distinguish between push and pull factors. **Push factors** are the reasons why people leave their country, such as poverty, famine, war, bad infrastructure, and natural disasters due to climate change. **Pull factors** are the reasons which make a country attractive to live in, such as a great variety of jobs, good social services, and access to education.
- It is also important to distinguish between migrants and refugees.

Migrants	Refugees
- Leave their countries of origin for a limited period of time or permanently, usually for economic reasons. - Might have job offers or have heard of good opportunities. - Examples are the emigrants from Europe to the US (19th century), from Poland to the Ruhr district (19th century), migrants within the EU today, migrants from Africa to the EU today. - Migrant seasonal workers go to other countries for a limited period, typically during the harvest season, e.g., people from Romania and Bulgaria who work on German and British farms.	- Usually flee their countries of origin to escape persecution, war, or other forms of violence. - Currently, many Ukrainian refugees are staying in Poland, Germany, and other countries. - Most of the world's refugees (as of 2021, 74 percent) are hosted in low- and middle-income countries. For example, there are large numbers of Syrian refugees living in Jordan and Lebanon.

- There were about 281 million migrants in 2020. Nearly two-thirds of them were labour migrants. The World Migration Report from 2022 states that Europe and Asia hosted the most international migrants (Europe: around 87 million, Asia: around 86 million), followed by North America, Africa, Latin America and the Caribbean, and Oceania. Migrants, for the most part, seek – and find – employment in the countries of destination. Quite a large number of them are illegal immigrants.
- The world is presently witnessing the highest levels of displacement on record. In mid-2022, UNHCR reported that there were about 103 million forcibly displaced people around the world. Among them were over 32.5 million international refugees. 74 percent of them are staying in neighbouring countries. Over 59 million were internally displaced people, i. e., people who have fled from one part of their country to another (e. g. in Nigeria), either as a result of conflict and violence (53.2 million) or as a result of disasters (5.9 million).
- In 2021, Turkey hosted the largest refugee population worldwide, with 3.7 million refugees and asylum seekers, followed by Colombia (2.5 million), Germany (2.2 million), Pakistan (1.5 million), and Uganda (1.5 million).

- 72 percent of refugees originate from just five countries: Syria (6.8 million), Venezuela (5.6 million), Ukraine (5.4 million), Afghanistan (2.8 million), and South Sudan (2.4 million).
- There are also over 4 million stateless people who have been denied nationality and access to basic rights such as education, healthcare, employment, and freedom of movement.
- Nearly one percent of the world's population has fled their homes.
- Nearly one person is forcibly displaced every two seconds as a result of conflict or persecution.
- The fact that most refugees seek help in neighbouring, not always wealthy countries can cause major problems there. The population of these countries has to share access to education, healthcare, and jobs with the newly arrived people. Compared to rich states like Germany, countries like Jordan or Lebanon find it far more difficult to cope with the situation. Colombia is another example. The country is only just beginning to overcome the effects of a civil war, but it also has to host over one million refugees from Venezuela.
- Migration also means enrichment. With time, the country of destination will integrate the new people. Their customs and beliefs will be incorporated into social life and bring about more cultural diversity.
- Many refugees want to return to their home countries when the living conditions have changed. Others decide to stay in their host countries and build a new life there.
- Migrant seasonal workers also go home when their jobs are finished.

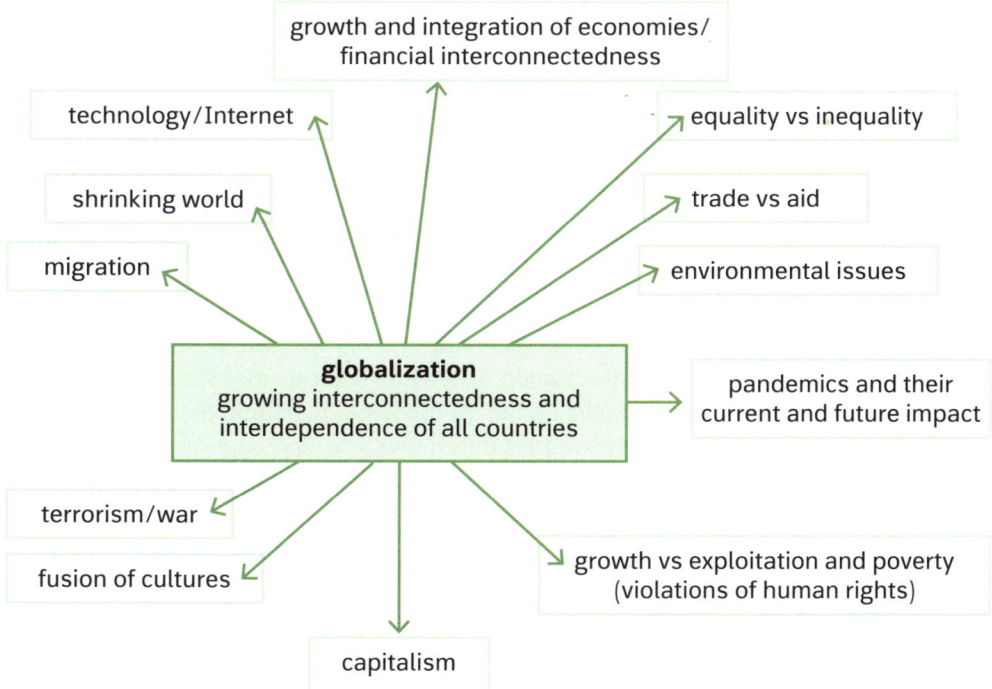

The Media in Times of Globalization

Important keywords:
Media literacy: refers to the ability of a recipient to analyse and evaluate the messages they receive through media. It enables users to decide what personal data to share with whom and it is also vital for producing their own messages.
Fake news: refers to organized, systematic misinformation campaigns often linked to governments and is regarded as one of the greatest threats to democracy, free debate and the Western order. The rise of social media is seen as central to the spread of fake news.
Conspiracy theory: refers to a belief that a group of people or an institution are covertly trying to harm people or things or are responsible for certain events. For instance, a group among the opponents of COVID-19 control measures may believe in conspiracy theories.
Propaganda: refers to pre-selected, often misleading or biased information, ideas or statements, half-truths or lies, which are used to promote a political point of view and help a cause, a political leader, or a government by influencing people's opinions. It is a systematic effort to manipulate beliefs, attitudes, or actions. Propaganda is often a key instrument in international armed conflicts, such as the war in Ukraine that started in 2014.

The influence of the media on society
- As **prime sources of information**, the media can influence the opinions of a whole society about certain topics.
- Before the Internet, it was much more expensive to distribute information and there were simpler definitions of news and media, making regulation easier.
- With the help of more or less open forms of **censorship**, public opinion can be strongly influenced. This was fictionalized by George Orwell in his famous novel *1984*, in which a totalitarian regime, among other means, represses its people by **controlling** and **manipulating** the **information** conveyed through the media.
- It is still being debated whether **images of violence** presented on **TV** and in **computer games** increase adolescent violence.
- Social media have undone many of the boundaries that prevented fake news from spreading in democracies. On Facebook, Twitter, Telegram, and other social media, people can easily share false information. There are agencies that specialise in disseminating disinformation to achieve certain purposes, e. g., manipulating an election.
- In consumer societies, **advertisements** determine to a high degree what is considered to be a desirable lifestyle. This can be seen as a form of **indoctrination** and **social control**.

Media and communication
- Social networking communities (e. g. Facebook, MySpace, etc.) enable their users to connect with people worldwide.

- Facebook founder Mark Zuckerberg's vision is to make the world a more open space (cf. https://www.facebook.com/zuck, August 8, 2012).
- On a political level, it is said that Facebook played an important role in the so-called Arab Spring (December 2010), as civil resistance was organized and coordinated with the help of the social platform.
- Social media platforms have become increasingly abused for hate posts, rumours, incitement to violence, and offensive posts.
- The protection of users' Internet privacy, as well as the storing and safekeeping of personal data, is a widely disputed point.
- In 2017, Donald Trump was described as "possibly the first 'social media' and 'reality TV' president" in an article on a CNN website. Trump often posted controversial and even false statements, which induced Twitter to become the first platform to add fact-check labels to comments containing misinformation about COVID-19 or the election process. In January 2021, Twitter, Facebook and Instragram banned Trump, but between November 2022 and January 2023 he was reinstated on these social media.

Glossary – The Media

access	Zugang, Zugriff
censorship	(politische) Zensur
credibility	Glaubwürdigkeit
inclination	Bereitschaft
indoctrination	Indoktrination, ideologische Beeinflussung
Internet fraud	Internetbetrug
literacy	Lese- und Schreibfähigkeit
mass communication; mass media	Massenkommunikation, Massenmedien
prime function	Hauptfunktion
public	öffentlich; Öffentlichkeit
spread	sich ausbreiten; Ausbreitung
unilateral	einseitig

Glossary – Globalization

Americanization	Amerikanisierung
anti-globalist	Globalisierungsgegner/-in
backwardness	Rückständigkeit
competition; competitive	Konkurrenz(kampf), Wettbewerb; konkurrenzfähig, konkurrenzorientiert
corporate identity	Firmenimage
crop diseases	Krankheiten von Pflanzen/Saatgut

debt relief	Schuldenerlass, Entschuldung
desertification	Wüstenbildung, Vordringen der Wüste
developing countries; development aid	Entwicklungsländer; Entwicklungshilfe
driving forces of globalization	Antriebskräfte der Globalisierung
drought	Dürre, Dürreperiode
(earth's) atmosphere	Erdatmosphäre
economic growth/prosperity	Wirtschaftswachstum/Wohlstand
emerging markets	Schwellenländer
environmental commitment	Umwelteinsatz
environmental damage	Umweltzerstörung
environmentally friendly	umweltfreundlich
expansion of capitalism	Ausbreitung des Kapitalismus
fair trade	fairer Handel
flood, flooding	Hochwasser, Überschwemmung
global interconnection	globale Querverbindung
global marketplace	globaler Marktplatz
global player/global superpower	Weltfirma/globale Supermacht
global warming	Erderwärmung
greenhouse gas	Treibhausgas
human rights	Menschenrechte
human-generated carbon dioxide	durch Menschen produziertes Kohlen- stoffdioxid
increase profit margins	die Gewinnspanne erhöhen
Industrial Age	Industriezeitalter
industrial nations	Industrieländer/-nationen
interdependence of economy and ecology	gegenseitige Abhängigkeit/Verflechtung von Ökonomie und Ökologie
international stock markets	internationale Börsenmärkte
investment climate	Investitionsbedingungen
labour laws; labour market	Arbeitsgesetze; Arbeitsmarkt
low-wage countries	Niedriglohnländer
mass tourism	Massentourismus
melting of glaciers	Gletscherschmelze
micro-credits	Kleinstkredite
NGO (non-governmental organization)	Nichtregierungsorganisation
outsourcing	Produktionsverlagerung
political turmoil	politischer Aufruhr, politische Turbulenzen

pollution	Verschmutzung
population overshoot, overpopulation, excess of population	Überbevölkerung
poverty	Armut
reduce the cost of production	die Produktionskosten senken
rise in global temperature	weltweiter Temperaturanstieg
robotized production	computergesteuerte Produktion
short-haul flights	Kurzstreckenflüge
surface transport	Bodentransport
supremacy	Vormachtsstellung, Überlegenheit
sustainability	Nachhaltigkeit, Zukunftsfähigkeit
sweatshop	Sweatshop, ausbeuterischer Betrieb
trade	Handel
trademark policy	Markenpolitik
undernutrition; malnutrition	Unterernährung; Mangelernährung
unemployment	Arbeitslosigkeit
working conditions	Arbeitsbedingungen

Science and Ethics

Current Scientific Issues

The beginnings of science date back to ancient societies such as China and Greece when scholars first sought to explain the world through observation and elaboration. During the Renaissance, science experienced a rebirth, and in the wake of the Industrial Revolution, it evolved into what it is today: the foundation of our modern way of life.

Challenges and opportunities

Scientific research aims to explore and explain the world around us and improve our means of coping with difficulties and obstacles. Technology, in turn, is the practical outcome of this research, namely the tools and machines we use to make our lives (seemingly) easier. However, each new technology also harbours risks and creates new dependencies. One simple example will suffice to illustrate this point:
- At the end of the 19th century, the first automobiles were produced. Within a few decades, they replaced horse-drawn vehicles and other means of individual transport. Motor vehicles made travel and transportation of goods easier and cheaper.
- The demand for cars increased during the 20th century, and their production became cheaper. Today, many households in Western societies own at least one car, and some jobs cannot be done without a car, especially in rural regions where public transport systems do not yet meet general mobility needs.
- The demand for cars has also grown in China and emerging markets such as India.

- The need for fossil fuels to run cars has led to increased drilling for oil on land and at sea. At the same time, more and more large roads, highways, and parking lots have been built. As a result, more and more natural habitats have been destroyed.
- The amount of carbon dioxide and other climate-changing exhaust fumes has increased dramatically, contributing decisively to the present climate crisis.

Using the example of the car, it is easy to see that one should always consider the positive and negative potential of technological developments.

Genetic engineering

> **Keywords:**
> **Genetics:** the scientific study of the ways living organisms inherit traits from their ancestors, e. g. a person's eye colour or size.
> **Genome:** the whole hereditary information of an organism encoded in its DNA.
> **Genetic engineering (GE):** a branch of applied biology in which an organism's genome is changed using biotechnology.
> **Genetically modified organisms (GMOs):** living things that have been created through genetic engineering.

Putting a new piece of DNA into a cell can produce a new trait. For example, crops such as cotton plants have been modified so they can poison harmful insects. There have also been experiments with crops that were given genes encoding antifreeze proteins from Arctic fish to make them frost-resistant.

People with genetic disorders can receive gene therapy. The idea is to modify cells or to repair or reconstruct defective genes.

Uses of genetic engineering:
- In agriculture (e. g., to produce stronger and more nutritious crops like golden rice)
- In industry (e. g., to produce biodegradable plastics)
- In biological and medical research (e. g., to create pharmaceutical drugs)
- In experimental medicine (e. g., to cure diseases with gene therapy)

Ethics

Pros and cons of genetically engineered food

In contrast to the classical form of modifying food plants through breeding, modern biotechnology can alter the genetic make-up of crops. Genetically engineered food, also known as genetically modified (GM) food, is made from organisms whose DNA has been changed.

What GM crops are being grown and where:
- In 2015, GM crops were grown in 28 countries, covering over 10 percent of the world's arable land.
- Commercially-grown GM crops include soybeans, maize, cotton, oilseed rape, potatoes, pumpkins, alfalfa, aubergines, sugar beets, and papayas.
- The largest users of GM crops are the US, Brazil, Argentina, India, and Canada.
- Five EU countries grow GM maize: Spain (the largest producer of GM crops in Europe), the Czech Republic, Slovakia, Portugal, Romania, and Poland.
- In Africa, GM crops are grown in South Africa, Burkina Faso, and Sudan, mainly cotton.

The ongoing debate about GM crops

Pros	Cons
GE can help to meet the world's growing need for food. Approximately 50 billion people will need food in 2050, which means agricultural production will have to double within the next few decades. However, the amount of farm land is shrinking. With the help of GE, crops can be altered to make them grow faster, so that they can be harvested in areas with shorter growing seasons. This can also allow introducing some food crops into new areas, or perhaps make two harvests possible in regions where presently there is only one.	**GE has no impact on world hunger.** The war on poverty and malnutrition will be lost if patent laws and intellectual property rights lead to genetically engineered food production being monopolized by a small number of private companies. The owners of the rights to produce GM foods may be reluctant to allow access to technology or genetic material, making developing countries even more dependent on industrialized nations. Commercial interests may override worthy and potentially achievable goals.
GE helps to handle the consequences of climate change such as floods, drought, infestation of pests, etc. because crops with greater stress tolerance can be produced. Moreover, plants that are more resistant to pests do not need to be treated with as much pesticides, which reduces environmental pollution. As farmers do not need to use their vehicles for spraying, the use of GMOs also helps to cut their fuel emissions.	**Variety, not GE, is the answer to climate change challenges.** Crop rotation is an old and proven method. Challenges have to be met by finding even more sustainable solutions.

GE crops are safe because they have to be tested, registered and approved before they are sold and used. They can be controlled and confined to certain areas.	**GE crops are not safe** since registration procedures are often not performed by independent institutions but paid for by GE companies. There are no facts about the long-term effects GM crops could have on humans and on the environment. Confinement to certain areas is not possible because fertilization by insects or wind cannot be controlled. Moreover, GMOs have impacts on the food chain. Scientists say they have reduced butterfly populations in the US, or led to birth defects among other animals.
Our health benefits from GM food. Plants and animals can be engineered to produce larger amounts of essential vitamins and minerals, such as iron. The amounts of protein, carbohydrates, and saturated and unsaturated fats can be altered. Plants and animals could produce useful medicines and even vaccines, solving nutrition and health problems in some parts of the world. In order to offer a healthy diet or even prevention or treatment of diseases for all consumers, specially designed food could be produced.	**GM food might turn out to be a threat to our health.** The many chemical compounds in foods behave in extremely complex ways in the human body. Combining plant genes can threaten allergy sufferers. People also fear links to cancer, reproductive problems and digestive disorders. If a food contains components that have not been part of human diet so far, it is hard to tell what its effects may be over time.
GM food tastes better. Foods can be genetically modified to have more flavour and better texture. GE can also make food last longer so there is less waste.	**Natural food tastes better and is better for your health.** A study suggested our taste buds and our consciences are intertwined. In tests consumers preferred eating food they believed to be organic or ethically produced.

TIPP

Sie finden viele Listen mit *pros and cons* zum Thema *genetic engineering* online. Wählen Sie ein oder zwei aus und schreiben Sie sich weitere wichtige Argumente und Formulierungen heraus.

Glossary – Science and Ethics

achievement of science	Errungenschaft/Leistung der Wissenschaft
artificial insemination	künstliche Befruchtung
development	Entwicklung
DNA (deoxyribonucleic acid)	DNA/DNS
double helix (DNA)	Doppelhelix (DNA)
error rate	Fehlerrate
genetic disorder	genetische Funktionsstörung
genetic engineering	Gentechnik, Genmanipulation
genetic fingerprint	genetischer Fingerabdruck
genetic make-up; genetic constitution	Erbgut; genetische Struktur
genetic modification (GM)	genetische Veränderung
heredity; inheritance	erblich; Vererbung
inherit	erben
insecticide	Insektizid
in-vitro fertilisation	In-vitro-Befruchtung
laboratory	Labor
to modify; modification	modifizieren, verändern; Modifizierung
molecule	Molekül
to mutate; mutation	mutieren; Mutation
non-polluting	umweltfreundlich
organ donor	Organspender
to pass on	vererben
pesticide	Unkrautvernichtungsmittel, Pestizid
progress (no article, no plural)	Fortschritt
reproductive cloning	Klonen von Lebewesen
research (into)	Forschung
research facility	Forschungseinrichtung
resistance	Resistenz
stem cell	Stammzelle
technology	Technologie, Technik
test-tube baby	Retortenbaby
therapeutic cloning	therapeutisches Klonen
transgenic	transgen; genetisch verändert

Schwerpunktthemen für das Abitur 2024

The Ambiguity of Belonging

Ambiguity

> **Keywords:**
> **Ambiguity:** the fact that something has more than one possible meaning and may be difficult to understand or cause confusion.
>
> **Ambiguity competence:** a person's ability to cope effectively with change, to recognise, understand, and productively manage ambiguity, heterogeneity, and uncertainty, as well as to act in different roles.
>
> **Belonging:** the feeling of being comfortable and happy in a particular situation or with a particular group of people because you have a good relationship with them and they fully accept you.

We are constantly challenged by ambiguity in our lives: situations, relationships, or events often leave room for more than one possible and plausible interpretation.
- When looked at from a negative point of view, ambiguity can cause doubt, uncertainty, lack of clarity, and obscurity.
- When looked at from a positive point of view, ambiguity can trigger creativity, inventiveness, and individual initiative.

Causes of ambiguity

There are a number of internal as well as external causes of ambiguity, for example:
- Shifts in perspective
- Clashes between individual needs and social expectations
- Clashes between the demand for conformity and the desire for individual freedom
- Differences between internal and external identification (labelling)

Belonging

In 1943, American psychologist Abraham Maslow presented a theory about a hierarchy of needs. According to Maslow, love and social belonging needs are psychological needs that rank above mere physiological and safety needs. A sense of belonging is the basis of self-esteem and confidence, regardless of whether the groups you belong to are large or small. Here are some aspects that explain the importance of belonging:
- Belonging to a group makes you feel comfortable and connected to other people because you are accepted, respected, or loved.
- Inclusion in a group gives you a feeling of security and support.

- Social belonging needs include family, friendship, intimacy, trust, and acceptance as well as love and affection.

In order to feel a sense of belonging, a person must make an active effort to regularly interact with others. Different experiences and surroundings also play an important part in this process. These factors keep changing, so the various facets of identity are constantly developing and reshaping.

A healthy sense of belonging usually results in a stable identity. It enables us to love ourselves and others, helps us achieve our goals and cope with painful experiences. However, if an individual, for either external or internal reasons, cannot develop a sense of belonging, psychological, physical, and social problems are very likely to occur.

The Ambiguity of Belonging

Cultural belonging has historical, social, and individual dimensions. Whether we belong to certain groups at all and in what ways we are part of them is due to changing factors that shape and reshape our personal, social, and cultural identity. Many aspects of that identity may be ambiguous, as disharmony or even conflicts will sometimes occur in the relationships it involves.

The following sections will help you understand why some people felt an ambiguity of belonging in certain historical and cultural contexts.

TIPP

To understand why the ambiguity of belonging can be a big challenge, it is helpful to look at the history, national identity, and culture of the US. This information will serve as a useful background for discussing the problems and challenges of its present-day multicultural society.

The USA

Over the last 230 years, the US has become the most powerful country in the world. Establishing a democratic nation during its early years was one of its greatest achievements, and the Constitution on which the nation was founded is still regarded as one of the most important political documents in world history. Today, the United States faces multiple challenges both domestically and in foreign affairs. Many people experience ambiguity about their sense of belonging in daily life. However, with its vibrant and multifaceted society, the US continues to hold a nearly mythical attraction for people from all over the world.

Colonization and the concept of the American Dream

On the following pages, you will explore some of the key concepts generally associated with the American Dream, many of which are often addressed in political speeches. Please note that these key concepts often overlap and are closely related.

Keyword:
The American Dream: There is no single definition of what the American Dream actually is, as it varies for each and every American.
The term was first used in 1931 by historian James Truslow Adams in his book *The Epic of America*. Adams defined the American Dream as "that dream of a land in which life should be better and richer and fuller for every man, with opportunity for each according to his ability or achievement."

Freedom

For many immigrants, the first thing they saw upon arriving in New York City by ship in the 19th and the first half of the 20th century was the Statue of Liberty, located on Liberty Island.

Journalist Roger Cohen calls immigration "reinvention", claiming that the countries of immigrants eliminate the anguish of the motherland and invite incomers to the selective forgetfulness of a new identity.[2]

The Statue of Liberty
- It was given to the USA by France in 1886 to celebrate the first 100 years of American independence from Britain (the first centennial).
- The statue is a robed woman holding a lighted torch in her right and a stone tablet in her left hand, displaying the date of the Declaration of Independence (July 4, 1776). She wears a crown with seven spikes representing the seven continents and seven oceans, and underneath her right foot is a broken chain.
- The statue is one of the most famous American icons, symbolizing freedom and enlightenment.

---

[1] Roger Cohen: https://www.nytimes.com/2013/11/29/opinion/cohen-the-quest-to-belong.html

Ellis Island
- This was the place where most immigrants first set foot on American soil.
- It was a federal immigration station from 1892 to 1954 and the gateway to a new and often better life for the majority of immigrants.
- Some immigrants were detained there for legal or medical reasons or even sent back to their home countries.
- It is called "Isle of Hope, Isle of Tears" in a song about the first person to enter the US through Ellis Island, 15-year-old Annie Moore from Ireland. The song is about the expectations of immigrants like Annie but also about the pain they felt after leaving home.

The Puritans
- Towards the end of the 16th century, a movement of English Protestants called Puritans felt that Protestantism in England was not much different from Catholicism.
- Their intention was to purify the Church of England, not to leave it.
- They wished to remain English subjects but free to worship God in their own way.
- In September 1620, a group of 102 people left England for America, sailing on a ship called the *Mayflower,* and arriving in America 65 days later in a place they named Plymouth Bay.
- The Puritans' beliefs and values had a lasting impact on New England society.

The New Canaan
- In the Bible, Canaan was the land God promised to the Israelites. God ordered Moses to lead the people from captivity in Egypt to Canaan – "a land of milk and honey."
- The United States sees itself in this tradition. The idea of America as the "New Canaan" is closely linked to the idea of "Manifest Destiny".
- In the early 1600s, thousands of colonists, sometimes entire families, were sent to America. Jamestown in 1607 (English), Quebec in 1608 (French), and settlements in the region of present-day New York (Dutch) were among the first colonies to be founded.
- Since different nations were contending with each other to explore and make use of America, the country's colonization can be described as a struggle among the leading European nations of the period.
- It is important to keep in mind that the process of colonizing the New World meant an invasion of territories that had been inhabited and controlled by Native Americans for many centuries. Called "Indians" by the settlers, they faced the challenge of dealing with the invasion. The superior arms of the invaders, as well as European diseases, led to the loss of their lands and rights.
- Another group of people also played an important role in the colonization process. Building a colony was hard work, and right from the beginning, the shortage of labour drove some colonizers – for example, the Spanish – to enslave the native population. The English turned towards Africa to find a supply of labour, thus launching the era of the African-American slave trade.

Timeline of immigration I: 1607 to 1802

1607	Colonial immigration begins; English settlers arrive in America.
1619	The importation of African slaves begins.
18th century	About six to seven million slaves are taken to the New World.
1717–1769	36,000 British convicts are transported to America for indentured service.
1790	The Alien Naturalization Act sets the first uniform rules for granting US citizenship by naturalization.
1798	The Alien and Sedition Acts (a set of four laws) give the US President the power to imprison and deport immigrants, as well as to detain non-citizens during times of war. The period of residency requirement is increased from five to 14 years.
1802	The Naturalization Law restores the provisions of the 1790 act by reducing the required residency period to five years again.

Naturalization
The 1790 Alien Naturalization Act distinguished between "citizens" and "not natural born citizens." Only a "free white person" of "good moral character" could be naturalized under this law. The 1802 law required a person to declare their intent to become a US citizen at least three years in advance. This law also granted citizenship to the children of naturalized citizens and to children of US citizens born abroad.

The ambiguity of belonging: 17th and 18th centuries

	Belonged to (in the past) and identified with	Had to cope with	Shaped a new identity due to
First Nations	– native American religions – their tribes/ nations – their natural environment/ settlements – their families and positions	– the European invaders – new illnesses, alcohol – a lack of food – compulsory settlement, involuntary Christianization, the prohibition of their own languages – racism, violence	– their exposure to foreign languages, unknown illnesses, weapons, drugs – the will to survive – subordination in armed conflicts, enslavement – life in reservations; the loss of aboriginal spirituality and the revival of it; the loss of native languages, the ensuing loss of their connection to indigenous culture and their new efforts at revitalizing native languages

The first settlers	– Western culture and Christianity – their ethnic communities – social backgrounds – their families and professions	– providing food, shelter, safety – a new environment – native inhabitants – a lack of work force – Great Britain's influence on the colonies	– a shared Protestant work ethic based on virtues such as hard work, discipline, moderation, honesty and self-improvement – the trial and error method, their learning from native peoples – armed conflict, subordination, treaties – the slave trade and the enslavement of native peoples – the Declaration of Independence, the Bill of Rights
Africans	– native African religions – their tribes/ nations – their natural environment/ settlements – their families and positions	– enslavement – compulsory settlement, involuntary Christianization, the prohibition of native languages – racism, violence	– their sharing the same fate – a new spiritual development of African American religions – the maintenance of African traditions – the creation of new traditions, rites, music styles, etc. and hence of a distinct African American culture

Declaration of Independence

– Written in 1776, one year after the beginning of the American Revolutionary War.
– Drafted by a committee consisting of John Adams, Benjamin Franklin, Thomas Jefferson, Robert Sherman and Robert Livingston.
– Edited by others and revised by the Second Continental Congress, a group of delegates from the 13 colonies.
– States the principles on which the American government and identity are based.
– Lists 27 complaints against King George III to assert the 13 colonies' right to rebellion.
– Declares a complete break with Britain and claims the United States as an independent country.
– Stresses equality: "We hold these truths to be self-evident, that all men are created equal, that they are endowed by their Creator with certain unalienable rights, that among these are life, liberty and the pursuit of happiness."
– Questions the rights of the British king, George III.
– Calls for every American to have the opportunity to pursue their personal dreams (note: at first, women were excluded from this statement).
– Stresses individual rights, while taking into consideration the rights of others.

American Constitution

- Written in 1787.
- The **preamble** of the Constitution declares the intention to form a more perfect union[2], establish justice, ensure domestic tranquillity, provide for the common defense, promote the general welfare, and secure the blessings of liberty for the American people.
- The Constitution established a new democratic form of government that was distinct from the British monarchy.

Bill of Rights

- Written by James Madison in 1791.
- It consists of the first ten amendments to the American Constitution.
- It was written to provide greater protection for personal freedom in response to calls from some states.
- The amendments guarantee unalienable rights for American citizens, such as freedom of religion, freedom of speech and the press, and the right to bear arms.

Going West

After the US government had bought the western part of the country (Louisiana Purchase, 1803), President Thomas Jefferson commissioned an expedition to explore the new territory. The Lewis and Clark Expedition, a group of 42 soldiers and civilians, found a route across the western part of the continent, mapped the newly-acquired region, studied its plants and animals, and established trade with Native American tribes.

Manifest Destiny/The Frontier

Manifest Destiny

- The term "Manifest Destiny" was first used by American journalist John L. O'Sullivan in 1845. In an essay, he pleaded for the annexation of Texas, not only because Texas wanted this, but because it was Americans' "manifest destiny to overspread the continent allotted by Providence for the free development of [their] yearly multiplying millions". In an article about an ongoing conflict with Britain about territories in the Northwest, he stated that the US had the right to claim the whole of Oregon. Sullivan wrote: "And that claim is by the right of our manifest destiny to overspread and to possess the whole of the continent which Providence has given us for the development of the great experiment of liberty and federated self-government entrusted to us."
- The phrase "Manifest Destiny" expressed the belief that the US was destined by God to expand across the North American continent.
- It was used to justify the forced removal of Native Americans from their homelands.
- It was used as a pretext to acquire land in Oregon, Texas, Mexico, and California.

---

[2] Barack Obama took up the idea of "a more perfect union" in a speech he delivered on May 28, 2008, in which he elaborated on the issues of race and inequality in the USA.

– After the Civil War, "the New Manifest Destiny" was invoked as the US purchased Alaska, annexed Hawaii and acquired territories in the western Pacific and Latin America as a result of the Spanish-American War.
– "Manifest Destiny" remained a key philosophy until the end of World War I.

Timeline of immigration II: 1800 to 1849

1807	The African slave trade is abolished, but the domestic slave trade within the US is not affected by the new law.
1814–1850	Native Americans are exempted from naturalization and forced from their tribal land. At the same time the slave population increases dramatically.
1816	Irish immigration to the US begins. Five million Irish immigrants will come to the US during the 19th century. There are Anti-Irish sentiments.
1848	The Treaty of Guadalupe Hidalgo ends the Mexican-American War. The US acquires land that eventually becomes all or parts of California, Nevada, Utah and Arizona, as well as the entire state of Texas, which still includes parts of Kansas, Colorado, Oklahoma, and New Mexico.

The Old West ("Wild West")
For hundreds of years, Native nomads had lived on the Great Plains – the vast flatland located between the Mississippi River and the Rocky Mountains, a landscape with prairie, steppe, and grassland, but hardly any trees and little water. The indigenous tribes knew how to deal with the different weather conditions, the strong winds, and the harsh winters.
At first, only few settlers had the courage and skills to settle down in such inhospitable regions, but after 1865 more people were willing to try. The Civil War had created severe economic problems, so people were forced to migrate to other places to survive. Thousands of settlers moved westward, taking the land from the indigenous peoples, often by brute force. They settled in the Midwest, on the Great Plains, in Texas, in the Rocky Mountains, in the Southwest, and on the West Coast.
The American sense of belonging and concepts of American masculine identity have deep roots in the westward movement.

The Frontier
– A frontier is the margin of land where people live and have built towns, and beyond which the country is wild and unknown.
– The American frontier was an advancing border which marked the lands that had been settled, and it was defined by the westward movement. The Pacific Coast was reached in the second half of the 19th century.
– In the 1960s, President John F. Kennedy used the term "New Frontier" to gain support for his domestic and foreign policies, e.g., to develop science and space exploration.

Life, liberty and the pursuit of happiness

Civil War, Reconstruction, and the rise of industrial America (1860–1900)

- The northern and southern states were very different socially, economically, and politically (North = increasingly industrial and commercial, South = largely agrarian).
- African American slavery was the central point of political crisis. Northerners wanted to limit the spread of slavery or abolish it altogether. Southerners generally wanted to maintain and even expand it.
- When Abraham Lincoln, an abolitionist, became president in 1860, eleven southern states decided to secede. They formed an independent government called the Confederate States of America in which slavery would be protected.
- The Northern states that remained loyal to the government were called the Union.
- Four states stayed in the Union even though they allowed slavery (Kentucky, Missouri, Maryland, and Delaware).
- The conflict resulted in the Civil War (1861–1865), which was won by the Union. Almost as many Americans were killed in the Civil War as in all the nation's other wars combined.
- Slavery was abolished in the entire US, and about four million slaves were freed (Emancipation).
- Reconstruction (1865–1877): The South rebuilt damaged property and changed its economy so that it no longer depended on unpaid slave labour. However, the "New South" remained largely agrarian.
- Many former slaves had no choice but to return to essentially the same lives as before Emancipation. Black farmers now worked for white landowners as so-called sharecroppers. The landowners allowed them to use parts of their land and, in return, received a share of the crops the tenants grew. Sharecroppers usually grew cotton, tobacco, rice, sugar, and some other crops. Landowners often dictated what they had to grow, manipulated prices, and put pressure on the tenants by threatening not to renew the lease.
- In the decades following the Civil War, the Northern economy experienced a boost: old industries such as railroad construction expanded to the West, and new industries such as petroleum refining, steel manufacturing, and electrical power production emerged.
- Rise of American capitalism: industrial growth produced a new class of wealthy industrialists and an affluent middle class in the Northern states. The working class grew as well (blue collar workers).
- Millions of newly-arrived immigrants and even larger numbers of migrants from rural areas formed the labour force that made industrialization possible.
- Technology and industrialization led to more competition and falling prices for farm products. Many young people from rural regions moved to cities to find jobs.

The 13th Amendment

The 13th Amendment to the Constitution was ratified in December 1865. It states that "neither slavery nor involuntary servitude" shall exist within the United States.

Timeline of immigration III: 1850 to 1899

1862	The First Homestead Act encourages westward migration. Public land is offered to citizens and immigrants at $1.25 per acre or less.
1863–1869	Some 10,000 Irish and 15,000 to 20,000 Chinese labourers are hired to help construct the first transcontinental railroad.
1875	The Supreme Court declares the regulation of immigration a federal responsibility.
1880s	Congress begins to pass immigration legislation.
1880s	The first great wave of European immigrants arrives. Anti-Chinese riots spread. In some areas, Chinese are not allowed to own land.
1882	The Immigration Act restricts certain groups from immigrating, such as criminals and people with mental illnesses. The Chinese Exclusion Act prohibits the immigration of Chinese labourers for ten years.
1886	The Statue of Liberty is unveiled. The "huddled masses yearning to be free" are invited to immigrate.

The 14th and 15th Amendments
- The 14th Amendment, ratified in 1868, granted citizenship to all persons born or naturalized in the United States, including former slaves.
- It guaranteed all citizens "equal protection of the laws".
- The 15th Amendment, ratified in 1870, granted voting rights to African American men.

From rags to riches
The increasing economic power of the USA was an important pull factor for people living in unstable conditions. The vision of starting with nothing and becoming a wealthy citizen, an essential part of the American Dream, often came true in the early days.
Here are some of the factors that fuelled economic growth:
- The discovery of plentiful natural resources (e.g. coal, copper, iron, oil)
- The gold and silver rushes (e.g. the California Gold Rush from 1849 to 1855 or the Silver Rush starting after the Comstock Lode was discovered in Nevada in 1859)
- The invention and manufacture of new products, e.g. the telephone, the refrigerator, and the sewing machine
- Manufacturing procedures made more efficient by commercial use of electricity
- The new possibility of mass production after the introduction of the assembly line by Henry Ford
- Cheap labour due to the steady influx of immigrants (cf. page 69)
- Growing infrastructure (e.g. railway systems) and increased distribution efficiency
- Increasing consumption of consumer goods by those who profited from the rise of capitalism

> During the later 19th century, vertical social mobility was more likely than later on. However, the dream of moving "from from rags to riches" remained unfulfilled for most poor people, and they continued to belong to the specific social, economic, and ethnic groups into which they were born.

The ambiguity of belonging: 19th century

	Belonged to/ identified with	Had to cope with	Shaped a new identity due to
White Americans	– Western culture and Christianity – their settlements – their social backgrounds – their families and their professions	– providing food, shelter and safety during the westward expansion – the nation's changing political landscape – issues between the North and the South, including slavery – the Civil War – the reconstruction of the South – unemployment and the economic crisis due to the Civil War – immigration	– the necessity of being brave, strong and skilled, and their enormous will power – the concept of "Manifest Destiny" – the right to vote, social and political reforms, the forming of political parties – the effects of the secession of the South – industrialization – new immigration acts – the Homestead Act – the activities of labour unions

The early 20th century and the "Roaring Twenties"

- The early 20th century was an era of business expansion and progressive reform in the US.
- Progressive Era (1896–1917): The Progressives strove to improve American society by addressing the problems caused by industrialization, urbanization, and immigration. They wanted to make big business more responsible through various kinds of regulations (such as fighting against corruption and improving the working conditions in factories), improve the living conditions in slums, conserve natural resources, protect the environment, and revitalize democracy. They initiated several election reforms, and one of the results was women's suffrage in 1920 (19th Amendment).
- Initially, the US wanted to stay neutral during World War I, but in 1917, it declared war on Germany because of the Germans' submarine warfare in the North Atlantic and their attempts to convince Mexico to form a secret alliance against the US.
- In 1918, Germany and its allies (Austria-Hungary, Bulgaria, and the Ottoman Empire) surrendered to the Allied Powers (Britain, France, Russia, Italy, Belgium, Serbia, Montegro, and the US).
- There was a sharp depression in the US in the second half of the 1910s.

- The 1920s were a decade of economic growth and new prosperity, but also a period of nationalistic policies, repudiation of internationalism, and rejection of the reforms of the Progressive Era.
- In 1924, the National Origins Act limited the number of immigrants to 164,000 per year, discriminated against immigrants from Southern and Eastern Europe and barred Asians completely.
- Automobile manufacturing was the most successful industry and had a massive influence on American society. Detroit was an important production site.
- The term "Roaring Twenties" is often used for the 1920s because many young people rebelled against conventions and adopted a more liberal lifestyle. New forms of popular culture and leisure activities boomed. However, the term is an exaggeration, as life continued along traditional lines in many places. Moreover, the decade witnessed the strengthening of a Christian fundamentalist movement, which in 1919 had achieved the prohibition of alcohol, and a revival of the Ku Klux Klan.

The Great Depression and World War II

- In October 1929, a stock market crash put an end to the phase of prosperity. The Great Depression began. People's jobs, savings, homes and farms were threatened.
- Eventually over a quarter of the American work force was unemployed.
- In 1933, Franklin Roosevelt became President and initiated the so-called New Deal, which was characterized by large-scale social programs and government participation in economic activities. It restored people's faith in democracy, but could not bring about complete economic recovery.
- In 1939, World War II broke out. At first the US did not want to become involved, but entered the war after the Japanese attack on Pearl Harbor (Hawaii) in December 1941. In 1945, the Allies (Britain, the US, the Soviet Union and 21 combatants) won the war against the Axis powers (Germany, Japan and Italy).

Postwar

America's participation in World War II influenced the country in almost every aspect of life:
- Millions were conscripted into the armed forces and sent across the globe.
- War industries created a huge demand for labour, so millions moved to the Atlantic, Pacific and Gulf coasts, where most defence plants were located.
- As a result, the US economy was doing better at the end of World War II than the economies of other countries.
- The government provided money for veterans to attend college and purchase homes and farms.
- American society began to prosper again.
- The white population experienced greater upward mobility than minority groups.
- Due to their exclusion from the American Dream, African and Hispanic Americans as well as women started to demand civil rights and full freedom more vehemently.
- Shortly after the end of World War II, the Cold War began between the US and the Soviet Union as well as their respective allies. In 1949, NATO was created and in

response the Soviet Union formed the Warsaw Pact. Several major crises occurred in the four decades that the Cold War lasted.

Consequences of the westward movement

The westward movement was often idealized, but had tragic consequences, especially the brutal treatment of the First Nations, the destruction of nature and the near extinction of some wildlife, such as the buffalo.

Land degradation due to false farming methods was one of the main factors that resulted in the Dust Bowl in the 1930s, a period of severe dust storms in some states in the Midwest and Southwest. Severe drought exacerbated the process. As a consequence, many farmers had to abandon their land and headed west to find work. For example, 15 percent of the inhabitants of Oklahoma fled the state, mostly using the newly built Route 66. Due to the Great Depression, competition was tough. A lot of people experienced homelessness, hunger and poverty.

As a consequence of the Dust Bowl the Soil Conservation Service was founded by the government, which to this day has been putting efforts into preserving and conserving natural resources.

The Dust Bowl became the subject of many cultural works. In his famous novel, *The Grapes of Wrath,* John Steinbeck described the lives of migrant workers who had been displaced, and folksinger Woody Guthrie sang many songs about the misery of the people who had to seek refuge from the storms. The federal government also hired numerous photographers to document the crisis. These artists captured the struggles of the migrants and made people in other parts of the country aware of the immense suffering caused by the Dust Bowl.

Push and pull factors for immigration

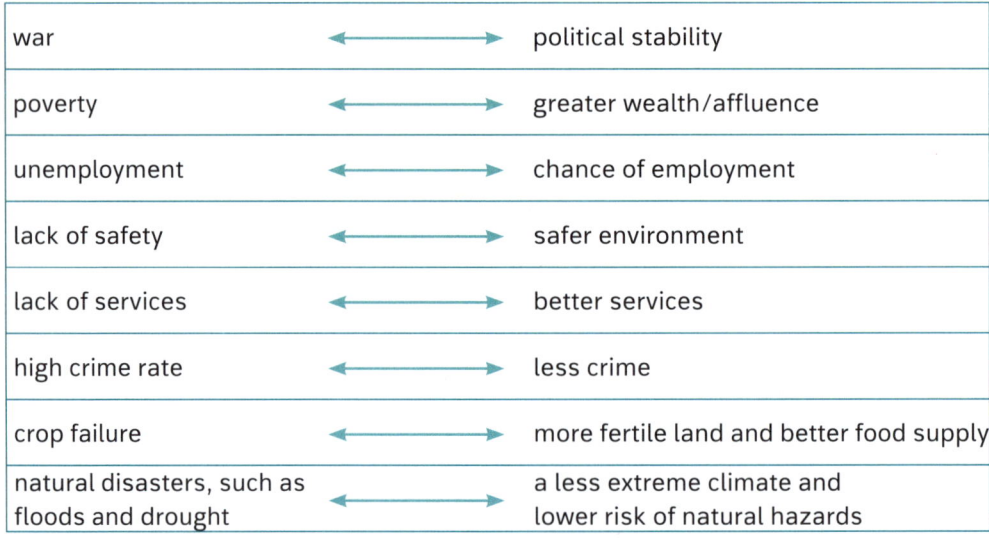

war	political stability
poverty	greater wealth/affluence
unemployment	chance of employment
lack of safety	safer environment
lack of services	better services
high crime rate	less crime
crop failure	more fertile land and better food supply
natural disasters, such as floods and drought	a less extreme climate and lower risk of natural hazards

The American Dream today

> **Keywords:**
>
> **Multicultural society:** a society that accepts various ethnic groups and their cultural heritages as equal.
>
> **Salad bowl:** an integration model that values cultural diversity and encourages immigrants to combine their cultures with others, while maintaining their traditions, values, and native languages ("unity in diversity").
>
> **Melting pot:** an integration model in which various ethnic groups do not retain their cultural heritage but amalgamate into one new nation. The term was first used by Jean de Crèvecoeur in his 1782 *Letters from an American farmer.*
>
> **Cultural assimilation:** the process by which ethnic minorities adjust to the dominant culture by acquiring new customs and attitudes through contact and communication.

Is the US a melting pot or a salad bowl?

The debate about whether the US is a melting pot or a salad bowl has been ongoing for quite some time. Some argue that it is a melting pot because many people with different backgrounds have adopted American traditions and speak English, even though no official language has been declared by the government. However, others see the US as a salad bowl because different groups maintain distinct cultures. For example, Chinese Americans still celebrate Chinese New Year, Indian Americans still celebrate Diwali, and Mexican Americans still celebrate the Day of the Dead. American culture is, in fact, a mix of hundreds of different cultures. It is so complex that it cannot be easily defined.

Inequality and the American Dream

For a long time, the American Dream made the United States the world's strongest magnet for immigrants, and many people still believe in it today. It promises that anyone who works hard and plays by the rules can achieve a good life. However, in recent decades, the concept of the American Dream has been viewed more critically as it has become clear that not many people of poor backgrounds are able to make it to the top. In 2017, a UN report stated that the American Dream was "rapidly becoming the American Illusion." The country now has the lowest rate of social mobility among rich countries. Income inequality is high, and many citizens live in poverty.

While in the past, the American middle class personified the American Dream, it has been shrinking in the last few decades. In 1971, 61 percent of adults lived in middle-class households, but in 2021 that number had fallen to 50 percent. This is partly due to the fact that incomes did not rise as much in middle-class households as they did in upper-income households. Another factor behind the decline is the outsourcing of classic white-collar jobs, such as data processing and accounting, to other parts of the globalized world.

In the United States, income inequality leads to disparities in health and healthcare. Studies have demonstrated that individuals with higher incomes have better health outcomes. One reason for this is the country's dependence on private health insurance. Inequality in education is also prevalent, with affluent schools spending far more money on students than their impoverished counterparts (in 2015, $1,500 more per student). High-income families can afford to reside in affluent neighbourhoods that provide excellent education, whereas children from low-income families are often confined to under-resourced schools.

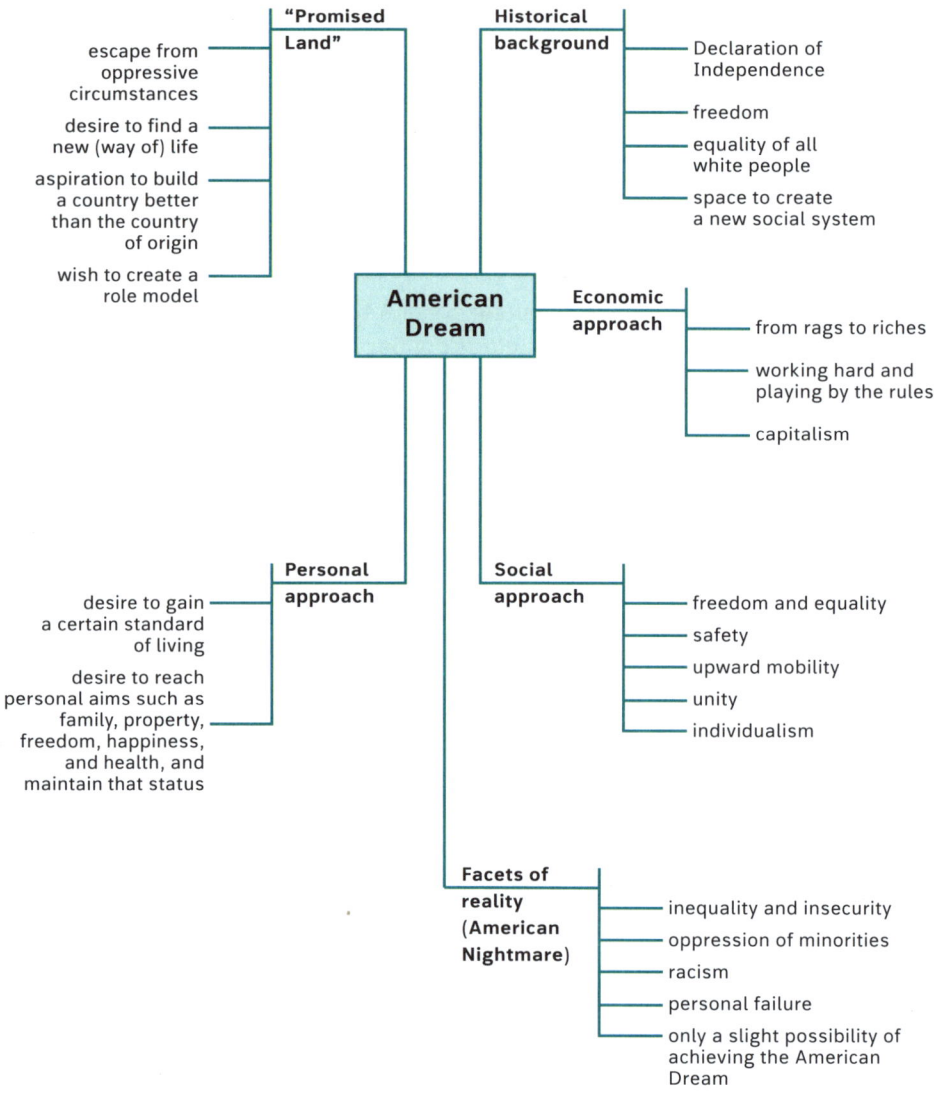

Diversity and its Consequences

Timeline of immigration IV: 1900 to 1949

1908	The play *The Melting Pot* opens in Washington, and its title becomes a metaphor for the United States.
1910	Angel Island Immigration Station opens in San Francisco Bay. Immigrants from 84 countries arrive. The largest groups come from China, Japan, India, Mexico, and the Philippines.
1922	The US Supreme Court decides that Asians cannot apply for citizenship because they are not considered "free white persons".
1924	Indian Citizenship Act: all Native Americans born in the US are citizens by birth. The Immigration Act (Johnson-Reed Act) shuts the "Golden Door" to America for many nations by limiting the number of immigrants to 164,000 per year, discriminating against immigrants from southern and eastern Europe and barring Asians completely.
1942	Bracero Program: Due to a labour shortage in agriculture, the US government issues temporary work permits to millions of Mexicans. The program continues until 1964. President Roosevelt signs Executive Order 9066, placing Japanese Americans into internment camps. The policy is upheld until 1944.
1943	Chinese Exclusion Repeal Act: China is placed under the same immigration regulations as European countries because it is the most important ally of the US in the Pacific war against Japan. Even though the act is regarded as a positive development, it is still restrictive.
1948	Displaced Persons Act: 200,000 displaced persons from Europe are admitted for permanent residence.

Passing a series of **alien land laws**, the US tried to discourage "non-desirable" immigrants from settling permanently by limiting their ability to own land and property. Although these laws did not name any specific groups, they mainly aimed to prevent Chinese and Japanese immigrants from becoming landowners.

Around the turn of the 20th century, resentment against Asians grew, and the idea of a "Yellow Peril" was cultivated. This racist metaphor was used in many Western societies at that time. After the Chinese Exclusion Act of 1882 had stopped immigration from China, a lot of new Japanese immigrants arrived in the states on the West Coast. Many of them took up tenant farming and became very successful, which increased antipathies against them and fuelled an exclusionary movement.

Social tensions and the ambiguity of belonging

The United States prides itself on its ethnic diversity and the ideal of a nation made up of people with various ethnic backgrounds, religions, values, traditions, and languages living peacefully together. However, the US is also a nation with severe social tensions, as revealed in 2021 by the Pew Research Center, which compared data from 17 advanced economies. In that survey, 90 percent of Americans said that there were conflicts between people who supported different political parties. 70 percent said that conflicts existed between people with different ethnic or racial backgrounds, and 74 percent stated that racial and ethnic discrimination was a serious problem in the US.

Major social issues in the United States

- Racism: The US has a long history of discriminatory policies, and systemic racism has never stopped. Presently, a conservative backlash to the progress sought by civil rights activists can be observed. There has also been growing violence against non-white people, including police brutality.
- Education: Some of the most common problems include overcrowding, budget cutbacks, lack of security in schools, school closures, lack of technical equipment, low income for teachers, outdated training methods, and lack of parental involvement.
- Healthcare: Most Americans agree that their health system urgently needs to be reformed, but they cannot agree on how to do it. The country spends more per person on health-care costs than any other developed country in the world, but health quality is quite low. Around 1 in 10 adults have medical debt, and some three million people owe more than $10,000. Black adults, people with disabilities, and people in poor health are most likely to have high medical debt. The US health system was not equipped to handle the COVID pandemic well.
- Wage inequality: In 2020, 90 percent of working Americans received only 60.2 percent of all wages. In 2021, the top 10 percent had 70 percent of all wealth in the country.
- Poverty: The problem of poverty is interconnected with issues such as homelessness, lack of educational opportunities, racism, and drug abuse. African Americans have the highest poverty rates.
- Voting rights: In 2013, the Supreme Court issued a new ruling with regard to the Voting Rights Act. Until then, states with a history of racial discrimination had to get certification that any election change they planned would not be discriminatory. The Supreme Court argued that such requirements were no longer necessary. Since then there have been repeated efforts at infringing voting rights. For example, in some states, stricter voter ID laws have been imposed, voting times have been shortened, and registration has been restricted.
- Hostility towards the LGBTQ+ community and their allies: In recent years, conservative media and politicans have increasingly targeted gay and trans people. The attacks have started seeping into the law. The most prominent example is the "Parental Rights in Education" bill, which was passed in Florida in 2022. It banned public school teachers from instructing their students about topics such as sexual orientation or gender identity, which is why opponents call it the "Don't Say Gay" bill.

Tasks and challenges for the US

- The 2020 Census showed a population growth to 331 million in the previous decade, revealing the second lowest growth rate ever recorded. The median age in the US today is 38, which means Americans are getting older. There are more citizens 80 years and older than two years old or younger. More than 40 percent of Americans identify as people of colour, and all of the nation's population growth is attributable to them. This demographic shift has to be widely recognized and measures against discrimination, anti-immigrant sentiments, and the increasing wealth gap have to be taken.
- The Biden-Harris administration must continue to address the impact of the COVID-19 pandemic, develop strategies for economic recovery, and increase efforts to tackle climate change. Moreover, they must navigate the complex geopolitical landscape, including the ongoing war between Russia and Ukraine, and work towards promoting peace and stability around the world.

Timeline of immigration V: 1950 to 2022

1954	Ellis Island closes.
1976	President Gerald Ford proclaims that the internment of citizens of Japanese origin during World War II was a national mistake.
1980	Some four million illegal immigrants (about half from Mexico) are estimated to be in the US.
2001	9/11: Terrorists attack the World Trade Center in New York and the Pentagon in Washington.
2002	The Enhanced Border Security and Visa Entry Reform Act regulates the inspection and admission of aliens and the issuance of visas.
2004	The Minuteman Project is founded, an organization of civilians that patrols the US-Mexico border.
2006	The Secure Fence Act allows 700 miles of fence along the Mexican border.
2007	The Department of Homeland Security estimates that there are 11.8 million illegal immigrants in the US, 59 percent of them from Mexico.
2010	Support Our Law Enforcement and Safe Neighborhoods Act: a restrictive immigration law in the state of Arizona is enacted. Among other things, officers are allowed to arrest people upon "suspicion" of illegal states. Many provisions are afterwards overturned by the Supreme Court.
2012	Iraqi citizens are granted special immigrant status for service during the Iraq War.
2014	The Emergency Afghan Allies Extension Act of 2014 grants immigrant visas for Afghans who supported the US in the War in Afghanistan.

Security
Social security and social welfare

The US social welfare structure has been shaped both by tradition and by changing economic and social conditions.

Important facts

- There is no national health insurance system in the US, and people are not obliged to have health insurance. In 2018, about 14 percent of the population was uninsured.
- Most citizens are insured by a combination of private insurance and several federal and state programs. Many Americans have group plans based on employer-sponsored health insurance. Medicaid (for the poor) and Medicare (for people aged 65 and older) are two of various healthcare programs funded by the government.
- In 2010, President Barack Obama's administration introduced the Affordable Care Act (ACA), commonly known as "Obamacare". Its primary goals were to make affordable health care available to more people, to expand the Medicaid program, and to support innovative medical care delivery. There have been attempts to repeal the law, but the Supreme Court has upheld it three times. Increasing numbers of people have selected ACA, and the Biden-Harris administration has strengthened the program. Healthcare costs have been lowered, maternity care has been improved, and a drug control strategy, as well as a new strategy to tackle the mental health crisis, has been released.
- The Temporary Assistance for Needy Families Program (TANF) provides cash assistance to poor families. The grant requires that all recipients of social welfare must find work within three years after joining the program and can only benefit from it for 60 months within their lifetime.
- The Supplemental Nutrition Assistance Program, previously known as "food stamps," is another form of aid for the needy.
- All the US states have individual unemployment insurance programs, and the benefit amounts vary from state to state. The standard duration of compensation is six months for people who have become unemployed through no fault of their own.

The gun debate

The US has an estimated 120.5 firearms per 100 residents and gun-related violence has steadily increased in recent years. According to statistics published by the Centers for Disease Control and Prevention, more Americans died of gun-related injuries in 2020 than in any other year on record, with more than half of the deaths resulting from suicides. Additionally, the FBI has reported an increase in active shooter incidents, such as mass shootings. In 2000, there were only three such incidents, but by 2020, the number had risen to 40. Despite the shocking figures, the debate over proposals to limit Americans' access to firearms is highly controversial, as gun ownership is a right protected by the Second Amendment to the Constitution, which states: "A well-regulated Militia, being necessary to the security of a free State, the right of the people to keep and bear Arms, shall not be infringed." Many Americans are in favour of enforced gun control, but the National Rifle Association (NRA) is a powerful gun lobby with a substantial budget that it is able to influence politicians.

Background information

- Historically, guns were necessary for pioneers to survive and protect their families from wild animals and marauding groups.
- As farming and hunting were the main ways of sustaining a family for a long time, the use of guns was a normal everyday activity, like using tools.
- Today, approximately 30 percent of American adults own a gun, with most of them being white males. Two-thirds of them say that protection is the major reason for owning a gun.
- There are three types of self-defense laws in the US. Stand-your-ground laws provide that people may resort to deadly force if they believe that it is necessary to defend themselves or others against certain violent crimes. Duty to retreat laws require a person who is attacked or defending someone else to not use deadly force but to avoid danger by retreating if they can do so safely. Castle doctrine laws allow people to use deadly force without retreating if they are attacked in their homes, yards, vehicles or places of work. Many states have enacted stand-your-ground laws, while others use a blend of self-defense laws. States that impose a duty to retreat also have castle doctrine laws.

What are the arguments for and against gun control?

Pro	Con
Since many crimes involve guns, restricting gun ownership would reduce the gun-related crime rate. It would also reduce the number of suicides.	Criminals will always be able to obtain weapons and rarely use legal ways to do so in the first place. Therefore, gun control laws would not reduce the gun-related crime rate. In addition, victims can at least defend and protect themselves and their families if they own guns. Gun control would leave them helpless.
Mass shootings committed by teen-agers, mentally disturbed people, or supporters of zero tolerance policies would no longer be possible or would at least be drastically reduced.	Police are simply unable to protect all citizens from violent crimes. Therefore, it is useful to allow citizens to carry weapons themselves.
A crime victim who has a gun might be killed instantly because the criminal feels threatened.	Crimes are often prevented because criminals suspect that possible victims might possess a gun.
The Second Amendment was written in order to protect the rights of armed militias, i.e. citizen-soldiers, which were organized by state and local governments. It was not meant to protect individual people's use of firearms.	The Second Amendment protects civilians' right to own a gun.

Legal private gun ownership increases the risk of guns falling into the hands of children and therefore leads to more fatal accidents.	Women, disabled people, pensioners, and children face a higher risk of becoming crime victims because they have no means of self-defense.
Suicides, crimes of passion, and other impulsive acts are easier to commit if guns are highly available.	Gun control laws give too much power to the government and may lead to tyranny.
Crimes that might not have been very harmful may lead to killings if guns are involved.	Banning guns will lead to a much larger and better-organized black market for illegal firearms.
More gun control laws are needed to protect women from domestic abuse and stalking.	Reasonable gun control and educational programs can replace bans on guns.
Legally owned guns are often stolen and used by criminals.	It is unfair to restrict the recreational and peaceful use of guns, such as hunting and sport shooting.

TIPP

You can find many detailed pro-and-con lists, as well as interesting articles on the gun debate online.
There are examples of possible exam tasks on gun laws on pages 158 and 174.

American Society and Human Rights

In a country in which "life, liberty and the pursuit of happiness" are anchored in the constitution, the question of human rights is crucial. One point of controversy is the death penalty, as the US is one of 55 (as of 2022) countries in the world still making use of it.

INFO

Check www.deathpenaltyinfo.org or www.amnestyusa.org for more information.

Human rights issues have been raised with regard to some policies introduced after the 9/11 attacks, including the treatment of prisoners at Guantanamo Bay Detention Camp.

Racial profiling
Racial profiling is a highly controversial issue. Amnesty International USA defines it as "the targeting of individuals and groups by law enforcement officials, even partially, on the basis of race, ethnicity, national origin, or religion [...]".
Examples of racial profiling have been documented and illustrated by governmental agencies and private groups. They suggest that minorities are much more often the subject of routine traffic stops and other security-related practices. A variety of federal

and state laws provide potential redress to individuals who claim that their rights are violated by race-based law enforcement practices and policies.

Black Lives Matter
After the shooting of an African American teenager called Trayvon Martin in 2013, the activist movement Black Lives Matter (BLM) started campaigning against racial prejudice and discrimination. In May 2020, George Floyd, an African American, was killed by a white police officer who knelt on his neck for over nine minutes. Worldwide protests followed. Even though President Donald Trump's reactions and measures divided the nation still further and fuelled escalation, the protests became a catalyst for some changes. Neck restraints have been banned by many large police departments. BLM still holds protests and organizes campaigns against police brutality, killings of black people, racial profiling, and racial inequality in the US.

INFO Capitol Hill riots

President Donald Trump lost in the 2020 presidential elections but refused to admit his defeat. On January 6, 2021, while senators were meeting to certify the election results, Trump addressed a large crowd of supporters and urged them to march "peacefully" to the Capitol. However, he also claimed there had been massive voter fraud and told his audience to "fight like hell". After that, hundreds of people broke into Congress, vandalizing offices and shouting death threats. Many of them were carrying weapons. It took the police about four hours to restore order. More than 140 people were injured in the storming. Five people died shortly before, during or after these events. President Joe Biden said that on that day the rioters had "held a dagger at the throat of America and American democracy."

Foreign Affairs

With a colonial history before its independence, the United States initially chose to stay out of global politics for more than a century. Its involvement in two world wars in the first half of the 20th century led to a change in its foreign policy from isolationism to interventionism:
- Following World War II, the American ideal of freedom and democracy became an outright **ideology opposing the communist system**. In 1947, President Truman formulated the **Truman Doctrine,** which would define US foreign policy in the coming decades. Truman stated that it was "the policy of the United States to support free peoples who are resisting attempted subjugation by armed minorities or by outside pressures."
- Between 1947 and 1989, the main aim of the US was to restrict the expansion of the Soviet Union. This period also shaped post-Cold War US policy and led to a new concept of **preemptive intervention** to protect national security, as seen in the wars in Afghanistan and Iraq.

- The key to American foreign policy is its self-image as a nation offering the promise of **freedom and democracy**, which is founded on the concept of **Manifest Destiny** (see page 68).
- Since the end of the Cold War with the Soviet Union, the United States has been the world's foremost power.
- Despite diplomatic and political controversies under former President Trump, the US remained Germany's most important partner outside the EU during his presidency.
- Since Russia's attack on Ukraine, the Biden administration has provided massive security assistance and economic support to Ukraine. All NATO states' actions are defensive and aimed at ensuring that the war does not escalate and spread beyond Ukraine.

Timeline of American foreign policy

The following table gives you an overview of the most important challenges and choices of US foreign policy.

1898	Spanish-American War	Conflict over Spain's Pacific possessions (Cuba, Puerto Rico, the Philippines, Guam and other islands).
1914–1918	World War I	1917: The US enters the war after Germany's return to unrestricted submarine warfare.
1939–1945	World War II (Pearl Harbor 1941)	The US enters the war after the Japanese attack on the American fleet in Hawaii.
1945	Hiroshima and Nagasaki	Atomic bombings by the US kill between 129,000 and 226,000 people, most of them civilians. Shortly afterwards Japan surrenders to the Allies.
1947	Truman Doctrine	President Truman (1945–1953) pledges support for anti-communist nations; beginning of the Cold War.
1950–1953	Korean War	Invasion of South Korea by troops from North Korea, a socialist state; UN troops are sent to support South Korea; the US provide about 90 percent of the military personnel.
1961	Bay of Pigs invasion	Attempted invasion of Cuba by Cuban exiles with the aim to overthrow Fidel Castro's communist government; the attempt is supported by the US, but fails.
1955–1975	Vietnam War	War between North and South Vietnam; the Soviet Union and the US are directly involved.
1991	Gulf War	Reaction to the Iraqi invasion of Kuwait by 35 countries led by the US; Kuwait is liberated.

1999	NATO bombardment of Yugoslavia	Aerial bombing campaign during the Kosovo War; the Yugoslav army withdraws; a UN peacekeeping mission ensues.
2001	Invasion of Iraq and Afghanistan	Reaction to terrorist attacks on New York and Washington by Al Qaeda (9/11).
2002	"War on Terror"/ "Global War on Terrorism (GWOT)"	Global counterterrorism military campaign initiated by the US.
2003–2011	Iraq War	A US-led coalition led by the US invades Iraq, claiming the country possesses weapons of mass destruction and supports terrorism; it overthrows the government of Saddam Hussein; an insurgency against the coalition forces and the new government ensues.
2011	Killing of Osama Bin Laden	Secret CIA-led operation by US Navy SEALs approved by President Barack Obama.
2013–present	Global surveillance disclosures	Leaked classified documents reveal NSA surveillance of both domestic and foreign nationals, including heads of government.
2013–2022	Syria crisis	US-led international coalition fights the Islamic State; US supports the Autonomous Administration of North and East Syria and its armed wing, the Syrian Democratic Forces.
2022	Russia-Ukraine War	US massively supports Ukraine.

9/11 – The war on terror

After the end of the Cold War and the collapse of the Soviet Union, the US was left as the world's sole superpower. However, as the timeline above illustrates, it has remained engaged in military actions abroad, either punitively or in peacekeeping efforts.

On September 11, 2001, four passenger airliners were hijacked by terrorists. Two were flown into the Twin Towers of the World Trade Centre in New York, causing them to catch fire and collapse. The third plane crashed into the Pentagon, and the fourth into a field in Pennsylvania. The attacks killed more than 3,000 people.

As a consequence, President George W. Bush declared a "War on Terror." In his address to a Joint Session of Congress on September 20, 2001, he announced that nations providing aid or shelter to terrorists would be pursued as enemies. This led to the invasions of Afghanistan in 2001 and Iraq in 2003, aimed at pre-empting and preventing attacks by taking offensive actions to ensure American security.

> **Pre-emption versus prevention**
> In international law, it is generally accepted that a state has the right to take action against another state that is manifestly about to attack (**pre-emption**). However, **taking action against** a state that could pose a threat in the future (**prevention**) is less accepted.

The USA Patriot Act (full title: "Uniting and Strengthening America by Providing Appropriate Tools Required to Intercept and Obstruct Terrorism Act") was passed six weeks after the 9/11 attacks. Its goals are to enhance American security by strengthening law enforcement and intelligence agencies so they can more easily identify terrorists. The Patriot Act has been widely and controversially discussed.

- Supporters claim that it has been helpful in a number of investigations and has led to the arrest of terrorists.
- Critics believe that the act gives the government too much power, threatens civil liberties, and undermines democracy.

Surveillance powers have been increased in four areas:

- Record searches: The government is allowed to check personal activity records.
- Secret searches: The government's right to search private property without giving notice to the owner has been expanded.
- Intelligence searches: The FBI can secretly conduct a physical search or wiretap on American citizens to obtain evidence of crime without proving probable cause.
- "Trap and Trace" searches: Investigators have more authority than before to survey the content of communication, such as recording the URLs that someone visited.

Homeland security has become even more important in the 21st century. After the 9/11 attacks, the anthrax attacks in 2001, and the Boston Marathon bombing on Patriot's Day in 2013, Americans have felt less safe. However, it has also become clear that increased surveillance comes at the cost of privacy and freedom.

Economy and Ecology in the USA

Capitalism

> **Two definitions of capitalism**
> An economic system in which investment in and ownership of the means of production, distribution, and exchange of wealth is made and maintained chiefly by private individuals or corporations. (Webster's Concise College Dictionary 1999)
>
> An economic system in which the means of production and distribution are privately or corporately owned and development is proportionate to the accumulation and reinvestment of profits gained in a free market. (American Heritage Dictionary 2009)

Prior to the Great Depression of the 1930s, the US was a capitalist economy focused on the free market and minimal government intervention. However, due to the widespread unemployment and poverty caused by the Depression, many believed that this capitalist economy had failed. In response, President Franklin D. Roosevelt introduced an economic bill of rights that granted certain basic rights to all citizens, such as education, healthcare and housing. As a result, the government assumed economic responsibility for its citizens. Today, the American economy is considered a "mixed economy", which means that while freedom of choice, competition, and private property remain important factors, government involvement has increased and now accounts for approximately one third of the nation's economy.

Currently, the degree of government involvement is a source of controversy, particularly given the persistent under-performance of America's economy. Critics argue that the present economic system seems unable to offer equal opportunities and choices to every American.

Wealth inequality is defined as the uneven distribution of assets within a population. The United States displays wider disparities of wealth between the rich and poor than any other major developed nation, and this gap continues to widen. Possible reasons for this include the impact of technology (resulting in fewer low-skill jobs and more jobs in low labour cost countries), current tax rates, and shifting social norms that seem to more readily accept soaring salaries than in the past

Climate change, global warming, and the energy question

Although scientists have known about the greenhouse effect of gases such as CO_2 for over 100 years, the debate over whether or not human activity is the cause of global warming and climate change continues.

One the one hand, supporters of the pro arguments, including the US National Academies of Science, NASA, and many others, contend that
- greenhouse gas levels are rising due to human activities such as burning fossil fuels and deforestation
- these activities result in significant climate changes, such as global warming, loss of sea ice, glacier retreat, more intense heat waves, stronger hurricanes, and more droughts
- immediate international action is required to prevent dire consequences.

On the other hand, associations such as the Heritage Foundation and the American Association of Petroleum Geologists, and many others, argue that
- human-generated greenhouse gas emissions are too small to significantly change the Earth's climate
- our forests and oceans can absorb these small increases, and 20th-century warming resulted from natural processes, including fluctuations in the sun's heat and ocean currents
- global climate change is based on bunk science and scare tactics.

Facts on US Energy
- After China, the US is currently the second-largest energy consumer worldwide, relying largely on fossil fuels, such as petroleum, natural gas, and coal, to meet its demands.
- As a result of burning these fossil fuels, the US ranks second in carbon-dioxide emissions worldwide.
- The country is also the largest producer of oil and natural gas globally.
- Imported oil accounts for approximately 40 percent of the US consumption.
- However, due to the development of new energy sources and changing uses of energy, the energy consumption patterns in the US have been evolving. While renewable energy sources contribute 12 percent to America's energy mix, the US did not sign the Kyoto Protocol, which was a worldwide agreement to lower greenhouse gas emissions, in 1997. Nonetheless, the country took part in the UN Climate Conference held in Paris in 2015, and an agreement came into effect in 2016.
- In 2023, the Biden-Harris administration announced the investment of approximately $6 billion in funding to accelerate decarbonization projects.

Ecology
- Former President Barack Obama recognized global warming as a significant threat to the world and expressed his determination to address it by unveiling "The Climate Action Plan" in 2013, a national initiative to tackle climate change. It included strategies to cut carbon pollution, prepare the US for the impacts of climate change, and lead international efforts to combat global warming.
- In contrast, Former President Donald Trump's "America First Energy Plan" failed to address the issue of global warming and, in fact, revoked the "Climate Action Plan" and the "Waters of the US Rule."
- In 2022, the Biden-Harris administration introduced the Inflation Reduction Act, which, among other ambitious measures, invests into domestic energy production while promoting clean energy. It intends to drive down consumer energy costs, increase energy security, and reduce greenhouse gas emissions. (EU governments worry that the act will undermine their economies' competitiveness in the large North American market.)

Facts abouts the US economy
- The US boasts the world's largest and most technologically advanced economy, with a market-oriented system that is relatively free from government intervention.
- As the world's largest producer of goods, the US economy is home to some of the world's most successful companies, including Apple, Google, IBM, McDonald's, and Microsoft. US companies are renowned for their cutting-edge technological advancements, particularly in the fields of computers, medical equipment, aerospace, and military technology.
- The US financial market is also one of the world's largest and most powerful. However, the gains in household income over the past several decades have disproportionately

benefited the top 20 percent of households, leading to income stagnation for lower-income families.
- The 2008 recession was largely attributed to the mortgage crisis, falling home prices, investment bank failures, tight credit, and the global economic downturn.
- Additionally, the US has faced long-term challenges such as deteriorating infrastructure, rapidly rising medical and pension costs for an aging population, energy shortages, and deficits in current accounts and the budget.
- The COVID-19 pandemic has had severe economic consequences, and the end is not yet in sight. Travel, financial markets, employment, shipping, and other industries have been seriously disrupted.

"Post-truth"

In 2016 "post-truth" was chosen as the Oxford Dictionaries' Word of the Year, due to its role in the context of Brexit and Donald Trump's election for president. It is an adjective defined as "relating to or denoting circumstances in which objective facts are less influential in shaping public opinion than appeals to emotion and personal belief." In times of post-truth, "fake news" has become a new problem (cf. page 54).

The ambiguity of belonging: 21st century

Americans ...		
belong to and identify with	**have had to cope with**	**have shaped a new identity due to**
– a nation that had never experienced a major attack on its own soil until September 11, 2001	– the terrorist attacks of 9/11	– homeland security measures – preemptive warfare, such as the invasions of Afghanistan and Iraq
– a society that strongly upholds constitutional and human rights	– the Patriot Act, which granted enhanced authority to intelligence agencies, such as the CIA, NSA, and FBI	– new surveillance measures, leading to a debate about freedom vs. security
– a society that values individual resilience	– a growing budget deficit – a debate on gun control – a debate on healthcare	– the ongoing struggle to strike a balance between individual enterprise and governmental intervention in the economy

– a society that often aspires to achieve the American Dream	– social inequality and the challenge of achieving the American Dream – racism and discrimination	– protests against racial discrimination, hate crimes, voter suppression tactics, and anti-immigrant sentiments – social reforms, such as ACA ("Obamacare")
– specific groups in a deeply divided country	– the consequences of the "America first" agenda – the events leading up to and following the election of Joe Biden	– the election of Donald Trump and his "America First" agenda – their attitudes towards the democratic system of the US

Glossary – the USA

an eye for an eye	Auge um Auge; jdm. etwas mit gleichen Mitteln heimzahlen
assimilation	Assimilation, Integration, Eingliederung
civil disobedience	ziviler Ungehorsam
cultural heritage	Kulturerbe
Declaration of Independence	Unabhängigkeitserklärung
deterrence; to deter	Abschreckung; abschrecken
deprivation; to deprive sb. of sth.	Entbehrung; jdm. etwas entziehen/vorenthalten
discrimination; to discriminate against sb.	Diskriminierung; jdn. diskriminieren
E pluribus unum (One from many)	lat.: aus vielen eines; Wappenspruch im Siegel der USA
enemy combatant	feindliche/-r Kämpfer/-in
entrepreneur	Unternehmer/-in
equality; equal opportunities	Gleichheit; gleiche Chancen
fame	Ruhm
freedom; freedom of speech; freedom of the press; freedom of religion	Freiheit; Redefreiheit; Pressefreiheit; Religionsfreiheit
frontier	Grenze (zwischen Zivilisation und Wildnis)
gold rush	Goldrausch
identity	Identität

immigrant; immigration; influx of immigrants; Immigration Act; to immigrate	Einwanderer/-in; Einwanderung; Zustrom von Einwanderern; Einwanderungsgesetz; einwandern
"In God we trust."	„Wir vertrauen auf Gott." (Offizieller Wahlspruch der USA)
inauguration; inaugural address	Amtseinführung; Amtsantrittsrede
liberation; to liberate	Befreiung; befreien
melting pot vs. salad bowl	„Schmelztiegel" vs. „Salatschüssel" (Konzepte, die das Zusammenleben von Menschen mit unterschiedlichem kulturellem Hintergrund in einer Gesellschaft beschreiben)
multiculturalism; multicultural	Multikulturalität; multikulturell
naturalization; to naturalize sb.	Einbürgerung; jdn. einbürgern
pioneer; pioneer spirit	Pionier; Pioniergeist
refugee; refugee camp	Flüchtling; Flüchtlingslager
retribution	Vergeltung
segregation vs. desegregation	Rassentrennung vs. Aufhebung der Rassentrennung
success; successful; to succeed	Erfolg; erfolgreich; erfolgreich sein
Civil Rights Movement	Bürgerrechtsbewegung
Promised Land; the land of milk and honey; God's own country; the New Canaan	das gelobte Land; das Land, in dem Milch und Honig fließen; Gottes eigenes Land; das neue Kanaan
the pursuit of happiness	das Streben nach Glück
to attain self-fulfilment	sich selbst verwirklichen
persecution; to persecute	Verfolgung; verfolgen
from rags to riches; from dishwasher to millionaire	vom Tellerwäscher zum Millionär
to pledge allegiance to the flag	den Fahneneid leisten
prosperity; to prosper	Wohlstand; florieren, gedeihen
settler; settlement; to settle	Siedler/-in; Siedlung; (be)siedeln
inalienable rights	unveräußerliche Rechte
unencumbered	unbelastet

Crooked Letter, Crooked Letter

Im amerikanischen Süden lernen Kinder mithilfe einer Eselsbrücke, wie man den Namen des Bundesstaats Mississippi buchstabiert: *„M – I – crooked letter – crooked letter – I – crooked letter – crooked letter – I – humpback – humpback – I".* Der „krumme Buchstabe" ist also das s. Gewunden verläuft auch die Handlung des gleichnamigen Romans von Tom Franklin aus dem Jahr 2010.

Aus zwei Perspektiven und in wechselnden Erzählzeiten entfaltet Franklin die Geschichte der Protagonisten Silas und Larry. Beide wachsen in den späten 1970er-Jahren in einer Kleinstadt in Mississippi auf und leben als erwachsene Männer in den frühen 2000ern noch immer im selben ärmlichen, von Arbeits- und Trostlosigkeit geprägten Ort. Der Roman, dessen Handlung um Kriminalfälle kreist, fokussiert vor allem den Themenkomplex der Freundschaft und des Verrats vor dem Hintergrund des von Rassismus und Diskriminierung geprägten und wirtschaftlich instabilen Südens der USA.

Im Folgenden wird die Charakterisierung der Figuren nur wenig Raum einnehmen, da Sie sich intensiv im Unterricht damit befassen und in den Interpretationshilfen Material finden können (siehe auch Materialien zum Englischabitur unter https://www.schule-bw. de). Vorrangig wird Ihnen hier Hintergrundwissen vermittelt, das es Ihnen ermöglicht, die Inhalte des Romans zum Schwerpunktthema „The Ambiguity of Belonging" und zu den weiteren abiturrelevanten Inhalten in Beziehung zu setzen. Diese Informationen werden zum Teil auf Deutsch angeboten, damit Sie die Möglichkeit haben, wichtige Aspekte voll zu erfassen. Die Ausführungen auf Englisch gewährleisten, dass Sie den für den Kontext relevanten Wortschatz festigen oder erweitern können.

Hintergrundwissen

In diesem Kapitel werden die Geschichte des Südens der USA, vor allem aber des Staats Mississippi, und die Bedeutung verschiedener Begriffe geklärt sowie Bezüge zur Handlung von *Crooked Letter, Crooked Letter* aufgezeigt.

Der amerikanische Süden und „the lost State" Mississippi

INFO Further information

https://www.info-usa.de/mississippi/
https://www.ms.gov
https://visitmississippi.org

„The Lost State" – so wird Mississippi, einer der ärmsten Bundesstaaten, von vielen Ostküstenamerikanern inoffiziell bezeichnet. Die folgende Zeitleiste hilft Ihnen zu verstehen, wodurch die Verarmung verursacht wurde und welche Faktoren das Leben der afroamerikanischen Bevölkerung in diesem Teil des Landes geprägt haben. Das

20. Jahrhundert wird ausführlicher dargestellt, da die Informationen es Ihnen ermöglichen, *Crooked Letter, Crooked Letter* im historischen Zusammenhang zu interpretieren.

vorkoloniale Zeit	– Gesellschaften der Choctaw (etwa 20.000), Natchez (rund 4.500) und Chickasaw (ungefähr 5.000) siedeln im Süden der USA. – Die indigenen Kulturen betreiben Ackerbau und gründen erste Siedlungen. Die Chickasaw sind Halbnomaden.
ab 17. Jhdt.	– Beginn der Besiedlung durch Frankreich, das sich große Teile des Mississippi-Tals sichert
18. Jhdt.	– Die Franzosen führen Viehzucht, Holzindustrie sowie den Anbau von Früchten, Reis, Tabak und einer wertvollen Baumwollart ein, ebenso das Plantagensystem und somit auch die Sklavenarbeit. – Nach der Niederlage Frankreichs im Siebenjährigen Krieg (1756–1763) erhält Großbritannien weite Teile von Mississippi. Es tritt sie ab, als die USA 1783 unabhängig werden. Spanien bekommt den südlichen Teil, der zwischen 1798 und 1812 an die USA übergeht.
19. Jhdt.	– Nach der Erfindung der Egreniermaschine *(cotton gin)* stellt die Landwirtschaft im großen Stil auf Baumwollanbau um. – 1808 wird der transatlantische Sklavenhandel verboten, nicht aber der inländische Sklavenhandel. – 1817: Gründung des Bundesstaats Mississippi (20. Bundesstaat) – 1830: Indian Removal Act: Die indigenen Chickasaw und Choctaw werden gezwungen, sich westlich des Flusses Mississippi anzusiedeln. Das freie Land wird von weißen Immigranten besiedelt. Die Reichen unter ihnen sichern sich die besten Gebiete für den Baumwollanbau in der Deltaregion, im Black Belt und um Natchez. – Mississippi gehört zu den sechs Staaten mit den meisten Sklaven. – 1822: Neues Sklavengesetz in Mississippi: Sklaven werden persönliches Eigentum ihrer Halter, die sie wie Tiere oder Werkzeuge behandeln dürfen. Sklaven dürfen keinen Handel treiben oder selbst Baumwolle anbauen. – 1865: Niederlage der Südstaaten im Bürgerkrieg. Danach erfolgt der ökonomische Niedergang des Südens, der bis nach dem Zweiten Weltkrieg weit hinter dem industrialisierten Norden zurückbleibt. – 1865: Mississippi lehnt den 13. Zusatzartikel der Verfassung (Abschaffung der Sklaverei) ab. Er wird dort erst 1995 ratifiziert.
20. Jhdt. (1. Hälfte)	– Das öffentliche Leben wird maßgeblich von Weißen geprägt, zum Teil noch immer den Idealen der Vorbürgerkriegszeit entsprechend. – Zahlreiche Lynchmorde (1877–1950: 581) an Schwarzen, ohne dass die Täter belangt werden – 1910–1970: *The Great Migration:* Rund sechs Millionen Schwarze aus den Südstaaten wandern aufgrund der schlechten Wirtschaftslage und der Diskriminierung *(Jim Crow laws)* in den Norden ab.

1950er	– 1954: Der Supreme Court erklärt, dass die Segregation an öffentlichen Schulen gegen die Verfassung verstoße. – 1955: Emmett Till, ein 14-jähriger schwarzer Junge, wird in Mississippi gefoltert und ermordet, weil er angeblich mit einer weißen Frau geflirtet hat. Die beiden weißen Täter werden freigesprochen. Till wird zu einer Ikone der Bürgerrechtsbewegung. – 1956: *Southern Manifesto:* Protestschreiben von 101 Kongressabgeordneten gegen die Rassenintegration, darunter alle Abgeordneten aus Mississippi
1960er	– 1963: Medgar Evers, ein berühmter Bürgerrechtsaktivist aus Mississippi, wird vor seinem Haus erschossen. Im Prozess sprechen die Geschworenen, allesamt weiße Männer, den weißen Täter frei. – 1964: Freedom Summer (Mississippi Summer Project): Bürgerrechtler reisen durch Mississippi und klären die afroamerikanische Bevölkerung über ihr Wahlrecht auf. Die Aktion wird von Freiwilligen aus allen Teilen des Landes unterstützt, auch von Weißen. – 1965: Voting Rights Act: Bundesgesetz zur Gewährleistung der gleichen Beteiligung von Minderheiten bei US-Wahlen, unter anderem, indem diskriminierende Analphabetismustests abgeschafft werden – 1967: Nach einem Urteil des Obersten Gerichtshofs muss Mississippi ebenso wie 15 weitere Bundesstaaten die dort bis dahin verbotene Mischehe zulassen.
1970er	– 1974: Der afroamerikanische Profi-Baseballspieler Hank Aaron bricht den legendären *Home-run*-Rekord von Babe Ruth. – 1976: Die Bürgerrechtlerin Unita Blackwell wird die erste afroamerikanische Bürgermeisterin Mississippis. Sie bleibt bis 2001 im Amt. – 1978: Der Kongress verlängert die Frist für die Ratifizierung des *Equal Rights Amendment* um weitere drei Jahre. Der Verfassungszusatz soll Frauen gleiche Rechte zusichern.
1980er	– 1989: Neue Beweise im Fall Medgar Evers tauchen auf und belasten den Täter erneut. Ranghohe Politiker werden beschuldigt, diesen gedeckt zu haben.
1990er	– 1994: Verurteilung des Mörders von Medgar Evers – 1995: Mississippi ratifiziert als letzter US-Bundesstaat den 13. Verfassungszusatz, was allerdings aufgrund eines Formfehlers ungültig ist.
21. Jhdt.	– 2005: Der Hurrikan Katrina verwüstet weite Teile der Südstaaten. In Mississippi sterben 238 Menschen. Der materielle Schaden beläuft sich auf rund 75 Milliarden Dollar. – 2013: Die Sklaverei tritt in Mississippi offiziell außer Kraft. – 2020: Im Zusammenhang mit der Rassismusdebatte nach dem Tod von George Floyd schafft Mississippi die bisherige Staatsflagge ab, die noch die Kriegsflagge der Konföderation enthält.

Segregation in the US

> **Keyword:**
> **Segregation:** the separation or isolation of a race, class, or ethnic group by enforced or voluntary residence in a restricted area, by barriers to social intercourse, by separate educational facilities, or by other discriminatory means (Merriam Webster). Examples: racial segregation in public in the US until the 1950s; the treatment of non-whites in South Africa during the apartheid era.

The practice of slavery in America lasted for almost 350 years. But discrimination and segregation continued even after slavery was officially abolished in 1865.

In the 1970s and 1980s, when parts of *Crooked Letter, Crooked Letter* are set, skin colour could still be decisive for privileges or disadvantages. At first sight it settled the question as to which part of society a person belonged to, regardless of their background, education or financial status. Quite literally, there only was a "black-and-white" answer to that question.

The American Dream and the issue of class

The prospect of social mobility is the central aspect of the American Dream and is still one of the pull factors for immigrants. However, quite a few studies have shown that vertical mobility is not as common as most Americans would like to believe. The chances of moving upward through the classes, from "rags to riches", seem no more likely today than they were some 35 years ago. Instead, the social gap seems to be growing wider. The question of class is rarely discussed in public, but plays an influential role in everyday life and politics. Sociologists disagree on the number of classes in the US, but a common view is that there are four: upper, middle, working and lower class. Many observers prefer the term "the poor" to the expression "the lower class".

In his novel, Tom Franklin creates a vivid image of the life of the lower class in the South and uses labels that are often applied to its members, such as "white trash" and "trailer trash".

> **Keyword:**
> **White trash:** a disparaging and offensive term for poor, uneducated white people (as opposed to poor Blacks), especially (but not exclusively) used in the rural areas of the southern United States.
> **Trailer trash:** an offensive term for people living in trailer parks.
>
> Both expressions imply not only poverty, but also moral failing, for example criminal behaviour, drug and alcohol abuse, self-neglect and unreliability.

INFO Further reading

Nancy Isenberg (2016). *White Trash: The 400-Year Untold History of Class in America.* (New York: Penguin)

Socio-economic status/background

This term means the net rating of a person's or family's social and economic status or position in comparison with others.

Categories/levels/positioning	– high (upper class) – middle (middle class) – low (lower class)
Variables on which positioning is based	– income – education – occupation – subjective perceptions of social status – subjective perceptions of social class

The historical and social context of *Crooked Letter, Crooked Letter*

Historical and social context	*Crooked Letter, Crooked Letter*	
Different ethnic groups	– Larry and his parents	white American
	– Silas and his mother	African American
	– Cindy, her mother and stepfather	white American
	– Wallace Stringfellow	white American
Segregation/racial issues: intolerance of interaction between African American and white people	– Friendship between Larry and Silas as boys – Affair between Carl Ott and Alice Jones – Affair between Silas and Cindy (Silas's mother refers to Emmett Till, see page 94) – White boys urge Larry to insult a black girl and Larry is beaten for doing so.	
Change of attitude, growing acceptance of Blacks in sports, entertainment, politics (see information on Hank Aaron and Unita Blackwell on page 94)	– Silas "32" Jones used to be a star baseball player at high school. – He is now Chabot's only police officer.	

(Socio)economic status/ background		
	– Larry, childhood	white middle class
	– Larry, adulthood	white lower class
	– Silas, childhood	black lower class
	– Silas, adulthood	black middle class
	– Cindy, childhood	white lower class
	– Tina Rutherford	white upper class
	– Irina Mott	white lower class
	– Wallace Stringfellow	white lower class
"White trash"	– Irina Mott and her neighbours (neighbourhood, appearance, language)	
	– Silas's name for Irina's neighbourhood, "White Trash Avenue", and his suspicions about criminal acts there (meth lab in an old trailer, etc.)	
	– Wallace Stringfellow (neighbourhood, appearance, behaviour)	

The Personal Quest for Belonging

Das folgende Kapitel beleuchtet die Suche der Romanfiguren nach Zugehörigkeit, ihre Entscheidungen und die Konsequenzen, die sich daraus ergeben. Die Unklarheiten oder Mehrdeutigkeiten im Hinblick auf die „Ambiguity of Belonging" sind jeweils in der farbig unterlegten Spalte aufgeführt.

The Teenagers' Quest for Belonging

Larry	
– belongs to the white middle class	– wants to belong to his age group but is not accepted by the other white boys
– does not live up to ideals of masculinity	– wants to be his father's beloved son but his father is disappointed in him (looks, physical appearance, interests) – due to his lack of physical strength he is not accepted by the boys whose friend he would like to be
– has interests which set him apart from others (reading horror stories, nature)	– wants to be accepted by his father, but Carl calls him a "momma's boy" and "on the girly side"; Larry knows that Carl would have preferred Silas as his legitimate son – can share his interests with Silas – wants to be Silas's friend, but then insults him during a fight because he wants to gain his father's respect – other boys laugh at him because of his interests
– wants to help Cindy and Silas	– wants to be Cindy's "knight", but lacks the courage to defend her when she is harassed by her step-father – wants to be Silas' friend, but lacks the courage to stand up to his father
– tries to be accepted	– insults a black girl to impress his white peers – brings snakes to school – wears the zombie mask (at the haunted house) – his attempts only increase his isolation (he is ridiculed, ignored, used)
– wants to do what is right (wants to help Cindy even when he finds out that she only uses him)	– wants to belong to a group of friends or have a relationship but due to his naivety and good-heartedness he is used by Cindy and Silas

Larry's challenges in his quest for belonging as a boy:
- troublesome relationship with his father, who rejects and manipulates him
- painful (school) experiences with peers, who ostracise, reject, manipulate and ridicule him

Silas	
– has family issues	– wants to belong to a complete family, but does not know who his father is
– is a city boy	– wants to belong to a place and has mixed feelings about having moved to Mississippi from Chicago, but then starts feeling at home in Chabot
– integrates into his new school, is the "cool kid"	– wants to belong to his age peers, but becomes friends with Larry, who is considered a misfit – ignores Larry after the haunted house party
– finds out that Carl is his father	– wants to belong to his family but is unsure now about who he really is and unconsciously blames his mother
– has a relationship with Cindy	– wants to be part of a relationship and is happier than ever during the first half of his junior high-school year – feels hurt when Cindy refers to their relationship as "messing around" – his mother finds out and warns him; he listens to her advice – wants to be part of middle or even upper-class society so he decides to pursue his baseball career instead of continuing his relationship with Cindy – loves Cindy and knows that Cecil is treating her cruelly, yet lets her run off alone after a fight
– leaves Mississippi for Oxford	– wants to move up in society so he chooses a baseball career instead of staying in Mississippi where he feels at home – chooses to ignore the consequences of not telling the truth about Cindy's disappearance because of his social ambitions – his need to belong to new social circles is stronger than his sense of justice; he therefore gladly accepts the "escape route" to the north which his mother arranges for him, even though he has to leave his friends, his team and his home behind

Silas's challenges in his quest for belonging as a boy:
- family issues: initially does not know who his father is, then finds out that Carl is his father, which leads to an identity crisis
- difficult relationship with his mother
- being uprooted and displaced
- racial issues

Cindy's quest for belonging ends abruptly before she has the chance to grow up.

Cindy	
– is a popular girl at school	– wants to belong to her peer group, but seems to keep up the image of a "rebel girl" ("cussing, smoking, messing with boys" [chapter 10]; drinking beer at the age of 15) – wants to be part of the community, yet risks her social status by dating a black boy
– has a relation-ship with Silas	– wants to be loved and respected (stepfather abuses her, mother does not help her) and finds this in her relationship with Silas; however, she refers to their relationship as "messing around" – Silas could offer her a way out of her situation at home – although she is afraid of Cecil, she endangers herself and Silas, knowing Cecil would never accept a black boyfriend – sees Silas as the person who can help her get away from her hometown; later it turns out that she may have been pregnant with his baby, so the idea of running away with him could also have been a plan to save them all from Cecil's wrath and violence
– is unstable	– seems to be precocious (experience with boys, drinking and smoking); however, her behaviour seems more to be a desperate way to seek attention or an act of rebellion – being severely threatened by Cecil's behaviour and fully aware of how dangerous he is, she recklessly manipulates Larry and inflicts further emotional damage, and indirectly social disaster, by forcing him into a life-changing situation
– is courageous	– tries to stand up to her stepfather Cecil, but is unable to tell her mother about his acts of violence because she is convinced that her mother would not believe her – seems to confirm what her mother thinks of her ("she, kind of, believes the worst about me")

Cindy's challenges in her quest for belonging as a teenager:
– a broken home (her mother's second husband abuses her)
– precocious and almost self-destructive behaviour (drinking and driving, provoking Cecil's rage)
– racial issues (dating a black boy, possibly becoming pregnant by him)

The Adults' Quest for Belonging

Larry	
– is an outcast with little connection to the outside world	– would like to be part of the Chabot community, but has come to terms with his isolated life even though he feels the impact of loneliness and being an outsider
– longs to have a friend	– wants to belong to a social group and so believes Wallace is his friend, although he senses that something is not quite right – even after he has found out that it was Wallace who shot him he feels responsible for him and wonders if he could have prevented Tina's death
– is known as "Scary Larry"	– even after his innocence has been proven he is unsure whether society will accept him or whether he will remain an outsider
– wants to find his own place in society after Silas's revelations	– wants to be himself again and not just people's "version of him" – although he wants to belong to the Chabot community again, he is unwilling to sacrifice his dignity – decides not to be the victim any longer and thus stops protecting his "friend" Wallace – discovers his true identity (as opposed to the version created by others) and finds the strength to stay true to that new-found identity by not forgiving Silas immediately

Larry's challenges in belonging as an adult:
– living in isolation, being a social outsider
– loneliness
– the burdens of the past which have led to his stigmatization

Silas	
– is still known as "32", which is the number on the baseball shirt he wore as a teenager (→ has not matured)	– still wants to be the popular cool kid in Chabot, but instead is the "sole law enforcement" without any real friends apart from his girlfriend Angie – his behaviour is immature until he realizes that guilt is preventing him from maturing
– is Chabot's police officer	– wants to be a respected member of society; however, he has lied to himself about past events and has kept vital information from the police – tries to solve the cases of Tina Rutherford's disappearance and M&M's murder because he wants to be respected; in the process realizes that he has to take responsibility for the past even if this might jeopardise his social standing
– has chosen to come back to Chabot	– wants to belong to his home community, but the past catches up with him and his guilty conscience finally forces him to confess the truth
– lacks courage	– wants to take responsibility, but finds it very difficult to admit his past failures; however, he risks his personal safety in order to arrest Wallace and thus clear Larry's name – almost lets Irina seduce him even though her neighbourhood scares him; leaves her place at the last minute just because there might be a witness

Silas's challenges in belonging as an adult:
- ambiguous sense of responsibility (being a police officer vs. the secrets from his past)
- lack of courage
- fear of risking his social status if he rights the wrongs of the past

Key Topics

Friendship	Larry → Silas	– shared interests as boys (different races and social status); outcast → popular person
	Silas → Larry	– shared interests as boys – does penance as an adult
	Larry → Wallace	– two outsiders
Betrayal	Larry → Silas	– calls him "nigger" when they fight
	Silas → Larry	– "house of horror" incident – does not confess that he was with Cindy the night she disappeared; keeps this a secret for years
	Cindy → Larry	– manipulates Larry (date) – forces him to help her
	Wallace → Larry	– is obsessed with Larry, who is the alleged murderer – copies Larry's alleged crime – tries to kill Larry
	Silas → Cindy	– chooses his baseball career over her – lacks the courage to have an interracial relationship with her – lets her run off in the dark even though her dangerous stepfather is probably waiting for her – by keeping his secret he prevents the discovery of her murderer
	Carl Ott → Ina Ott	– has an affair with their maid, Alice Jones – lets Alice and his illegitimate son live on their land and thus hurts Ina further
	Silas → Angie	– lies to Angie about his relationship with Cindy – almost accepts Irina's obvious offer to become intimate
Racial issues	Larry & Silas	– interracial friendship
	Silas & Cindy	– interracial relationship
	Carl & Alice	– interracial adultery
	Carl & Silas	– interracial family ties

Symbols and Motifs

Crooked Letter = S
- Synonym for Mississippi
- The story is "crooked", i.e. not told chronologically, and the truth is revealed only gradually.
- The protagonists' lives have gone adrift; they are "crooked".

Snakes
- Symbols of death, danger, betrayal and sin
- Larry tries to impress his peers with snakes.
- Wallace keeps snakes und puts one into Irina's mailbox.
- There is a snake next to Silas's body after the shooting.
- Silas asks about snakes when he meets Irina at a bar.

Books
- Symbols of escape from problems
- Larry is always reading, much to his father's contempt.
- Books are a connection between Larry and Silas as well as between Larry and the world.
- When Larry is an adult, his home is full of books.

Guns
- Symbols of ambiguity: for some characters, guns represent maturity and masculinity while others have a different attitude towards violence.
- Larry teaches Silas how to use a gun and lends him one of their father's rifles.
- Carl makes Larry, his legitimate son, and Silas, his illegitimate son, fight for the ownership of a gun.
- As an adult, Larry is not allowed to own weapons, but there is a gun in his hand when he is found shot.
- Being a constable, Silas carries a gun but has never used it so far.
- Wallace owns numerous firearms and sends one to Larry anonymously.
- Wallace shoots Larry with the gun he sent him.

The zombie mask
- Symbol of hidden identity, also represents horror
- Larry wears the mask at the "house of horror", hoping that he will be accepted, but as soon as the party is over he realizes that it has not changed anything.
- Represents horror: Larry's attacker wears it and probably wore it when he killed Tina Rutherford.
- By wearing the mask, Wallace assumes another identity; he pretends to be "Scary Larry".

Characters and their Profiles

Round characters are fully realized characters and usually play an important role in a story. They are complex and sometimes ambiguous personalities and often undergo a development which might surprise the reader.

Flat characters are two-dimensional and predictable. They do not change during the story.

In the following section the characters are described with ten adjectives each to give you a short overview of their traits and situations. The list also shows Larry's and Silas's character development during the course of action.

Larry as a boy	frail, introverted, weird, naive, obedient, cowardly, vulnerable, caring, loyal, courageous
Silas as a boy	uprooted, jealous, athletic, ambitious, popular, sensitive, venturesome, infatuated, ignorant, weak
Larry as a man	lonely, caring, passive, obedient, polite, guilty, humble, reflective, active, courageous
Silas as a man	lonely, scrupulous, frustrated, ambitious, immature, reflective, caring, conscience-stricken, mature, brave
Wallace Stringfellow	lonely, fascinated (by Larry), harmless, poor, weird, calculating, dangerous, obsessed, aggressive, desperate

Flat characters

Carl Ott	abusive, demanding, scornful, domineering, macho, irresponsible, ignorant, sadistic, uncaring, alcoholic
Ina Ott	devoted, religious, loving, protective, kind, cold, unforgiving, weak, powerless, demented
Alice Jones	attractive, hard-working, protective, lonely, dignified, unhappy, isolated, devoted, supportive, foresighted
Cindy Walker	pretty, popular, confident, rebellious, harassed (by Cecil), provocative, precocious, manipulative, uncaring, desperate
Cecil Walker	abusive, unemployed, cruel, mean, domineering, aggressive, poor, macho, calculating, alcoholic

Crooked Letter, Crooked Letter – Crime Novel or Coming of Age Novel?

Crime novel elements	Coming of age novel elements
– is about crimes and their detection (Cindy, Tina, M&M) – murderers cover up their crimes (Wallace, Cecil) – is suspenseful (pattern of a whodunit) – one protagonist is an investigator with a flawed, but likeable character (Silas) – features violence (M&M, Tina) – includes social issues (race, class, family structures, …)	– traces the psychological and moral growth of the protagonists from childhood to adulthood and maturity (Larry, Silas) – is based on a tragedy that disturbs the protagonists emotionally (Cindy's disappearance and Larry being blamed for it) – Silas matures gradually and with difficulty

Gran Torino

Der Gran Torino ist ein sogenanntes *muscle car,* ein Wagen mit einem großvolumigen Achtzylindermotor, der von Ford im Segment der oberen Mittelklasse in den Jahren 1972 bis 1976 gebaut wurde.

Der Titel des Films weist bereits auf das Setting hin: Detroit, einst blühende Metropole der Autoindustrie, erlebte seit den 1980er-Jahren einen dramatischen Niedergang und ist mittlerweile eine sterbende Stadt, in der viele Menschen im Elend leben. Die Kriminalitätsrate dort zählt zu den höchsten in den USA.

Der Protagonist Walt Kowalski (Clint Eastwood) fühlt sich nach dem Tod seiner Frau unwohl in seinem Viertel und hat sich von seiner Familie entfremdet. Nach und nach entwickelt sich dann aber eine Freundschaft zwischen dem griesgrämigen, häufig wütenden Kauz und den zunächst von ihm verachteten asiatischen Nachbarn. Vor allem Thao, der Sohn der Familie, wächst ihm ans Herz.

Eastwood gelang es mit diesem Film, komplexe Themen wie Migration, Gangkultur und Kriegstraumata miteinander zu verweben und darüber hinaus ein Gegenmodell zu der weitverbreiteten und zunehmenden Phobie vor dem Fremden, dem Anderen zu zeigen.

Der Film erschien 2008 inmitten der damaligen Finanzkrise, ist jedoch in Anbetracht der politischen und gesellschaftlichen Entwicklungen in den letzten Jahren immer noch hochaktuell.

Im Folgenden können Sie Hintergrundwissen zu diesem Schwerpunktthema rekapitulieren und sich Bezüge zum Film vergegenwärtigen. Erneut wird insbesondere der Aspekt „The Ambiguity of Belonging" beleuchtet. Die Figuren werden nur kurz charakterisiert, da Sie sich damit im Unterricht befassen und auch in den Interpretationshilfen ausführliche Erläuterungen dazu finden können. Die Informationen werden zum Teil auf Deutsch angeboten, damit Sie die Möglichkeit haben, wichtige Aspekte voll zu erfassen. Die Ausführungen auf Englisch gewährleisten, dass Sie den für den Kontext relevanten Wortschatz festigen oder erweitern können.

Hintergrundwissen

Im folgenden Kapitel finden Sie eine kurze Biografie Clint Eastwoods, einen Abriss der Geschichte Detroits als *motor city* im 20. Jahrhundert sowie Erläuterungen zu relevanten Begriffen. Zudem werden Bezüge zu den Figuren aus *Gran Torino* und bestimmten Handlungselementen aufgezeigt.

Clint Eastwood

Phases and developments in Clint Eastwood's career as an actor and director:

Phase		identified with
1959–1966: first westerns	– Began his career as a hero in westerns: a laconic, fearless gunfighter with strong morals, maintaining law and order using violence when necessary. – Played the role of The Man with No Name in three Italian westerns ("spaghetti westerns"), and became an international star.	– The Man with No Name: silent, ambiguous hero wearing a green poncho and smoking a cigarillo
1966–1992 *Dirty Harry* and Revisionist Westerns (a darker, more realistic illustration of the times when settlers often used brutal force to conquer the land)	– Played in American westerns. – Played the part of the cynical and tough police inspector "Dirty Harry". – Also started working as a director of westerns and thrillers. – His protagonists often have complex characters and sometimes seek redemption for past wrongdoings. Eastwood often acted these parts himself. – Is a devotee of jazz and a good pianist; directed *Bird,* a film biography of Charlie Parker, and produced a documentary about Thelonious Monk.	– Dirty Harry, a police inspector with a .44 magnum revolver (is still often identified with this character today)
1992–today	– Has made films on a large variety of subjects. – Some films focus on the question of what happens to the "lone wolf" (previously the hero in American glorifications of the past) once he starts getting old.	– aging male hero without any emotional ties

The development in Eastwood's work seems to reflect the changes that the American self-image has undergone.

Motor city ("Motown") Detroit – from boom to bust

Several factors prompted Detroit's decline from a prosperous metropolis to a shell of its former glory (cf. https://archive.nytimes.com/www.nytimes.com/interactive/2013/08/17/us/detroit-decline.html).

INFO

Passend zu diesem Thema finden Sie auf S. 158f. einen Text mit einer Klausuraufgabe.

Causes of decline	Details
– Reliance on a single industry	– By 1950, the population was almost 1.85 million. – The Big Three motor companies – Ford, General Motors and Chrysler – attracted many workers. – Decentralization: due to strikes led by the unions and the refusal by blacks and whites to work side by side, factories were built in the suburbs and in neighbouring states. – Automation (replacement of assembly-line jobs with machinery) cost tens of thousands of jobs. – Energy crisis (1970s), recession (1980s) and foreign competition made profits decrease. – Lack of diversification caused Detroit to suffer more than other cities.
– Racial tensions	– Black population: 1950: 16%; 1967: about 33%; today: about 82% – Severe conflicts between black and white people; fear and hatred have remained since riots in 1967 and have hindered growth.
– Failed leadership	– City leaders did not react adequately to the deep-rooted structural problems; some were involved in various scandals.
– Lack of efficient public-transport system	– The focus was on the car industries and investments went into road and highway construction rather than public transport. – People did not travel together on buses, subways, etc., which is now seen as a missed opportunity to ease tensions. – The lack of public transport prevents people from commuting.
– Conse-quences of poverty	– 36% of the population live below the poverty line. – As few residents pay taxes, it is hard for the city to maintain social services. The city is full of dilapidated buildings. – The unemployment rate is about 20% (February 2022). – The crime rate is high; there is increasing gang violence.

Angry white men

In the first part of *Gran Torino,* protagonist Walt Kowalski is shown as a typical "angry white man". This stereotype refers to a group of white males without higher education who were once blue collar workers but now face unemployment or only have minimum-wage jobs. Especially in the so-called Rust Belt (the former industrial region in the Northeast) deindustrialization has had a massive negative impact on the working class since the 1980s, causing a fear of identity loss. Many people there feel abandoned by the government and overwhelmed by the changes that have been taking place throughout society. They believe in a strong national identity and the concept of American masculinity. They are suspicious of globalization, emancipation, multiculturalism and gun control and they often direct their anger towards African Americans, feminists, immigrants and the LGBTQI+ community. Their anger, ignored or underestimated for years, finally helped to put populist Donald Trump in the White House in 2016.

> **Angry white man**
> A cultural stereotype for a conservative or right-wing white man who is frustrated about his (real or imagined) loss of status in society. The voting bloc of angry white men emerged in the 1990s as a reaction to affirmative action (the policy of making sure that certain groups such as women, ethnic minorities, people with disabilities or older people get a fair share of the opportunities available).

> **Blue-collar workers**
> Wage earners who perform manual labour and need to wear work clothes or other protective clothing, e. g. mechanics, welders, longshoremen and miners.

American masculinity

For many years the concept of American masculinity was based on the following traits and behaviours:
- being strong and silent
- being a protector and provider
- being stoical and brave at all times (not expressing emotions)
- using violence to deal with problematic issues

Many people still believe in traditional masculine ideology. However, there are also many who think it is bad that society tolerates this sort of masculinity.

Gran Torino focuses on two very different concepts of masculinity: the conservative one described above and a more reflective, caring version that includes a sense of responsibility for past and present actions.

History of the Hmong

The story of the Hmong, one of the most recent Asian immigrant groups in the US, is very tragic, but seldom discussed in public. Here is some information about the Hmong people's origin and their reasons for migrating to the States.
- The Hmong are an indigenous group living chiefly in East and Southeast Asia (Southwest China, Vietnam, Laos, Thailand and Myanmar).
- During the Vietnam War, Hmong people from Laos were trained by the CIA to fight against the North Vietnamese Army in what has been called a "secret war" in Laos. They made great sacrifices to help American soldiers.
- In 1975 Laos was taken over by a communist government and the Hmong were persecuted on account of their support of the US. More than 100,000 of them fled to refugee camps in Thailand from where they were resettled to different countries including the US.
- Over 170,000 people of Hmong origin live in the US today.

The trauma of war

> **Post-traumatic stress disorder (PTSD)**
> A condition of enduring anxiety after experiencing shock, acute danger or other frightening or threatening ordeals. Many war veterans suffer from PTSD.

Veterans from the Korean War (1950–1953), known as the "Forgotten War" or "Unknown War" because World War II and the Vietnam War were more prominent in the public's perception, frequently suffered from PTSD and also from a lack of recognition for their sacrifices and stamina while serving their country.

The Historical and Social Context of *Gran Torino*

Context	*Gran Torino*
– Detroit	– Walt used to work in the automobile industry. – He has seen Detroit's better days. – He is living in a multicultural, impoverished neighbourhood. – People in his neighbourhood are being terrorized by a gang.
– Angry white man	– First part of the film: Walt's world has collapsed completely but he refuses to move house. – His anger is directed toward his neighbourhood. – He uses racial slurs.
– Blue collar mentality	– Walt used to be a committed and well-paid worker and was proud of his job; he still keeps his Gran Torino.
– American masculinity	– The Gran Torino is a symbol of his masculine ideals. – Walt was a soldier in the Korean War. – First part of film: Walt represents the typical angry white man. – Second part: Walt represents other ideals; e.g., he acts a mentor to Thao and is very caring. – He keeps his main masculine traits until the end: protective, brave, solving problems with violence. – Thao represents the opposite: he does the washing up, likes gardening, lets his sister "boss him around." – Thao's adaptation to American masculinity: he gets a job as a constructor (considered typically male), has a girlfriend (dates Youa) and at the end inherits Walt's Gran Torino.
– the Hmong	– Walt's neighbours: Hmong family – Culture clash at the beginning
– PTSD	– Walt fought in the Korean War and killed 13 people, among them an innocent Korean teenager; he probably suffers from PTSD. – The presence of his Asian neighbours triggers old memories and guilt.

The Ambiguity of Belonging

Das folgende Kapitel beleuchtet die Zerrissenheit der Charaktere in Bezug auf ihre Zugehörigkeit und ihre Entscheidungen sowie die Konsequenzen, die sich daraus ergeben.

Aspekte der Ambivalenz	Walts Zerrissenheit
Zugehörigkeit zur Familie	– fühlt keine emotionale Verbindung mehr zwischen sich und seinen Kindern und Enkeln, lernt aber den Umgang innerhalb der Hmong-Familie und später auch mit ihm zu schätzen
Nachbarschaft	– ist in seinem Viertel verwurzelt, fühlt sich jedoch gleichzeitig isoliert und fehl am Platz in der von den Hmong dominierten Umgebung – entdeckt dann, was er mit den Hmong gemeinsam hat
Religion	– ist Katholik, hat sich aber von seiner Kirche distanziert; trotzdem entwickelt er ein Vertrauensverhältnis zu Pater Janovich
Werte	– glaubt an traditionelle Werte (being "a real American with decent values") – hält am „alten" Patriotismus fest, doch leidet unter seinen Erfahrungen im Koreakrieg – fühlt sich von seiner Familie nicht respektiert, erkennt aber, wie die Hmong die Familie achten und der älteren Generation großen Respekt entgegenbringen, und entdeckt dadurch Gemeinsamkeiten
amerikanisches Männlichkeitsideal	– hat starke rassistische Vorurteile, leidet aber unter Schuldgefühlen wegen seiner Taten im Koreakrieg – ist unfähig, seine Gefühle zu zeigen und anzuerkennen, geht aber eine emotionale Verbindung mit der Hmong-Familie ein – möchte unabhängig sein, aber fühlt sich für Sue und Thao verantwortlich – ist bereit, Gewalt als Mittel einzusetzen; dies führt aber auch dazu, dass er zuletzt sich selbst opfert, um der Gerechtigkeit Genüge zu tun und seine früheren Taten zu sühnen

Walts Ambivalenz im Hinblick auf seine Zugehörigkeit zeigt sich auf mehreren Ebenen:
– Isolation in Zeit (er ist den Werten der 1950er verhaftet) und Raum (multikulturelle Nachbarschaft überfordert ihn) → kulturelle Ebene
– Entfremdung von seiner Familie und ebenso von sich selbst aufgrund der Kriegserfahrungen → soziale und emotionale Ebene
– Distanzierung von seiner Glaubensgemeinschaft → persönliche und spirituelle Ebene

Aspekte der Ambivalenz	Thaos Zerrissenheit
Zugehörigkeit zur Kultur der Hmong	– wird den Werten der Hmong entsprechend erzogen, verweigert aber die Teilnahme an einer traditionellen Geburtsfeier und kleidet sich wie ein amerikanischer Teenager – will sich an die amerikanische Kultur anpassen, trägt jedoch ein traditionelles Gewand bei Walts Beerdigung; hat eine Freundin, die auch Hmong ist
Familie	– hat kein männliches Vorbild in seinem Ringen um Anpassung, findet jedoch in Walt eine Vaterfigur
amerikanisches Männlichkeitsideal	– hat feminine Züge (Erscheinung, verrichtet „Frauenarbeit", ist passiv), entwickelt sich aber durch Aneignung einer derberen Ausdrucksweise, die Arbeit auf einer Baustelle, seine Freundin und schließlich den Besitz des Gran Torino mehr zu einem „typischen Mann", allerdings ohne sich selbst untreu zu werden oder plötzlich unauthentisch zu wirken

Thaos Ambivalenz im Hinblick auf seine Zugehörigkeit zeigt sich auf mehreren Ebenen:
– Zerrissenheit zwischen der Kultur der Hmong und der amerikanischen Lebensweise
– Unsicherheit in Bezug auf seine Rolle als Mann

Key topics

Family	Walt	– is estranged from his own family. – is not respected by his sons.
	Thao and Sue	– belong to the big Hmong family that have strong bonds and support one another. – Thao has a difficult position in his female-dominated family, not having a male role model.
	Walt → Thao	– Walt becomes a father figure for Thao.
Racism in the multicultural American society	Walt	– suffers from the effects of the white flight from Highland Park. – uses racial slurs:
	Sue and Thao	– feel tied to the social norm of staying with their own people (Sue is an exception, briefly dating a white boy)
Guilt and redemption	Walt	– killed 13 people in Korea, among them a teenager – contributes to the spiral of violence and its impact (drive-by shooting, the gang's revenge in raping Sue) – sacrifices his life in order to make the neighbourhood safer for Thao, Sue and their family and to atone for his past and present guilt

American masculinity	Walt	– at first resembles the stereotype of the angry white man. – then develops a different kind of masculinity, although certain traits remain.
	Thao	– is almost the opposite of the ideal of American masculinity. – is "manned up" by Walt (job, girlfriend, car).
(Gun) violence		– Walt owns at least two guns. – The Latino and Hmong gangs use guns.
Ambiguity of belonging		– See page 112

Symbols and Motifs

The Gran Torino
– represents conservative American values
– is a "muscle car" that underlines Walt's (American) masculinity
– is an outdated model and therefore also a symbol of Walt's position in his family and in society
– is one of the elements that create a growing bond between Walt and Thao

Walt's lighter and his Silver Star Medal
– are reminders of Walt's Korean war experiences
– are symbols of his ever-present guilt
– Walt uses the lighter at the end to provoke the gang into shooting him, thus changing the symbol of guilt into one of redemption.

Cross
– is a symbol of Walt's salvation

Motif: life and death
– are juxtaposed (funeral ceremonies vs. birth ceremony, Walt's death vs. peaceful life for Thao and Sue)
– The film is framed by two funerals.
– Father Janovich often focuses on "life and death".
– Walt's war experience is a central theme.
– There is a final shoot-out.

Dilapidation vs. refurbishment
– The run-down neighbourhood reflects the loss of values and traditions.
– Thao's job of refurbishing houses helps him to gain self-confidence.
– Thao and Walt working together and helping each other with repairs causes them to become friends and is an act of building new relations.

Character Profiles

Here the three main characters are described with ten adjectives each to give you a short descriptive overview of their personality traits.

Walt	lonely, conservative, masculine, racist, self-reliant, practical, conscience-stricken, determined, considerate, caring
Thao	insecure, gentle, torn, lost, weak, persistent, willing (to change, to work), humorous, self-confident, positive
Sue	strong, assimilated, friendly, self-confident, open, considerate, courageous, intelligent, emancipated, mature

Gran Torino and *Crooked Letter, Crooked Letter*

Das Diagramm zeigt thematische Schnittstellen zwischen dem Film und dem Roman.

race
- cross-cultural relationships
- time and place (setting)
- racial prejudice

family
- parent-child relationships
- position in the family
- estrangement
- blood-related vs. heart-related bonds

friendship
- happiness vs. lack of friendship
- true friendship
- limits of friendship

(gun) violence
- guns as means of empowerment
- guns as means of violence
- guns as means of protection

(American) masculinity
- different concepts of masculinity
- gender identity

religion
- as a substitute for social contacts
- the role of religion in creating a sense of belonging

Shared characteristics between the protagonists

Die Tabelle listet Gemeinsamkeiten der Protagonisten im Roman und im Film im Hinblick auf ihre Zerrissenheit in der Frage der Zugehörigkeit auf.

	Larry	Walt
Why is there ambiguity in the characters' sense of belonging?	– craves emotional bonds but is a social outcast – has difficulties finding his male identity – feels guilty (supposed murder in the past)	– alienated from his sons but becomes a father figure for Thao – lives "outside time and place" in his neighbourhood – forms close bonds to the Hmong family – feels guilty for the past (war)
What strategies do they choose?	– at first: struggles to gain friendship (tutoring, snakes, mask) – then: resignation, isolation, prayer, reading – end: courage, strength, hope	– at first: isolation, anger, stoicism – then: mentoring Thao, caring, protecting – end: reflection, atonement
What is the outcome?	– at first: feels lonely – end: sacrifices friendship to overcome the past and develop a sense of self again	– at first: feels lonely – end: sacrifices himself to save his new friends and to atone for the past

	Silas	Thao
Why is there ambiguity in the characters' sense of belonging?	– is black – is the poor outsider, then the "cool kid", later an adult without friends – feels guilty for the past (Cindy)	– has no friends but rebels against the gang – is insecure about his position in the family but finds a father figure in Walt – has difficulties finding his male identity
What strategies do they choose?	– at first: integration through baseball, later through law enforcement job – denies his involvement in a crucial past event – end: takes responsibility	– at first: reads, studies, is passive, is persuaded by the gang to steal Walt's car – then: develops his own specific male identity
What is the outcome?	– at first: is satisfied – end: atones for past wrongs	– at first: is lonely – end: adopts a more American male identity (job, girl, car)

Methoden der Textanalyse

Literarische Texte

Narration

Elements of narration

Plot

INFO Elements of a complete plot

exposition → rising action → climax/turning point → falling action → ending

---

A **plot** does not necessarily need to be complete, and it can have an open ending.

The **sequence** of events does not need to be chronological.
There may be foreshadowing or flashbacks, and sometimes the plot may be presented in reverse narration (umgekehrte Chronologie).
Especially in an excerpt from a longer text, which is the most common sort of text in the final exam, not all the elements of the plot may be included.
Certain **key events** within the story's action will increase tension, create suspense, and lead to a climax or turning point. After that, there will be a falling tension or relief.

INFO Tension curve

rising tension → climax or turning point → falling tension or relief

---

Theme
The **theme** of a story is always abstract. Some frequent themes are love, poverty, racism, childhood and youth, or death.
The **subject matter** of a story is the concrete realization of the theme.

Example
Two stories may have the same theme, such as racism. However, the subject matter of one story may be the murder of an African American person, while the subject matter of the other story may be the bullying of a female black student.

Character

When asked to characterize a figure from a narrative text, you must consider different aspects. Some key questions can guide you.

Direct characterization
- What does the narrator explicitly state about the character?
- What do other characters say about the character?
- What does the character say about himself/herself?
- How objective are these statements? Be aware of words with negative or positive connotations.

Indirect characterization
- How does the character behave?
- What does the character say and how does he/she say it?
- What kind of language does he/she use?

To aid your analysis, it might be useful to create a table with the following headings:

Character's outward appearance	Character's language	Character's actions	Character's statements	Other characters' statements (or actions)
...	...	...	...	...

Narrator/point of view

INFO Narrator

There are first-person and third-person narrators.
It is important to note that a first-person narrator is not the same as the author.

Limited point of view				Unlimited point of view
First-person protagonist narrator	First-person witness narrator	Third-person objective narrator	Third-person selective narrator	Third-person omniscient narrator
The central character captures the events from their point of view.	The narrator is part of the action, but not always at its centre.	The narrator confines the story to neutral descriptions and dialogue.	The narrator only describes the thoughts and feelings of some of the characters.	The narrator provides comprehensive portrayals and interpretations.

Modes of presentation

Panoramic presentation (telling) vs. scenic presentation (showing)

In narratives, there are two distinct modes of presentation: the panoramic mode and the scenic mode.

The **panoramic** mode is employed when the narrator provides a summary of several events, whereas the **scenic** mode is used when the narrator offers a detailed description of a scene.

Interior monologue is a specific type of scenic presentation that portrays a character's thoughts and feelings in real-time. In **reported thought**, thoughts are presented as reported speech, which is a stylistic device that allows a narrator to convey a character's mental processes indirectly.

These modes are closely connected with the concepts of **narrated time** and **narrating (or acting) time**:

The narrated time is longer than the narrating time.	Usually a summary of events is given.
The narrated time is identical with the narrating time.	One example is direct speech.
The narrated time is shorter than the narrating time.	Examples are stream of conscious-ness, interior monologue, or a detailed description of a scene that is comparable to slow motion in a film.

INFO Functions of the point of view and the mode of presentation

An omniscient narrator who remains neutral, observing the action and the characters while using a panoramic mode of presentation, tends to be detached. This creates a distance between the reader and the action. On the other hand, a narrator who adopts a character's point of view creates immediacy and directly involves the reader in the action.

Setting

The setting refers to the place and time in which the action of a story takes place. It is crucial for creating the right atmosphere and conveying symbolic meaning.

Atmosphere

Atmosphere is established through various means, including the setting, objects, colours, lighting, and references to a character's mood and language used in the story. The right atmosphere sets the tone for the story, creating a certain mood that evokes a particular emotion in the reader.

Symbolism

Symbolism is a literary device that uses symbols to represent ideas. A symbol is a thing that represents something else. Symbols can be objects, images, characters, names, or places, and they are used in every art form.

INFO Symbols

Established symbols are conventional symbols that have been used for a long time and are universally known. Examples of established symbols include the rose as a symbol of love, the cross as a symbol of Christianity/faith, water as a symbol of life, and autumn as a symbol of the middle age of humans. Readers understand the meaning of these symbols because they have been used repeatedly in literature and the visual arts.

Created symbols are things that become symbolic within a certain context because they are closely connected to an event, a situation, or a character. An author may create connections between two things and show how the two represent each other.

Symbols, metaphors, and similes
It is important to note that symbols are different from metaphors and similes.
A metaphor is an expression that describes a person or an object by referring to something that has similar characteristics.
A simile is an expression that compares one thing with another, always including the words "as" or "like".
Examples:
Symbol: Jackson gave Eliza a deep red rose.
Metaphor: Eliza was a beautiful rose.
Simile: Eliza was like a rose.

Language and style

When analyzing the style of a text, it is crucial to examine various aspects such as the register, diction (choice of words), tone, stylistic devices, and sentence structure.

Register refers to the level of language used in a particular situation, and it can be formal, neutral, informal, or vulgar. The text may contain a lot of slang words, taboo words, technical terms, or jargon.

Tone expresses the emotional attitude of the text and can be ironic, sarcastic, sad, humorous, serious, playful, angry, or any other emotion. The tone is determined by the choice of words, level of speech, rhythm, and sentence length.

Stylistic devices, such as metaphors, similes, imagery, and alliteration, can also contribute to the style of a text. These devices will be explained in the chapters on poetry and non-fictional texts (pages 123, 127–128).

Poetry

Poetry is a form of literature that emphasizes the **aesthetic function** of language and appeals to the senses. This is achieved through various elements, such as
- the sound and rhythm of words and phrases
- the choice of words
- sentence structure
- composition
- imagery.

In your final exam, you will be expected to analyze the meaning and effect of the language used in a poem.

How to proceed

To analyze a poem, you can start by asking a series of questions.
- Who is the speaker, and where is he/she?
- What is the speaker trying to convey? Is it a story, description, contemplation, or argument?
- Can you classify the poem as a certain type of poetry, for example with regard to the theme, such as love or nature poetry, or the speaker situation, such as introspective or experiential poetry?
- What is the speaker's attitude, and what is he/she saying?
- How is the poem structured, and does the structure correspond to the speaker's thoughts?
- What is the significance of the title?
- Which stylistic devices does the speaker use, and what is their function?
- Is there a rhyme scheme and if so, what is its effect?
- How do the perception, feeling and thinking of the speaker develop?
- Does the poem have abrupt changes in content?
- Is the sentence structure simple or complex?

Elements of poetry

The structure of a poem is typically composed of **stanzas** and **lines**.

> **INFO** Speaker and author
>
> It is important to note that the speaker in a poem is not necessarily the author. While a poem may be autobiographical, it is still necessary to refer to the "speaker in the poem" rather than assuming that the speaker and the author are the same.

Poems often have a specific **rhyme scheme** in their stanzas.

Rhyme

Rhyme schemes

Pair rhyme	a a b b
Alternate rhyme	a b a b
Embracing rhyme	a b b a

Lines within a poem may have a certain rhythm, with the smallest unit being the foot, which consists of at least one stressed and one or two unstressed syllables. The pattern of stressed and unstressed syllables is known as **metre,** and it reflects the natural rhythm of the English language. The poet's skill lies in selecting words that create a regular metre within the poem.

Types of foot

foot	stresses		example
Iamb/iambic metre	– /	(da-**dum**)	compare
Trochee/trochaic metre	/ –	(**dum**-da)	lovely
Spondee/spondaic metre	/ /	(**dum dum**)	drop dead
Anapest/anapestic metre	– – /	(da-da-**dum**)	lemonade
Dactyl/dactylic metre	/ – –	(**dum**-da-da)	elephant

Lines

End-stop	A pause at the end of a line, usually marked by punctuation, such as a period, comma, semicolon, or question mark.	"Shall I compare thee to a summer's day?" (William Shakespeare, Sonnet 18)

Run-on lines (enjambment)	A phrase that extends past the end of a line, with no punctuation so that one must continue reading to reach the conclusion of the thought.	"When yellow leaves, or none, or few, do hang Upon those boughs which shake against the cold, [...]" (William Shakespeare, Sonnet 73)
Caesura	A metrical pause in a poetic line. Poets indicate such a pause with a comma, a tick, or two lines, either slashed (//) or parallel (||).	I hear lake water lapping // with low sounds by the shore (William Butler Yeats, "The Lake Isle of Innisfree")

Imagery

Imagery is a powerful tool that poets use to convey meaning and create vivid, sensory experiences. By going beyond the literal, dictionary meaning of words, imagery uses figurative language to evoke images, sounds, tastes, smells, and sensations that engage the reader's or listener's imagination. In fact, all figurative language is a form of imagery, and it is this quality that makes poetry and other forms of creative writing so rich and engaging. Whether it is a description of a beautiful sunset, a poignant metaphor for the passage of time, or a vivid portrayal of a character's emotions, imagery is an essential component of effective communication in literature.

INFO Watch out

"Imagery" is an abstract noun, and it refers to the collective use of images in language. Although there is no plural form of the word itself, you can refer to multiple images within the context of discussing a particular work or body of literature.

Types of imagery

Metaphor	A word or phrase used to describe a person or a thing, in a way that is different from its normal use, in order to show that the two people or things have the same qualities. "All the world's a stage." (William Shakespeare, *As You Like It*)
Simile	A comparison explicitly using the words 'like' or 'as'. "My love is like a red, red rose" (Robert Burns)
Personification	The representation of animals, plants, inanimate objects, or abstract ideas as humans. "Busy old fool, unruly Sun,/Why dost thou thus,/Through windows, and through curtains, call on us?" (John Donne, "The Sun Rising")
Symbol	A thing that represents something else. "The caged bird sings/with fearful trill/of the things unknown/but longed for still" (Maya Angelou, "Caged Bird". The bird is a symbol of oppressed African Americans.)

Drama

When analysing a dramatic text, it is important to focus on particular elements that are characteristic of plays.

Elements of drama
Structure
Plot

In drama, the audience is confronted with the action on stage directly, and although there is no narrator, the same plot elements can be identified as in narrative texts. These elements include:

INFO Elements of a dramatic plot

exposition → rising action → climax or crisis → falling action → denouement or catas-trophe

---

In a tragedy, the antagonists gain the upper hand in the falling action, which ultimately leads to a catastrophe. In contrast, a comedy has a happy ending where conflicts are resolved (denouement).

Text

A drama consists of **two kinds of text**: the parts spoken by the characters and the stage directions.

The **text spoken by the characters** is more crucial. It can be in the form of dialogue or monologue, with asides being a specific type of monologue.

Stage directions provide instructions regarding stage design, visual effects, sounds, the characters and their behaviour, as well as how some parts of the dialogue should be spoken. Visual and acoustic elements contribute to portraying characters and creating atmosphere, and sometimes they also add symbolic meaning to a scene.

Actor directions		Stage design directions	
visual	vocal	visual	aural
facial expressions	intonation	set	music
gestures	volume	scenery	sound effects
movements	pace	stage decoration	noise
makeup and hair	accent	lighting	other sounds
costumes	non-verbal sounds	props	volume and intensity

Characters

Characters are presented through their actions, interactions, dialogue, and their outward appearance.

There are **flat** characters who act in predictable ways and **round** characters who are fully developed.

Language/Dialogue/Communication

A drama operates on two levels: the inner system of communication, which refers to the communication among the characters, and the outer system of communication, which is the interaction between the playwright and the audience.

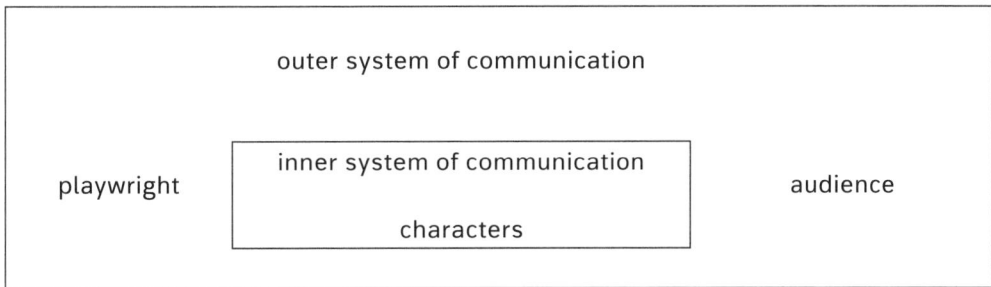

Dramatic irony is an important effect that is created by the two levels of communication in drama. When the audience knows more than a character, an utterance will be perceived as ironic when it sharply contrasts with reality.

In **comedy**, the audience's awareness of facts that the characters do not know, created through dramatic irony, can serve as a comic effect.

An **aside** is a dramatic technique where an actor speaks directly to the audience, providing information about their thoughts, feelings, or intentions. The other characters on stage are supposed to be unaware of what is being said.

Glossary – Useful Phrases for Analysing Literary Texts

The narrator tells the story of …/shows/relates/reveals …
The narrator takes X's point of view/takes sides with …
The narrator is omniscient.
The story is told in the first person/third person.
The narrator uses/employs metaphors/similes/comparisons/…
This metaphor shows/stands for/suggests/…
The tone is ironic/satirical/detached/matter-of-fact/serious/…
The story is about/deals with/focuses on/…
Atmosphere is created through various light effects/…
Tension/Suspense is created/built up through …
The poem is composed of four stanzas/verses.
You read/say/recite a poem.
The recital of the poem was very moving.
The poem is by Shakespeare.
It is a song by Genesis.
The speaker in the poem/the poetic I/the poetic persona
The poem consists of/is composed of/is arranged in three/… stanzas.
The comedy ridicules/mocks/satirizes …
The exposition sets the action in motion.
The action moves towards and culminates in a turning point.
The play has a simple/complex/tight plot.
The drama has a happy/unhappy ending.
X and Y are main/major/minor characters.
The protagonist is in conflict with his/her opponent.
The antagonist fights the protagonist.
The spectator/audience follows the play.
The play is performed/produced/staged in …
The scenery is shifted to …
Actors perform/enact a story or a play.
Actors play roles.
An actor enters the stage/makes an entrance.
An actor exits/makes his exit/makes her exit.

Language and style
Important literary devices

Literary device	Definition	Example
alliteration	a repetition of a consonant at the beginning of words that are close together	"From forth the fatal loins of these two foes […]" (Shakespeare, *Romeo and Juliet*)
allusion	an indirect reference	Poetry is great. Just think of the most famous writer of sonnets in English.
analogy	a comparison betwen things with similar features	The heart is simply a pump propelling the blood round the body.
anaphora	a repetition of the same word at the beginning of several sentences	Be bold. Be brief. Be gone. Stay safe. Stay well. Stay happy.
antithesis	a juxtaposition of two contrasting ideas through a parallel syntactical structure	"To err is human; to forgive is divine." (Alexander Pope)
assonance	the repetition of similar sounds, especially vowels, in two or more words that are close together	How now brown cow?
blank verse	an un-rhyming verse written in iambic penta-meter (a consistent meter with ten syllables in each line)	"The king has happily received, Macbeth,/The news of thy success, and when he reads […]" (Shakespeare, *Macbeth*)
chiasmus	the reversal of word order in two parts of a sentence	"Fair is foul, and foul is fair" (Shakespeare, *Macbeth*)
tricolon	a series of three words, phrases or sentences that are parallel in structure, length and/or rhythm	Friendship, affection, love. And when the night grows dark, when injustice weighs heavy on our hearts, when our best-laid plans seem beyond our reach, let us think of Madiba […] (Barack Obama)
ellipsis	an incomplete sentence	A good choice!
enumeration	a list of details	Macbeth is disloyal, greedy and obedient to his wife.
euphemism	the replacement of a word or phrase by one that is more agreeable	"Civilizing" Australian Aboriginal children meant forcibly removing them from their families.

hyperbole	exaggeration	I have told you a thousand times.
inversion	reversal of word order	"In Xanadu did Kubla Khan/A stately pleasure-dome decree: […]" (Samuel Taylor Coleridge, "Kubla Khan")
✓ irony	statements or situations that portray reality in a different way from what appears to be true	Stating during a thunderstorm, "Beautiful weather today." Entering a messy house and saying, "Nice place you have here."
✓ metaphor	a word or phrase that creates an implicit comparison between two non-similar things	I am the black sheep in the family. He has a heart of stone.
✓ onomatopoeia	a word that imitates the sound it stands for	Bang! Swoosh! Ding-dong. "It went zip when it moved and bop when it stopped,/ And whirr when it stood still." (Tom Paxton, "The Marvelous Toy")
oxymoron	a combination of contradictory words	"O heavy lightness, serious vanity, Misshapen chaos of wellseeming forms, […]" (Shakespeare, *Romeo and Juliet*)
paradox	an apparent contradiction	This statement is true and false at the same time.
parallelism	a repetition of grammatical elements, e.g. sentence structure	"We shall not flag or fail. We shall go on to the end. We shall fight in France […]" (W. Churchill) "[…] and that government of the people, by the people, for the people shall not perish from the earth." (A. Lincoln)
✓ personification	a common form of metaphor in which human characteristics are attributed to objects or abstract ideas	"Too hot the eye of heaven shines" (Shakespeare, Sonnet 18)
✓ rhetorical question	a question that does not require an answer	Do you think I'm stupid?
simile	a comparison using the words "like" or "as"	"My love is like a red, red rose." (Robert Burns, "A Red, Red Rose"))
tautology	a phrase or an expression that states the same thing more than once, often in a different way	While I nodded, nearly napping, suddenly there came a tapping,/As of someone gently rapping, rapping at my chamber door." (E. A. Poe, "The Raven")

Sach- und Gebrauchstexte

Argumentative Texts: How to Analyse (Political) Speeches

> **Keyword:**
> **(Political) speeches** aim to convince the audience of the speaker's position, in an effort to win them over to their side. Very often, speakers try to persuade the listeners by appealing to their emotions. In some cases, the orator may even attempt to manipulate the audience.
> It is crucial to note that the speaker wants to present their point of view as positively as possible.

When analysing a political speech, it is important to focus on the topic and characteristic features.

How to proceed

Reading the text

1. Read the (political) speech or extract and identify the main topic (reading for gist).
2. Re-read the text several times, paying close attention to certain characteristic features of speeches. Highlight relevant words or phrases and take notes (reading for detail).

Pay special attention to:

- Keywords and key phrases
- References to historical events
- References to famous people
- References to works of literature
- Stylistic devices

Questions to ask

While analysing a (political) speech, consider the following questions:

- What is the main topic of the speech?
- What is its political, historical, and social context?
- What do you know about the speaker's biography and political orientation?

Elements of a (political) speech
Structure

(Political) speeches typically consist of three parts: **an introduction, a main part**, and **a conclusion.** Each of these parts serves a specific purpose.

> **INFO** Introduction
>
> In the introduction, the speaker announces the topic or purpose of the speech and explains why it is important. The speaker also wants to capture the audience's attention, encouraging them to follow the speech closely and accept their arguments.

There are several ways to make listeners interested:
- The speaker can open by **sharing something about their personal history or a recent experience,** highlighting that the topic of the speech is of personal importance to them. By relating a **story** to the audience, the speaker will also appear less remote.
- Another common way of starting a speech is to **begin with a question** that refers to the main topic and will be answered later in the speech. By asking the audience a question, the speaker actively involves them, prompting them to think more deeply about the topic.
- A speaker may **present visual material to the audience,** such as pictures, objects, or a short clip from a film. This also helps to grab the audience's attention. Listeners will want to find out in what ways the visual material is related to the content of the speech.

[handwritten margin note: rhetorical questions]

> **INFO** Main part of a speech
>
> In the main part of the speech, the orator needs to maintain the audience's interest and ensure that they can follow the line of argumentation.

Several techniques are particularly effective:
- **Using short and simple sentences** to develop the argumentation step by step, ensuring that the audience can follow.
- **Quoting reliable sources, referring to statistics, and providing the audience with facts and background information.** This shows that the speaker is well-informed and has researched the subject.
- **Pointing out problems and providing solutions** to them, demonstrating the speaker's competence.
- **Including personal experiences** and vivid, concrete events, aiming for a personal relationship with the audience, **often using personal pronouns like "we", "us", or "our".**

INFO Conclusion

In the conclusion, the speaker restates the main points of the speech and provides a final argument or call to action. This is the last opportunity for them to persuade the audience and leave a lasting impression.

Towards the end of a speech, the speaker might use the following strategies:
- Revisit a question posed at the beginning of the speech.
- Appeal once more to the audience's convictions and emotions.
- Develop a compelling vision for the future.
- Ask for support, giving the listeners the feeling that their support is of major importance.

Language and style

Certain stylistic devices are often used in (political) speeches to make them lively and interesting.

Important stylistic devices
You can find the definitions of these stylistic devices on pages 127–128.

Stylistic devices	Examples
analogy	"In a sense we have come to our nation's capital to cash a check. When the architects of our republic wrote the magnificent words of the Constitution and the Declaration of Independence, they were signing a promissory note to which every American was to fall heir. This note was a promise that all men, yes, black men as well as white men, would be guaranteed the unalienable rights of life, liberty, and the pursuit of happiness." (Martin Luther King, "I have a dream")
simile	He fought like a lion in the battle.
metaphor	He was a lion in the battle.
alliteration	"Let freedom ring from the <u>m</u>ighty <u>m</u>ountains of New York." (Martin Luther King, "I have a dream")
repetition	"The answer to the slavery question was already embedded within our Constitution – a Constitution that had at its very core the ideal of equal citizenship under the law; a Constitution that promised its people liberty, and justice […]." (Barack Obama, "A More Perfect Union")
parallelism	"Let us be our sister's keeper. Let us find that common stake we all have in one another, and let our politics reflect that spirit as well." (Barack Obama, "A More Perfect Union")

antithesis	"It's a story that hasn't made me the most conventional candidate. But it is a story that has seared into my genetic make-up the idea that this nation is more than the sum of its parts – that out of many, we are truly one." (Barack Obama, "A More Perfect Union")
rhetorical question	How long shall this suffering continue?
irony	"Insert joke here, as Jeremy Corbyn would say." (Boris Johnson, speaking about the leader of the Labour party and mocking his inability to joke because his speeches were very serious.)

Glossary – Useful Phrases for Analysing Speeches

By telling the audience something about himself, the speaker attempts to establish a personal relationship with them.	Indem der Sprecher/die Sprecherin seinem/ihrem Publikum etwas über sich selbst erzählt, versucht er/sie, eine persönliche Beziehung zu ihm aufzubauen.
She attempts to win her listeners over to her side.	Sie versucht, das Publikum auf ihre Seite zu ziehen.
He draws a comparison between … and …	Er zieht einen Vergleich zwischen … und …
He puts emphasis on the meaning of his words by using parallelism/repetition/…	Er verleiht seinen Worten Nachdruck, indem er einen Parallelismus/eine Wiederholung/… verwendet.
He refers to well-known historical events, such as …	Er bezieht sich auf allgemein bekannte historische Ereignisse wie …
He wants to draw the audience's attention to the fact that …	Er möchte die Aufmerksamkeit des Publikums auf die Tatsache lenken, dass …
His frequent use of rhetorical questions is intended to show that …	Sein häufiger Gebrauch rhetorischer Fragen soll verdeutlichen, dass …
Her use of metaphorical language is intended to make her speech more lively and interesting.	Ihr metaphorischer Sprachgebrauch soll ihre Rede interessanter und lebendiger machen.
In line … she openly criticizes her political opponents.	In Zeile … kritisiert sie offen ihre politischen Gegner.
The frequent use of the personal pronoun "we" gives the audience the impression that the speaker regards himself as one of them.	Der häufige Gebrauch des Personalpronomens „wir" vermittelt den Menschen im Publikum das Gefühl, dass der Sprecher sich als einer von ihnen betrachtet.

The speaker appeals to the audience's emotions by ...	Der Redner/Die Rednerin spricht die Gefühle des Publikums an, indem er/sie ...
The speaker begins by ...	Der Redner/Die Rednerin beginnt mit ...
The speaker makes frequent use of metaphors/similes/symbols/examples to point out/to underline that ...	Der Redner/Die Rednerin macht häufig Gebrauch von Metaphern/Vergleichen/ Symbolen/Beispielen, um herauszustel- len/zu unterstreichen, dass ...
The speaker tries to convince his/her audience of his/her point of view by ...	Der Redner/Die Rednerin versucht sein/ ihr Publikum von seinem/ihrem Stand- punkt zu überzeugen, indem er/sie ...
The speaker aims to convince/persuade/ manipulate the audience.	Der Redner/Die Rednerin intendiert, das Publikum zu überzeugen/überreden/ manipulieren.

Expository Texts: How to Analyse Essays

Keyword:
Essays: The most common types of essays are:
– **Comments:** essays which reflect the author's opinion on a certain topic
– **Discussions:** essays in which the author weighs the pros and cons of a subject
– **Expository essays:** essays that present a topic logically without the author's opinion.
There are many other possible categories and subcategories of essays, depending on their purpose, audience, and content.

How to proceed

To analyze an essay effectively, it is important to determine which type of essay you are dealing with. For analyzing comments, you can refer to the section on political speeches above.
When it comes to **dicussions**, consider the following aspects:

Structure

– In the **introduction**, the author expresses the main idea of the essay. Instead of giving a personal opinion, they might provide background information or begin with a question that serves as a guideline and is answered in the essay.
– In the **main part**, the author can use different approaches. An **enumerative approach** involves listing all the aspects of the topic in a neutral way. A **dialectical approach** can present all the arguments in favour of a position before focusing on the counter- arguments or it can present the pros and cons alternatingly.
– Each **new aspect** is usually presented in a new paragraph. The various **arguments** can be supported with examples from real life, established facts, expert opinions, or

other reliable sources. These pieces of evidence are important to make the argument convincing and persuade the reader.
- In the **conclusion**, the author summarizes the arguments and may also restate their opinion and refer to future developments.

Glossary – Useful Phrases for Analysing Essays

The author discusses the pros and cons of ...	Der Verfasser/Die Verfasserin diskutiert die Vor- und Nachteile von ...
The author gives their personal opinion on the problem of ...	Der Verfasser/Die Verfasserin äußert seine/ihre persönliche Meinung zum Thema ...
He/She believes/is convinced/assumes that ...	Er/Sie glaubt/ist überzeugt/nimmt an, dass ...
She/He wants to persuade the reader of ...	Sie/Er möchte die Leser von ... überzeugen ...
One can easily follow his train of thought.	Man kann seinen Gedankengang leicht nachvollziehen.
At the end of her essay she draws the conclusion/comes to the conclusion that ...	Am Ende ihres Essays kommt sie zu dem Schluss, dass ...
His/Her arguments are (not) convincing.	Seine/Ihre Argumente sind (nicht) überzeugend.
The main topic of the essay is ...	Das Thema des Essays ist ...
The tone of the essay is humorous/ neutral/ironical/serious.	Der Ton des Essays ist humorvoll/ neutral/ironisch/ernst.
The author uses forceful/powerful/compelling examples to convince her readers.	Die Verfasserin verwendet schlagkräftige/starke Beispiele, um ihre Leserschaft zu überzeugen.
The author's choice of words shows/ emphasizes that he is for/against ...	Die Wortwahl des Verfassers zeigt/unterstreicht, dass er für/gegen ... ist.
She uses a rhetorical question in the opening paragraph as a thread to guide the reader through the rest of the essay.	In der Einleitung stellt sie eine rhetorische Frage, die den Leser wie ein roter Faden durch den weiteren Text leitet.
The author uses adjectives with positive/ negative connotations to support his/her point of view.	Der Verfasser verwendet Adjektive mit positiven/negativen Konnotationen, um seinen Standpunkt zu verdeutlichen.
Her attempt to persuade the readers backfires/works very well.	Ihr Versuch, die Leser zu überreden, misslingt/gelingt.

Factual Texts: How to Analyse Reports

> **Keyword:**
> A **report** is a specific type of newspaper article that presents only the facts of current events. It aims to inform readers rather than manipulate or influence them. A report answers the five "W" questions (Who? What? Where? When? Why?) and the "How" question (How did it happen?).

Sometimes students struggle to differentiate between a report and an article. The latter can also cover current events but is usually a mix of fact and opinion. **Articles** often have a more personal style and aim to entertain readers. They use adjectives, adverbs and direct addresses, often by asking readers hypothetical questions, such as "How would you feel if you discovered that someone had stolen your brand-new car?"

Reports, on the other hand, have the following characteristics:

Elements of a report
Structure

- Reports have **headlines** that provide basic information to arouse the reader's curiosity without providing too many details.
- The first paragraph is an **introduction** that provides the essential information.
- The **main body** consists of several paragraphs, each containing one piece of information.
- The last paragraph serves as a **conclusion.**

Language and style

- Reports are written in a factual style that does not reflect the author's personal opinion or contain any speculation.
- The paragraphs are relatively short with simple sentences to ensure that the reader understands the information.
- Experts or people with first-hand experience of the topic may be quoted, but the author does not provide any personal comments on their statements.

Glossary – Vocabulary for Analysing Reports

The report [title], written by [author], deals with/is about/describes ...	Der Bericht [Titel] von [Verfasser/-in] beschäftigt sich mit/handelt von/ beschreibt ...
The topic(s) of the report is (are) ...	Das Thema/Die Themen des Berichts ist/ sind ...
In the introduction, the reader learns about/gets to know ...	In der Einleitung erfährt der Leser/die Leserin ...
The report can be divided into ... paragraphs.	Der Bericht kann in ... Absätze gegliedert werden.
The report consists of ... paragraphs.	Der Bericht besteht aus ... Absätzen.
The author intends to inform the reader about ...	Es ist das Anliegen des Autors/der Autorin, den Leser/die Leserin über ... zu informieren.
The second/third paragraph provides information on ...	Der zweite/dritte Absatz enthält Informationen über ...
The author quotes an eye witness/ expert who says that ...	Der Autor/Die Autorin zitiert einen Augenzeugen/Experten, der sagt, dass ...
The author describes how ...	Der Verfasser/Die Verfasserin beschreibt, wie ...
The author does not give his/her personal opinion on the topic/problem/ question but merely relates facts.	Der Verfasser/Die Verfasserin äußert nicht seine/ihre eigene Meinung zum Sachverhalt/Problem/zu der Frage, sondern gibt lediglich Fakten wieder.
The factual style of writing shows that it is the author's aim to inform the reader and not to entertain him/her.	Der sachliche Sprachgebrauch verdeutlicht, dass es das Anliegen des Autors/ der Autorin ist, den Leser zu informieren und nicht, ihn zu unterhalten.

Visuelle Materialien

Das Schwerpunktthema im Abitur 2024 umfasst unter anderem auch den Film *Gran Torino*. In der Prüfung und den vorausgehenden Klausuren können Ihnen in den verschiedenen Anforderungsbereichen nicht nur Texte, sondern auch Bildimpulse vorgelegt werden. Um die Aufgaben zu diesen visuellen Materialien sinnvoll bearbeiten zu können, müssen Sie sich vorab mit den verschiedenen Arten von Bildimpulsen und den grundlegenden Begriffen zur Filmanalyse befassen.

How to Analyse Films

Filmarten

Spielfilm	(feature) film/ movie	erzählt meist eine Geschichte (fiktional oder realen Personen oder Ereignissen nachempfunden)
Dokumentar-film	documentary	konzentriert sich auf Fakten, um Informationen zu vermitteln
Werbefilm	commercial	ein kurzer Film, der für ein Produkt oder eine Dienstleistung wirbt und zum Kauf bzw. zur Nutzung animieren soll

Genres

Actionfilm	action film	enthält spektakuläre Elemente wie Explosionen, Verfolgungsjagden und Kämpfe
Abenteuerfilm	adventure film	handelt meist von einer Reise und spielt an fantastischen oder exotischen Schauplätzen
Komödie	comedy	intendiert, die Zuschauer zum Lachen zu bringen
Drama	drama	handelt häufig von Lebenskrisen oder lebensverändernden Ereignissen
Fantasyfilm	fantasy film	enthält Elemente, die nur in der menschlichen Fantasie existieren
Historischer Film	historical film	handelt von historischen Ereignissen oder zeigt eine fiktive Handlung in einem historischen Kontext
Musikfilm	musical film	enthält viele (oder ausschließlich) Lieder, die Teil der Handlung sind; häufig wird auch getanzt
Liebesfilm	romance	thematisiert die Liebe zwischen Menschen
Science-Fiction-Film	science fiction film	handelt vom Einfluss fiktionaler Technologien und wissenschaftlicher Leistungen auf die Zukunft
Thriller	thriller	ist durch anhaltende Spannung gekennzeichnet
Western	western	spielt im amerikanischen Westen im 19. Jhdt.

Schritt 1: Basisinformationen

– Benennen Sie zuerst die Filmart oder das Genre.
– Geben Sie Basisinformationen zum Film an: **Titel, Regisseur/-in, Produktionsjahr, Herkunftsland, Thematik** und ggf. **Drehbuchautor/-in** oder **literarische Vorlage, Produzent/-in, Schauspieler/-innen, Soundtrack.**
   (Gran Torino is a feature film/a drama directed by Clint Eastwood and was produced in the USA in 2008. It touches complex issues such as racism in a multicultural society, American masculinity, and the ambiguity of belonging.)

Schritt 2: Überblick

– Fassen Sie die Handlung zusammen und nennen Sie dabei a) den Handlungsort und den Zeitraum sowie b) die wichtigen Charaktere.
   (The film tells the story of a racist veteran of the Korean War who lives in a troubled Detroit neighbourhood.)

Schritt 3: Filmsequenzen analysieren

– Beschreiben Sie zunächst Ihren **ersten Eindruck** der ausgewählten Sequenz.

Beschreibung des ersten Eindrucks	When I first saw the sequence I thought … The scene is shocking/beautiful/tragic because …

– Beschreiben Sie im Folgenden, **worum es in der Szene geht** und wo sie im **Gesamtkontext** steht. Achten Sie dabei auf den **Handlungsverlauf** (Was passiert?), den **Handlungsort** und die **Handlungszeit** (Wo und wann findet die Szene statt?), die **Charaktere/Darsteller/-innen** (Wer ist daran beteiligt?), den **Spannungsaufbau** (Wo liegt die Interaktion, der Konflikt?) und die **Atmosphäre** (beispielsweise friedlich, heiter, düster oder bedrohlich?)

Situation	The sequence is about … The sequence reminds me of …
Zusammenhang im Gesamtkontext	The sequence is set in … after/before …. The sequence introduces new characters/… The sequence represents a turning point because …
Handlungsverlauf	It deals with the problem of … It presents/shows/mirrors/reveals/…. Suspense is created by/arises from … The main cause of suspense is …
Spannungsaufbau	Everything changes when … There is a conflict between … At first …, but then …
Atmosphäre	The atmosphere in this sequence is peaceful/serene/somber/depressing/scary/terrifying/…

– Gehen Sie auf **die Charaktere** ein und achten Sie dabei auf ihr Aussehen und ihre Körpersprache sowie ihr Verhalten und ihre Beziehungen untereinander. Achten Sie auch auf die Sprache und die Art der Kommunikation.

Charaktere	The audience is introduced to …/gets to know … There are three main characters: …	
Aussehen (appearance)	He/She is …	attractive/slim/tall/…
	He/She …	is wearing clean/dirty/tidy clothes. looks neat/groomed/cultivated/…
Verhalten (behaviour)	He/She is … There is something … about him/her.	*Positive:* gentle/quiet/brave/honest/open-minded/optimistic/self-confident/suave/sophisticated *Negative:* aggressive/dangerous/threatening/anxious/dishonest/narrow-minded/rude/shy/dominant/sinister
Beziehungen (relationships)	This character represents … He/She finds himself in a conflict with/has an inner conflict because… X and X are friends/have a relationship/…	
Sprache	His voice is …	loud/quiet/soft/pleasant
Kommunikation	There is a lot of/almost no/(very) little dialogue in this sequence. The character's monologue is about … There is a dialogue/a heated discussion/a quiet conversation/ … about … between X and Y. The scene presents an important dialogue/a key monologue/…	

– Gehen Sie auf die **Gestaltungselemente** ein und achten Sie dabei auf die Kamera-perspektive und -bewegung, die Beleuchtung, den Schnitt sowie den Ton, die Musik und Spezialeffekte. Erwähnen Sie auch wiederkehrende Objekte mit Symbolcharakter.

Kameraabstände (camera position and movement)	The scene is shot from X's point of view/a high angle/eye-level./The scene is seen from the perspective of ...
	The director uses a long shot/static shot/over-the-shoulder shot/high-angle shot/low-angle shot/helicopter shot/ a lot of close-ups/many brief shots/...
	The camera shoots from a high/low angle/pulls back/moves in/closes in on .../fades in on .../fades out from .../pans from left to right/tilts up and down/zooms in on .../zooms out from ...
	This shot is taken from a bird's eye view/worm's eye view.
	The hand-held camera underlines .../gives the scene an unsteady quality/aims at authenticity/...
	There is a tracking shot as the camera follows ...
Schnitt (cut), special effects (colour, fast or slow motion, freeze frame ...), Bildteilung (split screen)	The use of slow motion/black and white/intense colour emphasizes ...
	The director's use of fast motion/black-and-white/fast cuts/ freeze frames stresses ...
	To contrast the characters, the director makes use of warm red and cold blue/...
Beleuchtung (lighting)	The use of bright light/low-key lighting/backlighting/ semi-darkness/darkness/artificial illumination creates/...
	The director uses low-key lighting/high contrast lighting in order to ...
Ton und Musik (sound)	The film music/repeated melody/background noise creates/ contributes to/provides/...
	The upbeat/gloomy/aggressive/slow/fast-paced/... sound-track contributes to the atmosphere of the scene.
	There is a voice-over.

How to Describe Pictures

Im Folgenden finden Sie thematisch zusammengefasste und einzelnen Arbeitsschritten zugeordnete Redemittel. Die kursiv gedruckten Begriffe können innerhalb der Formulierungen ausgetauscht werden.

TIPP zum Punktesammeln

Achten Sie auf einen natürlichen und authentischen Sprachfluss und wählen Sie Formulierungen, die zu Ihrem persönlichen Schreibstil passen und sich harmonisch einfügen.

Schritt 1: Erster Eindruck

– Beschreiben Sie zunächst die Bildart.
   (The picture is an advertisement ...)
– Beschreiben Sie kurz, welche Situation das Bild zeigt.
   (The picture is a photograph/photo showing a group of athletes surrounded by armed police offficers.)
– Nennen Sie den Titel und (wenn angegeben) die Quellen des Bilds (Künstler/-in oder Fotograf/-in, Entstehungsdatum, Veröffentlichungsort, Veröffentlichungsdatum).
   (It was taken by an unknown artist and published in National Geographic.)
– Möglicherweise gibt es auch einen Hinweis bezüglich des Anlasses der Veröffentlichung (z. B. Olympische Spiele, Wahlen, aktuelle Diskussionen) oder der Motive des Künstlers/der Künstlerin.
   (The photograph was published during the Olympic Games in London.)

Beschreibung des ersten Eindrucks	The *picture* gives the impression that ...	Das Bild vermittelt den Eindruck, als ob ...
	When I first saw the *photo/ photograph* I thought ...	Als ich das Foto zum ersten Mal sah, dachte ich ...
	The *collage* reminds me of ...	Die Collage erinnert mich an ...
	When looking at the *painting*, my first association is ...	Meine erste Assoziation beim Betrachten des Bildes ist ...
Beschreibung der gezeigten Situation	The *photograph* shows ...	Das Foto zeigt ...
	This is a *painting* showing a typical scene ...	Das Bild zeigt eine typische Szene ...
	This *digital image* illustrates ...	Dieses digitale Bild zeigt ...
	This is a still *(from the film ...)* showing the scene/situation in which ...	Dies ist ein Standfoto (aus dem Film ...), das die Szene/ Situation zeigt, in der ...
	In this *illustration* you can see ...	Auf dieser Abbildung kann man ... sehen.

Schritt 2: Beschreibung des Bilds

Verwenden Sie bei der Bildbeschreibung stets das *present tense*.
Beispiel: *In the foreground there **is** a group of people.*
Wenn Sie aber beschreiben, was Personen im Bild gerade tun, verwenden Sie das *present progressive/present continuous*.
Beispiel: *They **are sitting** around a table.*

Betrachten Sie das Bild genau und wählen Sie je nach Art des Bilds eine der beiden nachfolgend erläuterten Methoden zur Beschreibung. Beantworten Sie in Ihrer Beschreibung möglichst die W-Fragen „Wer?", „Wo?" und „Was?".
Zeigt das Bild eine markante Situation, z. B. mit einer Person in einem Raum oder einem Gebäude in einer Landschaft, dann beginnen Sie mit der detaillierten Beschreibung des Hauptaspekts im Vordergrund. Geben Sie danach eine Beschreibung des Hintergrunds. Besteht keine ersichtliche Dominanz einer Person oder eines Gegenstands, dann empfiehlt es sich, mit einer Beschreibungsrichtung zu arbeiten, das heißt, Sie arbeiten sich von links nach rechts oder von oben nach unten oder umgekehrt vor.

Beschreibung der Anordnung von Objekten oder Personen im Bild	In the foreground/background/centre *you can see* ...	Im Vordergrund/Hintergrund/Zentrum sieht man ...
	At the top/At the bottom *there is* ...	Oben/Unten befindet sich ...
	In the upper right-hand corner/bottom left-hand corner *you can see* ...	In der oberen rechten/unteren linken Ecke sieht man ...
	On the left/right ... can be seen/are depicted.	Auf der linken/rechten Seite kann man ... sehen/werden ... dargestellt.
	In the lower left hand corner *the viewer finds* ...	In der unteren linken Ecke ...
Beschreibung der Bildart	The picture is a(n) ...	... photograph/photo/painting/digital image/advertisement/cartoon/film still/chart

Beschreiben Sie auch die **Körpersprache** der abgebildeten Personen:
- Gestik *(gestures)*,
- Mimik *(facial expression)*,
- Körperhaltung *(posture)*,
- Ausdruck *(expression)*.

| Beschreibung der Gestik, Mimik, Körpersprache | The person's body language indicates that he/she is ... | ... in pain/self-confident/ scared/insecure/helpless/ enjoying himself/herself ... |
| | His/Her facial expression suggests that he/she is ... | amazed/frightened/nervous/ annoyed/calm/happy/... |

Nennen Sie die Techniken, die der/die Künstler/-in verwendet. Beschreiben Sie den Einsatz von Licht und Schatten. Gibt es verschwommene, unscharfe Bildbereiche? Wie wird Farbe eingesetzt?

Beschreibung der künstlerischen Techniken	The colours are bright/brilliant/vibrant/vivid/bold/intense/ rich/dark/deep/light/soft/muted/pale/pastel/soft/...
	The photograph is ... clear/blurred/blurry/out of focus/full of contrasts.
	The artist used oil paint/watercolours/crayons.
	The technique of using light brush strokes/only outlines/a mix of materials/... creates ...
	The photographer used a close up/a soft focus/a sharp focus/... to stress/attract attention to/...
Beschreibung der Atmosphäre	The colours/... create a cosy/friendly/warm/lively/peaceful/ dark/depressing/scary/serious/terrifying/... atmosphere.
	These factors contribute to the atmosphere being exotic/ hectic/mysterious/confusing/...
	The ... in the photo convey(s) an atmosphere of great happiness/sadness/confusion/...

Schritt 3: Die Beschriftung

Beachten Sie die Bildunterschrift *(caption)*, die Überschrift *(heading)* bzw. den Titel *(title)* und erläutern Sie den Bezug zum Dargestellten.

Schritt 4: Analyse, Interpretation und Intention

Bei der Bildanalyse bzw. Bildinterpretation verwerten Sie die Informationen, die Sie durch die Bildbeschreibung gewonnen haben, d.h., Sie ziehen Schlussfolgerungen aus dem Beschriebenen bezüglich der Intention *(intention)* des Künstlers/der Künstlerin und bilden sich abschließend eine persönliche Meinung über das Bild, die Sie überzeugend begründen (siehe Schritt 5, Seite 144).

Schließen Sie die Schlussfolgerungen an Ihre vorangegangenen Betrachtungen an. Folgende Fragen können hierbei richtungsweisend sein:
- In welcher Beziehung stehen die Menschen in dem Bild zueinander? Welche Interpretationen lassen die Körperhaltung, Mimik und Gestik der Personen zu und was ist die Botschaft dahinter? Werden die Personen positiv, negativ oder neutral dargestellt?

- Bezieht sich das Bild auf etwas Bestimmtes (ein historisches Ereignis, eine soziale Fragestellung, eine politische Entwicklung ...)?
- Welchen Eindruck versucht das Bild zu vermitteln? Was soll den Betrachtenden suggeriert werden?
- Was ist die Absicht des Künstlers/der Künstlerin? Welche Botschaft möchte er/sie vermitteln und was soll dadurch bewirkt werden?
- Gibt es eine Zielgruppe *(target group)* und wenn ja, welche?

Interpretation und Intention	The collage suggests ...
	The painting gives you the impression that ...
	The photograph arouses feelings of ...
	X's facial expression suggests ...
	From the look of the woman, you can assume that ...
	The artist wants to express his/her approval/disapproval of ...
	The artist wants to illustrate the problem of ...
	Perhaps his/her intention is .../It seems to be his/her intention to ...
	The illustration is aimed at ...
	The photograph mainly targets ...
	... are the target group.

Schritt 5: Wirkung und persönliche Meinung

Im abschließenden Teil der Bildanalyse beschreiben Sie die Wirkung, die das Bild auf Sie hat, und begründen Ihre persönliche Meinung.

Wirkung und persönliche Meinung	I think/I believe the painting is meant to ...
	The impression I get from this illustration is that ...
	The painting makes me feel ...
	To my mind, it would be better/clearer/more impressive/... if the artist had used more/less/...
	It touches/moves me.
	It does not appeal to me.
	I like/don't like/dislike it because ...
	In conclusion I can say ...

How to Describe Cartoons

Karikaturen *(cartoons)* bestehen meist aus einer Illustration o. Ä. und einem kurzen Text, der entweder in Form von Sprechblasen *(speech bubbles)* oder als Bildunterschrift *(caption, punch line or written comment)* erscheint. Karikaturen sind satirische Darstellungen von Personen oder Situationen. Ziel ist es, gesellschaftliche Zustände, Institutionen oder Persönlichkeiten durch Übertreibung und Verformung auf humorvolle Weise kritisch darzustellen. Sie werden häufig in Zeitungen und Zeitschriften veröffentlicht.

Häufige Stilmittel

- **Exaggeration** (Übertreibung): Eigenschaften werden überzogen und überspitzt dargestellt.
  Beispiel: *The artist chose to reduce President Sarkozy's height to that of a child, whereas President Obama's height is drastically increased, thus stressing the difference in strength by exaggerating their physical appearance.*
- **Irony** (Ironie): Das Gegenteil des Gesagten ist gemeint.
- **Pun** (Wortspiel): Wörter werden verdreht und Doppel- oder Mehrdeutigkeiten bewusst eingesetzt.
- **Simile** (Vergleich): Ein direkter Vergleich zwischen zwei Dingen, in dem „like" oder „as" verwendet wird, um sie in Beziehung zu setzen.
  Beispiel: *She was as light as a feather.*
- **Symbol** (Symbol): Ein wahrnehmbares Zeichen bzw. Sinnbild (Gegenstand, Handlung, Vorgang), das stellvertretend für etwas nicht Wahrnehmbares (auch Gedachtes bzw. Geglaubtes) steht
  Beispiel: *The young man is holding a globe, a symbol of globalization, in his hands.*

Die Analyse einer Karikatur gliedert sich in vier Schritte und ist ähnlich aufgebaut wie die Bildbeschreibung/Bildanalyse. So können auch Redemittel zur Bildbeschreibung und -analyse übernommen und entsprechend angepasst werden. Im Folgenden sind zusätzliche und spezifische Redemittel aufgelistet.

Schritt 1: Thema und Beschreibung der Karikatur

Es gibt verschiedene Arten von Karikaturen:
- Karikaturen, die aus einem Bild und einer entsprechenden Bildunterschrift bestehen, werden **single-panel cartoon** genannt.
- Karikaturen, die ähnlich einem Comic aus einer inhaltlich verbundenen Serie von Illustrationen bestehen, werden **comic strip** genannt.
- Karikaturen, die in Zusammenhang mit einem (Leit-)Artikel stehen, werden **editorial cartoon** genannt und sind häufig ernster in Ton und Thematik als die oben genannten. Metaphern *(metaphors)* und Ironie *(irony)* werden eingesetzt, um soziale oder politische Situationen oder Zustände satirisch darzustellen *(to satirize)*.
- Benennen Sie klar das Thema der Karikatur, bevor Sie diese beschreiben.

	The topic of the cartoon is .../The cartoon deals with .../ The cartoon is about ...
Beschreibung der Karikatur	The cartoonist shows ...
	The cartoon consists of an illustration/a single panel/two panels showing ...
	The comic strip shows ...
	The caption/punch line is presented as direct speech in speech bubbles/as a general statement which reads: "..."
	The situation reminds one/you/me of ...

Die Aussagen in den Sprechblasen können auch in indirekter Rede wiedergegeben werden.

Beispiele: *The younger woman asks, "Could I perhaps borrow that buggy? I'd look so multi-taskable!"*

The younger woman asks if she could perhaps borrow the buggy so she would appear more "multi-taskable", meaning more competent due to her multi-tasking abilities.

Schritt 2: Interpretation/Analyse der Karikatur

Bei der Analyse einer Karikatur ist es wichtig, folgende Fragen zu berücksichtigen:

Setting – Ort und Zeit
- In welchem räumlichen und zeitlichen Kontext steht die Karikatur?
- In welchem thematischen Zusammenhang muss die Karikatur betrachtet werden?

Characters – Figuren
- Welche Haltungen und Werte repräsentieren die Figuren?
- Welche Aktionen und Gefühle werden durch die Körpersprache der Personen zum Ausdruck gebracht *(to communicate through body language)*?
- Welche Gefühle werden durch Mimik zum Ausdruck gebracht?
- Was wird anhand der Körpersprache hinsichtlich der Beziehung zwischen den Personen angedeutet oder suggeriert?

Action – Ereignisse
- Was geschieht gerade?
- Wie wird das Geschehen dargestellt?

Language – Sprache
- Welches Sprachregister wird verwendet? Was wird tatsächlich gesagt?
- Wird Interpunktion verwendet, um Emotionen zu verdeutlichen?

Stereotypes and symbols – Klischees und Symbole
- Verwendet der/die Karikaturist/-in Klischees *(stereotypes)*?
- Setzt er/sie Symbole ein, um eine Aussage zu vermitteln?

Irony and exaggeration – Ironie und Übertreibung
- Verwendet der Cartoonist/die Cartoonistin eine Übertreibung? Wenn ja, wo? Welche Wirkung hat der Einsatz dieser Übertreibung?
- Wird etwas im Cartoon ironisch dargestellt? Wenn ja, was? Welche Wirkung hat die Ironie?

Interpretation und Analyse	The character/... resembles ...
	He/She is a caricature of ...
	The cartoonist exaggerates character traits by ...
	The person's body language conveys/shows/reveals/... that ...
	The person's formal language hints at ...
	His/Her facial expression suggests that ...
	... symbolizes/stands for/is a symbol of ...
	The cartoonist uses irony to .../The use of irony makes it clear that ...

Schritt 3: Botschaft und persönliche Meinung

Bei diesem Schritt ist es ratsam, sich nochmals auf die politischen und sozialen Umstände zu besinnen, in deren Kontext die Karikatur zu verstehen ist. Möglicherweise besteht die Prüfungsaufgabe auch darin, die Karikatur in Bezug zu einem Text zu setzen. Versuchen Sie dann, die Botschaft und die Absicht des Karikaturisten/der Karikaturistin darzulegen. Abschließend werten Sie die Karikatur hinsichtlich Wirkung und Effekt.

Botschaft der Karikatur	The cartoonist is making a sarcastic comment on ...
	He/She is making fun of ...
	He/She wants to ridicule/draw attention to/caricature ...
	The artist criticizes the behaviour of/...
	The intention of the cartoonist is to show that ...
	The artist's point seems to be ...
	Probably he/she wants to reveal what is behind ...
	He/She wants to make the reader aware of ...
	The real point the cartoon is making seems to be ...
	The message is accentuated by ...

Darlegung der persönlichen Meinung	I think the cartoonist successfully exposes/conveys/...
	I think the cartoon achieves an impressive effect because ...
	The cartoon convincingly/impressively conveys the message that ... because ...
	The cartoon is effective/not effective in its presentation/portrayal/... of ... because ...
	I think the cartoon is difficult to understand because ...

Informationen zur Sprachmittlung

Ziel der Sprachmittlungsaufgabe ist die Überführung eines Inhalts von einer Ausgangs-sprache (Deutsch) in eine Zielsprache (Englisch). Es ist wichtig zu beachten, dass hierbei keine Übersetzung erwartet wird, sondern die sinngemäße Wiedergabe bestimmter Informationen eines Textes.

Wichtige Fertigkeiten zur Bewältigung einer Mediationsaufgabe

1. In Bezug auf den Ausgangstext sollten Sie die Methoden *skimming* und *scanning* sowie Markierungstechniken anwenden können.
2. In Bezug auf den Zieltext erfordert die Sprachmittlung einen souveränen Umgang mit der englischen Sprache, sodass Ausdrücke und idiomatische Redewendungen nicht wörtlich übernommen, sondern in korrektes und dem Kontext entsprechendes Englisch umgesetzt werden müssen.
3. Sie sollten Wichtiges von Unwichtigem unterscheiden und sowohl inhaltliche als auch sprachliche Vereinfachungsstrategien anwenden können.
4. Eine weitere Voraussetzung ist ein gewisses Maß an soziokultureller Kompetenz, das heißt, dass Sie erkennen, was jemand aufgrund seines kulturellen Hintergrunds nicht wissen kann und was ihm somit erklärt werden muss. (Beispiel: *„Spiegel online" is a political internet magazine.)*
5. Es ist empfehlenswert, sich intensiv mit *connectives* sowie Redemitteln und Idiomen auseinanderzusetzen (siehe Seite 24f.).

Analyse des Ausgangstextes

Folgende Aspekte sollten bei der Analyse des Ausgangstextes berücksichtigt werden:

1. Bei Sachtexten als Ausgangstext:
   Aus wessen Sicht ist der Ausgangstext geschrieben? Wer „spricht"?
   Was ist die Aussage des Ausgangstextes?
   Was ist die Absicht des Autors/der Autorin?
   Warum wurde der Text geschrieben?

2. Bei literarischen Ausgangstexten:
   Wer sind die Protagonist/-innen?
   Wie können sie charakterisiert werden?
   Wie agieren und interagieren sie?
   Was ist das Hauptthema des Textes?
   Wie ist die Atmosphäre?

3. Die Aufgabenstellung:

Welche Rolle spielen Sie bzw. welche Funktion haben Sie?

Für wen schreiben Sie Ihren Text?

Warum sollen Sie diesen Text schreiben? Was sind die Umstände?

Was ist der Zweck?

Welche Textform ist gewünscht?

Beispiel: *During his stay in Germany, your American exchange partner was surprised about the way German schools handle security issues, especially since he/she is used to very intensive security checks in his/her high school in New York City, including armed guards using metal detectors. After his/her return to the US he/she contacted you asking for your help in a presentation he/she has to give on his stay in Germany. He/She wants to inform his fellow students on the discussion about school security and surveillance in Germany. You have found this article in "Spiegel online". Write an email to your friend in which you summarize the most important aspects explained in the article.*

Ihre Rolle:	Austauschpartner/-in des/der amerikanischen Schülers/Schülerin
Adressat:	Ihr/-e amerikanische/-r Austauschschüler/-in
Thema:	Argumente bezüglich Überwachungs- und Sicherheitsmaßnahmen an Schulen in Deutschland
Kontext:	1. Ihr/-e Austauschpartner/-in war überrascht über den Umgang mit Sicherheit an Ihrer deutschen Schule im Vergleich zu den strikten Maßnahmen an seiner/ihrer Schule in den USA.
	2. Im Rahmen einer Präsentation über seinen/ihren Aufenthalt in Deutschland möchte er/sie seine Mitschüler/-innen über die Diskussion zu diesem Thema in Deutschland informieren.
Zieltextformat:	E-Mail
Sprache:	gepflegtes Englisch, aber nicht förmlich, da Sie an eine gleichaltrige Person schreiben, die Sie gut kennen

Vorgehensweise – Schritt für Schritt

Die folgende Arbeitsweise hilft Ihnen, die Mediation zu meistern.

1. Lesen Sie sorgfältig die Aufgabenstellung und notieren Sie, welche Information Sie dem Ausgangstext laut Aufgabenstellung entnehmen sollen (siehe Seite 149). Sie müssen also für die Aufgabe wesentliche Informationen von irrelevanten Informationen unterscheiden können. Finden Sie Schlüsselbegriffe.

2. Arbeiten Sie den Text Absatz für Absatz durch und markieren Sie die wesentlichen Sätze und Passagen (gemäß Aufgabenstellung).
   Weglassen können Sie
   - Informationen, die nicht zum Verständnis beitragen (etwa Beispiele, Anekdoten, persönliche Erfahrungen des Autors/der Autorin)
   - Detailinformationen
   - Wiederholungen.
   Ordnen Sie die gefundenen Schlüsselbegriffe und überprüfen Sie, ob Sie noch etwas hinzufügen oder weglassen können. Lesen Sie dafür am besten nochmals die Aufgabe.

3. Schreiben Sie Ihren englischen Text passend zum Kontext und zur adressierten Person. Achten Sie …
   - auf die Rolle, die Sie gemäß der Aufgabenstellung einnehmen
   - auf das erforderliche Sprachregister
   - auf den Zweck Ihres Textes (Sollen Sie informieren, kritisieren, erklären …?)
   - auf die formalen Aspekte des geforderten Textformats (z. B. Grußformeln in einer E-Mail).
   Lesen Sie Ihren Text nochmals durch und verfeinern Sie den Stil und das Register durch passende Redemittel.

4. Überprüfen Sie, …
   - ob Ihr Text dem erforderten Kontext entspricht und korrekt adressiert ist
   - ob Sie alle markierten Teile des Ausgangstextes in Ihrem Text erfasst haben
   - ob Sie die Details zum Textformat bedacht haben
   - ob Ihr Text klar strukturiert ist
   - ob Ihr Text flüssig formuliert ist
   - ob die Argumentation logisch aufgebaut ist
   - ob Sie die Zeiten korrekt verwendet haben
   - ob die Rechtschreibung korrekt ist.

Beispiele für Prüfungsaufgaben

Trainingsaufgaben

Aufgaben zum Hörverstehen (Prüfungsteil A I)

Tipps und Informationen

Das Hörverstehen ist im Leistungsfach der erste Teil der schriftlichen Abiturprüfung. Dabei wird authentisches Audiomaterial aus dem englischsprachigen Raum verwendet. Bitte bedenken Sie, dass Sie den Hörverstehensteil direkt vor dem Teil II Leseverstehen bearbeiten. Hier einige Tipps zum Ablauf:

- In der Klausur hören Sie die Aufzeichnung zweimal. Die Dauer des Beitrags liegt normalerweise zwischen vier und sechs Minuten. Sie sollten die Aufgabenblätter vor dem ersten Hören bereits vor sich liegen haben, durchgelesen haben und die Bedeutung schwieriger Formulierungen und Wörter mithilfe des *dictionary* herausgefunden haben.
- Als problematisch hat sich das Ausfüllen von Aufgaben mit Bleistift erwiesen. Im Abitur dürfen nur dokumentenechte Stifte verwendet werden. Wenn Sie die Lösungen beim ersten Hören mit Bleistift eintragen, bleibt Ihnen während des zweiten Hörens und danach sehr wenig Zeit, alles bisher Geschriebene wegzuradieren und mit einem dokumentenechten Stift erneut zu schreiben. Empfohlen wird der Einsatz eines Bleistifts daher nur bei den Multiple-choice- oder Zuordnungsaufgaben, bei denen relativ wenig geschrieben werden muss.
- Es ist hilfreich, während des ersten Hörens nur den ersten Buchstaben oder die erste Silbe eines Lösungsworts zu notieren (z. B. bei *gap-filling tasks*). Die Zeit zwischen dem ersten und zweiten Hören können Sie dann dazu nutzen, die Wörter zu vervollständigen und zum Beispiel mit einem Textmarker zu kennzeichnen, welche Teile Sie noch gar nicht, nur unvollständig oder eher unsicher bearbeitet haben. Dies hilft Ihnen, Ihre Konzentration beim zweiten Hören auf die Lücken zu richten.

Es ist auch eine gute Übung, sich selbst Hörverstehenstexte (zum Beispiel auf www.bbc.co.uk/sounds/play) zu einem abiturrelevanten Themengebiet anzuhören und dazu Fragen aufzuschreiben. Die Audios sollten zwei bis sechs Minuten lang sein. Hören Sie einen Text wie in der Abiturprüfung zweimal. Im zweiten Durchgang beantworten Sie die Fragen. Sie können auch mit einem Trainingspartner oder einer Trainingspartnerin arbeiten und sich gegenseitig Fragen zu unterschiedlichen Audios vorlegen.

Beispielaufgabe 1: *Mum's cooking makes jobs*

Quelle: https://www.bbc.co.uk/sounds/play/p018zgpl
(last accessed: 18 April 2023)

AUFGABENSTELLUNG

You will hear a radio programme about Asians in Britain.
You can listen to the recording twice. Read the tasks before listening to the recording.
Finalize your answers while listening a second time.

Task 1

Complete the sentences.
You do not have to write complete sentences. See the example (0).

0	The speaker's mother had always wanted to start a food business but did not do it because of … (Give two answers.)	*a) lack of confidence* *b) lack of formal qualifications (and language barriers)*
1	Things started to change when the speaker … (Give two answers.)	*a)* *b)*
2	After the children have left the house, women in the South Asian community consider themselves …	
3	Women from these ethnic minority backgrounds are not usually found in the statistics and do not claim …	
4	Their behaviour can be misinterpreted as …	
5	Irene motivated herself to be a part of 'Mummy's Cooking' because she thought she … (Give two answers.)	*a)* *b)*
6	At first she … how she was going to be perceived.	
7	Having done training makes her feel good because …	
8	Irene believes it is a barrier that older people think that the kind of training she received …	

Task 2

True or false? Tick the correct box.

		true	false
1.	The speaker set up 'Mummy's Cooking' together with some members of his family.	☐	☐
2.	Unemployment is rising especially among women from ethnic minority backgrounds.	☐	☐
3.	The fear of failing is one reason why Irene lacked confidence at first.	☐	☐

Lösungen

Task 1

1. a) was studying at university.
   b) had to eat bad food there.
2. too old to find employment.
3. unemployment benefit.
4. lack of willingness to work.
5. a) was a good candidate.
   b) could be independent.
6. feared
7. she can make good food and present it.
8. is for young people.

Task 2

1. false   2. true   3. false

Beispielaufgabe 2: *Climate change*

Dies ist eine anspruchsvolle Aufgabe. Sie können die Tonaufnahme mehrfach hören.
Quelle: https://www.npr.org/2022/02/28/1083580995/some-effects-of-climate-change-are-irreversible-but-theres-still-hope (last accessed: 18 April 2023)[1]

Task 1

Match the speakers to the statements.

Speaker		Statement no.
A	Mr Shapiro	
B	Mr O'Neill	
C	Mr Guterres	

1. ... believes that we have failed to address climate-related issues effectively.
2. ... states that fatalities and destruction are finally being related to climate change.
3. ... says it is possible to limit global warming to 1.5 degrees, but we should be prepared for failure to achieve this goal.

[1] Sie können die Tonaufnahme auf der Seite von finaleonline.de anhören. Geben Sie dazu den Code von Seite 2 in diesem Buch ein.

Task 2

Complete the sentences.

1. Due to climate change, poverty …
2. The damage to people, building and infrastructure will be high in …
3. At the same time, however, experts expect …

Task 3

Tick the correct answer.

Mr O'Neill states that nowadays scientists understand much better that in order to protect those who will suffer most …
a) there has to be special training to teach them how to build resilience. ☐
b) international cooperation and aid programmes are necessary. ☐
c) it is important to improve living conditions in addition to taking climate-specific measures. ☐

Lösungen

Task 1

Speaker	Statement no.
A Mr Shapiro	2
B Mr O'Neill	3
C Mr Guterres	1

Task 2
1. Due to climate change poverty will increase massively/tens or hundreds of millions of additional people will live in poverty.
2. The damage to people, buildings and infrastructure will be high in low-lying areas close to the coast.
3. At the same time, however, experts expect progress with regard to such outcomes to continue.

Task 3
c) Mr O'Neill states that nowadays people in charge understand much better that in order to protect those who will suffer most, it is important to improve living conditions in addition to undertaking climate-specific measures.

Im Folgenden finden Sie Trainingsaufgaben zu den verschiedenen Aufgabenformaten, die Ihnen nach dem Hörverstehen gestellt werden können.

Es ist empfehlenswert, nicht nur das Lösen der Aufgaben zu trainieren, sondern auch Ihr Zeitmanagement für die Prüfung selbst zu optimieren. Dazu können Sie sich aus den verschiedenen Aufgabentypen jeweils eine Aufgabe auswählen und dann versuchen, Ihre so zusammengestellte Prüfungsklausur in 225 Minuten zu bearbeiten.

Aufgaben zum Leseverstehen (Prüfungsteil A II.1)

Aufgabe 1: Sachtext/Politische Rede

AUFGABENSTELLUNG

Summarize US Vice President Kamala Harris's view on the status of democracy as well as the status of women, and outline the measures she specifies to improve both.

Materialgrundlage

Kamala Harris, "Remarks by Vice President Kamala Harris As Delivered to the Commission on the Status of Women", March 16, 2021 (speech held at that UN Commission) https://www.whitehouse.gov/briefing-room/speeches-remarks/2021/03/16/pretaped-remarks-by-vice-president-kamala-harris-as-delivered-to-the-commission-on-the-status-of-women/ (last accessed: 18 April 2023)

Remarks by Vice President Kamala Harris As Delivered to the Commission on the Status of Women *Kamala Harris*

Mr. Secretary-General, Mr. Chairperson of the Commission, Madam Executive Director, Distinguished Ministers, Excellencies, civil society members – it is an honor
5 to address this esteemed commission.

Since 1947, this commission has documented the realities women face, shaped global standards on women's rights, and stood for gender equality.

10 That work is as urgent now as it was at the start.

On behalf of the United States, thank you.

This year, in considering the status of women, especially as it pertains to the par-
15 ticipation of women in decision-making, we must also consider the status of democracy.

At its best, democracy protects human rights, promotes human dignity, and upholds the rule of law. 20

It is a means to establish peace and shared prosperity. It should ensure every citizen – regardless of gender – has an equal voice.

And free and fair elections that will 25 respect the will of the people.

At the same time, democracy requires constant vigilance, constant improvement.

It is a work-in-progress.

And today, we know that democracy is 30 increasingly under great strain.

For 15 consecutive years, we have seen a troubling decline in freedom around the globe.

35 In fact, experts believe that this past year was the worst on record for the global deterioration of democracy and freedom.

So, even as we confront a global health crisis and an economic crisis, it is critical 40 that we continue to defend democracy.

To that end, the United States is strengthening our engagement with the United Nations and the broader multilateral system.

We are also rejoining the Human Rights 45 Council.

Because we know the status of democracy depends on our collective commitment to those values articulated in the Universal Declaration of Human Rights.

50 The status of democracy also depends fundamentally on the empowerment of women.

Not only because the exclusion of women in decision-making is a marker of a 55 flawed democracy, but because the participation of women strengthens democracy.

And that's true everywhere.

Looking around the world, I am inspired by the progress that is being made.

60 And I am proud to report that, while the United States still has work to do, we, too, are making progress – and that women strengthen our democracy every day.

In every presidential election for the last 65 56 years, in the United States, more women have voted than men.

More women than ever before serve in the United States Congress.

More women than ever before are their 70 family's breadwinner.

And just last week, the President nominated two women to take the helm of two of our 11 combatant commands.

Women in the United States lead our 75 local, state, and national governments, make major decisions regarding our nation's security, and drive major growth in our economy.

80 These are signs of progress. These are signs of strength.

But, friends, we cannot take this progress for granted.

Especially now.

85 COVID-19 has threatened the economic security, the physical security, and the health of women everywhere.

As women struggle to get the healthcare they need, the pandemic appears to be reversing the global gains we've made in 90 the fights against HIV/AIDS, tuberculosis, malaria, malnutrition, and maternal and child mortality.

That's why, on the first day of our Administration, the United States re-en-95 gaged as a member state and leader in the World Health Organization.

And we are revitalizing our partnership with UN Women, to help empower women worldwide.

100 Here's the truth:

When women face obstacles to obtaining quality healthcare …

When women face food insecurity …

When women are more likely to live in 105 poverty, and therefore disproportionately impacted by climate change …

More vulnerable to gender-based violence, and therefore disproportionately impacted by conflict …

110 Well it's harder for women to fully participate in decision-making.

Which, in turn, makes it that much harder for democracies to thrive.

Eleanor Roosevelt, who shaped the Uni-115 versal Declaration on Human Rights, once said, "Without equality, there can be no democracy."

In other words, the status of women is the status of democracy.

120 For our part, the United States will work to improve both.

We are committed to upholding the democratic values embedded in the Declaration.

125 And we firmly believe that, when we work together globally, we can achieve the vision within it.

We look forward to partnering with all of you in the days and years ahead.

Thank you. 130

(704 words)

Beispiellösung

In her speech to the UN Commission on the Status of Women delivered in March 2021, US Vice President Kamala Harris declares that democracy is increasingly under pressure because freedom is in decline around the world, meaning that human rights, the protection of human dignity, the rule of law, gender equality, and free and fair elections are guaranteed in fewer countries nowadays. She stresses twice that the status and the empowerment of women and the status of democracy are closely interconnected. As far as the United States is concerned, not everything is perfect, but there has been progress concerning women's rights. Nowadays women are actively shaping democracy. They are using their right to vote, working and providing their families' income, holding public offices and succeeding in business.

However, the global COVID-19 pandemic and the resulting economic crisis have threatened the progress that has been made in respect of women's health and their economic and physical security, which is why it is all the more important to defend democracy. To that end, the US is strengthening its bond to the UN and other multinational organizations and has become a member of the Human Rights Council and the World Health Organization as well as a partner to UN Women again. Harris stresses that her country is committed to the ideas of the Universal Declaration on Human Rights and intent on improving both democracy and the status of women. She finishes her address by emphasizing her strong belief that worldwide cooperation on these issues will lead to achieving the vision of the Declaration.

Aufgabe 2: Sachtext/Politischer Zeitungsartikel

AUFGABENSTELLUNG

Summarize the author's ideas of the American Dream and the reasons he gives for Detroit's failure to live up to this dream.

Materialgrundlage

Emilio DeGrazia: "Our American Nightmare: Detroit", in: *Twin cities: Daily Planet, Twin Cities Enterprise,* 11 April 2013
https://www.tcdailyplanet.net/our-american-nightmare-detroit/ (last accessed: 18 April 2023)

TIPP

Dieser Text über Detroit passt gut zum Schwerpunktthema "Gran Torino".

Our American Nightmare: Detroit *Emilio DeGrazia*

[...]

I'll risk being denounced as anti-American here by suggesting that the American Dream has a tragic flaw that has made a
5 nightmare of Detroit. Central to this American Dream narrative we are routinely fed at school, at work, and through the media is that America is the land of boundless opportunity. We keep repeating the myth that
10 everyone can succeed here if they work hard enough. That they can do it on their own. That losers are losers because they're little engines that didn't try hard enough.

Tell that silly tale to a single mother with
15 three kids and no money to pay the rent or heat. Tell it to an unemployed father whose unemployed son wanders the streets, angry and depressed. Tell it to the teenaged girls who refuse to go to school because they're
20 afraid of what might happen there. Tell it to the thousands of Detroiters who don't go to doctors because they have no health insurance, and often no doctor willing to spend ten minutes with them.

25 Tell them with a straight face that they'll succeed if they try harder, without asking for help. Convince them they won't be shamed by asking for help.

That we all should be hard-working
30 little engines is a nice idea, necessary for teachers and parents to repeat as they try to inspire individuals to live up to their potential, and also useful to successful types who feel a need to congratulate themselves. But
35 it is not a credible groundwork for public discourse or public policy. At the core of the American Dream narrative is its tragic flaw, a cancerous radical individualism that expresses itself politically on both the right
40 and left, especially among libertarians. The cancer lurks in one of our favorite words – "freedom" – repeated like a meaningless mantra, drearily by preachers and politicians. The American Dream fiction claims
45 that an individual alone is responsible for his or her fate, and that the individual is "free to choose" this fate. An individual's failure, a whole city's failure, is not to be explained in terms of a failing economy, or
50 Wall Street greed, or mismanagement of its major industries, or corrupt politicians, or drug users outside Detroit's city limits who

enable those trapped inside to participate in the city's alternative and illegal econo-
55 my. And certainly nobody wants to hear anyone explain Detroit's problems in terms of race. [...]

The American Dream fiction, like the steady diet of melodramas we're routinely
60 fed by Hollywood, has good guys and bad. The moral of this simplistic story is that those who make it are good, and those who don't are bad and deserve to lose. What's wrong with them?
65 It's this flawed narrative, widespread and profound in the many who live outside our Detroits, and invoked by those who do great damage from outside, that makes victims of so many Detroiters. What we as outsiders don't see is that we're victims too 70 of the American Dream story we routinely tell ourselves. We have plenty of technical expertise, a lot of knowledge of systems, hoards of wealth, and, I think, a profound need for the gratification that comes from 75 collective response tied to worthwhile pur-poses. Detroit, its many versions through-out the U.S., will require us to pay and pay and pay for our collective failure to respond. 80

Beispiellösung

In his article "Our American Nightmare: Detroit", published in April 2013, Emilio DeGrazia explains why it is inappropriate to refer to the American Dream narrative when talking about the decline of Detroit. This narrative conveys the idea of the US as a country of unlimited opportunities in which you can be successful without any support if you only work hard enough, which means that individuals are responsible for their own fate and are to blame for personal failure.

To DeGrazia, this is a "silly tale" and a "fiction" because it judges failure without con-sidering social and economic factors. The problems of Detroit and its citizens are not understood with reference to a failing economy, the influence of Wall Street, mis-management of the city's important companies, corruption in politics, drug trafficking and racism. Instead those who are not able to live up to the American Dream are viewed as people who deserve to lose. Therefore DeGrazia thinks that the narrative has a "tragic" flaw which he calls "a cancerous radical individualism". This attitude prevents outsiders from empowering Detroit and its citizens to tackle their problems.

Aufgaben zur Textanalyse (Aufgabenteil A II.2)

Sachtexte/Politische Reden

AUFGABENSTELLUNG

Choose one of the following inaugural addresses. Analyse how the respective US President tries to convince his country of his vision.

Materialgrundlage

M1: https://trumpwhitehouse.archives.gov/briefings-statements/the-inaugural-address/ (last accessed: 18 April 2023)
M2: https://www.whitehouse.gov/briefing-room/speeches-remarks/2021/01/20/inaugural-address-by-president-joseph-r-biden-jr/ (last accessed: 18 April 2023)

M1 President Donald Trump: Inaugural Address
January 20, 2017 Washington, D.C.

[...] Today's ceremony, however, has very special meaning. Because today we are not merely transferring power from one administration to another, or from one
5 party to another – but we are transferring power from Washington, D.C. and giving it back to you, the American People. For too long, a small group in our nation's Capital has reaped the rewards of government
10 while the people have borne the cost. Washington flourished – but the people did not share in its wealth. Politicians prospered – but the jobs left, and the factories closed. [...] That all changes – starting right here,
15 and right now, because this moment is your moment: it belongs to you. [...] For many decades, we've enriched foreign industry at the expense of American industry; subsidized the armies of other countries
20 while allowing for the very sad depletion of our military; we've defended other nations' borders while refusing to defend our own; and spent trillions of dollars overseas while America's infrastructure has fallen
25 into disrepair and decay. We've made other countries rich while the wealth, strength, and confidence of our country has disappeared over the horizon. [...] From this moment on, it's going to be America First.
30 Every decision on trade, on taxes, on immigration, on foreign affairs, will be made to benefit American workers and American families. We must protect our borders from the ravages of other countries mak-
35 ing our products, stealing our companies, and destroying our jobs. Protection will lead to great prosperity and strength. [...] I will fight for you with every breath in my body – and I will never, ever let you down.
40 America will start winning again, winning like never before.

We will bring back our jobs. We will bring back our borders. We will bring back our wealth. And we will bring back our dreams. We will build new roads, and high-
45 ways, and bridges, and airports, and tunnels, and railways all across our wonderful nation.

We will get our people off of welfare and back to work – rebuilding our country with
50 American hands and American labor. We will follow two simple rules: Buy American

and hire American. We will seek friendship and goodwill with the nations of the world – but we do so with the understanding that it is the right of all nations to put their own interests first. We do not seek to impose our way of life on anyone, but rather to let it shine as an example for everyone to follow. [...] So to all Americans, in every city near and far, small and large, from mountain to mountain, and from ocean to ocean, hear these words: You will never be ignored again. Your voice, your hopes, and your dreams will define our American destiny. And your courage and goodness and love will forever guide us along the way. Together, we will make America strong again.

We will make America wealthy again. We will make America proud again.

We will make America safe again. And yes, together, we will make America great again.   (494 Wörter)

M2 President Joseph Biden: Inaugural Address
January 20, 2021 Washington, D.C.

[...] This is America's day.

This is democracy's day.

A day of history and hope.

Of renewal and resolve.

[...] Today, we celebrate the triumph not of a candidate, but of a cause, the cause of democracy.

[...] We have learned again that democracy is precious.

Democracy is fragile.

And at this hour, my friends, democracy has prevailed.

So now, on this hallowed ground where just days ago violence sought to shake this Capitol's very foundation, we come together as one nation, under God, indivisible, to carry out the peaceful transfer of power as we have for more than two centuries.

[...] This is a great nation and we are a good people. [...] Few periods in our nation's history have been more challenging or difficult than the one we're in now.

A once-in-a-century virus silently stalks the country. [...] Millions of jobs have been lost. Hundreds of thousands of businesses closed.

A cry for racial justice some 400 years in the making moves us. [...]

And now, a rise in political extremism, white supremacy, domestic terrorism that we must confront and we will defeat.

To overcome these challenges – to restore the soul and to secure the future of America – requires more than words.

It requires that most elusive of things in a democracy:

Unity.

Unity.

[...] Today, on this January day, my whole soul is in this: Bringing America together. Uniting our people. And uniting our nation.

I ask every American to join me in this cause.

Uniting to fight the common foes we face:

Anger, resentment, hatred. Extremism, lawlessness, violence. Disease, joblessness, hopelessness.

With unity we can do great things. Important things.

We can right wrongs.

We can put people to work in good jobs.

We can teach our children in safe schools.

We can overcome this deadly virus.

161

We can reward work, rebuild the middle class, and make health care secure for all.

We can deliver racial justice.

60 We can make America, once again, the leading force for good in the world.

[...] We can treat each other with dignity and respect.

[...] And so today, at this time and in this 65 place, let us start afresh.

All of us.

Let us listen to one another.

Hear one another.

See one another.

70 Show respect to one another.

[...] To all those who did not support us, let me say this: Hear me out as we move forward. Take a measure of me and my heart.

And if you still disagree, so be it.

75 That's democracy. That's America. The right to dissent peaceably, within the guardrails of our Republic, is perhaps our nation's greatest strength.

Yet hear me clearly: Disagreement must 80 not lead to disunion.

And I pledge this to you: I will be a President for all Americans.

[...] Recent weeks and months have taught us a painful lesson. There is truth 85 and there are lies.

[...] This is a time of testing.

We face an attack on democracy and on truth.

A raging virus.

Growing inequity. 90

The sting of systemic racism.

A climate in crisis.

America's role in the world.

Any one of these would be enough to challenge us in profound ways. 95

But the fact is we face them all at once, presenting this nation with the gravest of responsibilities.

Now we must step up.

All of us. 100

It is a time for boldness, for there is so much to do.

[...] And together, we shall write an American story of hope, not fear.

Of unity, not division. 105

Of light, not darkness.

An American story of decency and dignity.

Of love and of healing.

Of greatness and of goodness. 110

May this be the story that guides us. [...]

(598 Wörter)

Bewertungskriterien

Ihre Aufgabe ist es, den gewählten Auszug zu analysieren. Das bedeutet, dass Sie nicht nur auf die Inhalte eingehen, sondern auch die Sprache, vor allem Wortwahl und Stilmittel, und deren Wirkung untersuchen sollen.

TIPP zum Punktesammeln

Achten Sie auf eine klare Struktur Ihrer Textanalyse.
- Schreiben Sie eine zur Aufgabenstellung passende Einleitung.
- Präsentieren Sie im Hauptteil als Erstes die wichtigen Themen der Rede und die Hauptaussagen dazu. Nennen Sie anschließend die stilistischen Besonderheiten und analysieren Sie deren Wirkung.
- Beenden Sie Ihren Text mit einer Zusammenfassung.

TIPP Reden

Auf Seite 155 finden Sie eine Rede von Kamala Harris, die Sie anhand der Kriterien zur Analyse von Reden (Seite 129ff.) zur Übung ebenfalls untersuchen können.

Analysis of Donald Trump's inaugural address

Introduction of analysis
- Given on January 20, 2017 in Washington, D.C.
- Main purpose: to outline his vision of a better future for America

Main part of analysis
Main topics and structure of the speech:
- Failures of past administrations (ll. 7–13, ll. 16–28)
- New policies: America First, protectionism (ll. 28–37), reform plans (ll. 37–60)
- End of the speech: promises of a better future (ll. 60–73)

Stylistic devices:
- Parallelism: "Washington flourished – but the people did not share in its wealth. Politicians prospered – but the jobs left, and the factories closed." (ll. 10–13) → parallel sentence structure makes the content more memorable
- Repetition of the word 'right': "starting right here and right now" (ll. 14–15) → stresses the urgency of the measures he is planning
- Enumeration, parallelism: "For many decades, we've […] while […] " (ll. 16–27) → emphasizes the idea that the US has served other countries more than itself
- Alliteration: "disrepair and decay" (l. 25) → underlines his criticism that America's infrastructure has been neglected
- Inclusive "we" → creates a feeling of unity and solidarity; conveys that he identifies with American citizens
- Addressing the audience: examples: "transferring power from Washington, D.C. and giving it back to you, the American People" (ll. 5–7); "this moment is your moment: it belongs to you" (ll. 15–16); "You will never be ignored again" (ll. 63–64) → presents himself as a servant of the people; wants to convey that he empathizes with citizens and to show his solidarity with them
- Repetitions of "American": examples: "American workers and American families" (ll. 32–33); "American hands and American labor" (l. 51); "Buy American and hire American" (ll. 52–53) → illustrate his foreign-policy doctrine of "America first"
- Enumerations: examples: "the wealth, strength and confidence of our country has disappeared" (ll. 26–28); "other countries making our products, stealing our companies, and destroying our jobs" → Trump emphasizes how dramatic the situation is in his opinion.
  "Your voice, your hopes and your dreams", "your courage and goodness and love" (ll. 64–66) → Trump wants to convey that he cares about the welfare of the people.

- Anaphora: four times "We will bring back [...]"; four times "we will"+verb:"We will seek friendship [...]" (ll. 42–53); five times "we will make America [...] again" (ll. 67–73) → anaphora underline his determination to bring about change, and have a persuasive effect on the audience
- Simple sentence structure → easy to understand, used to get his message across to everyone

Choice of words:
- "today's ceremony", "today" (ll. 1, 2); "right here, and right now" (ll. 14–15); "from this moment on" (ll. 15, 28-29) → wants to emphasize that the day of his inauguration is a major turning point in American history; wants to earn people's trust in his presidency and his political programme
- "the ravages of other countries" (l. 34): sombre metaphor to make international partners the object of hatred, also used to emphasize the desolate condition of the US
- "our wonderful nation" (ll. 47–48); "your courage and goodness and love" (l. 66): uses positive adjectives and nouns to describe the US and its citizens; wants to express patriotism and nationalism as well as love and respect for the American people

Tone of the speech:
- First accusatory (ll. 7–28)
- Then determined and optimistic (ll. 28–53), later reassuring, appeasing (ll. 53–60)
- At the end: full of solemnity, even pomposity, but also consideration (ll. 60–73); examples: "all our across our wonderful nation" (ll. 47–48) → expresses nationalism; "I will fight for you with every breath in my body – and I will never, ever let you down." (ll. 37–39) → wants to come across as a strong leader who takes his office very seriously and feels obliged to serve the people; also presents himself as a loving and caring person

Student's evaluation/interpretation:
- Listening to Trump's description of conditions in the US, you might think that the country is completely run-down. He depicts politicians as the people's enemies and identifies international obligations as the major cause of the desolate conditions. According to him, other countries have profited from the commitment of the US. This has been to the cost of American citizens.
- Evaluation of these aspects, using background knowledge,such as the following facts: Trump is a right-wing politician who cultivated populism during his presidency and used the media to manipulate people; his policies and his behaviour put democracy at risk; true that US economy recovered during his presidency, but this trend had begun during the Obama presidency; it is an extreme exaggeration to state that the American people had been ignored before his presidency; other presidents put more emphasis on improving social welfare (example: Obamacare)

Conclusion of analysis
Summary of the main aspects

Analysis of Joe Biden's inaugural address

Introduction of analysis
– given on January 20, 2021 in Washington, D.C.
– main purpose: call for unity

Main part of analysis
Main topics and structure of the speech:
– Democracy, legitimate transfer of power (ll. 1–18)
– Multiple challenges (ll. 19–31, ll. 83–98)
– Unity as the most important requirement to overcome the challenges (ll. 35–51)
– Possible achievements through unity (ll. 52–63)
– Call for a fresh start with different social attitudes and general acceptance of pluralism (ll. 64–82)
– Call for action (ll. 99–111)

Stylistic devices
– Parallelism: "This is America's day. This is democracy's day." (ll. 1–2); "an American story of [...] goodness" (ll. 104–110) → makes the statements more memorable
– Very short sentences, often ellipses; examples: "Let us listen to one another. Hear one another. See one another." (ll. 67–69) → easy to understand, emphasis on keywords
– Repetition of "unity" (ll. 37, 38, 50, 105) and "uniting" (l. 41 [twice], l. 45) → strong emphasis on this aspect because the US is undergoing a severe crisis and the attack on the Capitol has shown that the nation is divided
– Anaphora: eight times "We can [...]" (ll. 52–62) → repetitive use of the same structure puts emphasis on what can be achieved together and is intended to convince the audience of Biden's goals; modal verb *can* expresses his confidence in Americans' ability to overcome their troubles
– Inclusive "we"; examples: "we celebrate the triumph [...] of a cause" (ll. 5–6); "We have learned that democracy is precious." (ll. 8–9); "we come together as one nation" (ll. 15–16); "we are a good people" (ll. 19–20) → creates a sense of community, of shared values and perceptions and of joint responsibility; this is the basis for unity; Biden also wants to convey that he will be focusing on the American people, not on himself
– Enumerations of present problems (ll. 47–49; ll. 89–93) → emphasize the fact that there are numerous challenges that must be dealt with simultaneously; Biden indicates that is he aware of many citizens' daily struggles
– Alliteration: "A day of history and hope. Of renewal and resolve" → underlines the importance of the event after the attack on the Capitol by Trump's followers
– Antitheses: examples: "hope, not fear" (l. 104), "unity, not division" (l. 105), "light, not darkness" (l. 106) → emphasis on most important attitudes and values; implicit criticism of the Trump administration
– Metaphors: "hallowed ground" (l. 13) → expresses great respect for the Capitol and thus for American democracy; "restore the soul [...] of America" (ll. 32–34) → conveys

that American citizens are in need of spiritual healing; "raging virus" (l. 89), "sting of systemic racism" (l. 91) → Biden creates images for the audience that emphasize that Americans are dealing with grievous problems
- Personification: negative attitudes such as anger, resentment and hatred, and bad conditions such as disease, joblessness and hopelessness described as "common foes" (l. 45) → foes (= people) are easier to deal with than abstract concepts; personification adds life to the words that describe the American crisis
- Several appeals: "let us start afresh" (l. 65); "Let us listen to one another. [...]" (ll. 67–70); "Hear me out as we move forward. Take a measure of me and my heart." (ll.72–73); "Yet hear me clearly" (l. 79) → suggest that citizens can actively shape the future of the US

Tone of the speech:
- Solemn when he speaks about the value of democracy and the importance of the peaceful transfer of power to him (ll. 1–18)
- Determined, hopeful, optimistic, encouraging when he talks about tackling problems and about the abilities of a unified American people (ll. 32–63)
- Conciliatory when he elaborates on the importance of unity (ll. 35–42) and a common effort to write a new American story (ll. 99–110)

Student's evaluation/interpretation:
Evaluation of these aspects, using facts about the achievements and failures as well as the current situation of the Biden administration

Conclusion of analysis
Summary of the main aspects

Aufgaben zu Composition (Aufgabenteil A II.3)

Aufgabe 1: Sachtext/Politischer Zeitungsartikel

AUFGABENSTELLUNG

Comment on Jean Guerrero's view of "mixedness" (l. 77).

Materialgrundlage

Jean Guerrero: "I used to be confused by my mixed identity. But mixedness will heal America", *The Guardian,* 28.10.2020; https://www.theguardian.com/commentis-free/2020/oct/28/i-used-to-be-confused-by-my-mixed-identity-but-mixedness-will-heal-america (last accessed: 18 April 2023)

I used to be confused by my mixed identity. But mixedness will heal America *Jean Guerrero*

Multiculturalism doesn't threaten civilization; it threatens extremism. As the US grows more mixed, it will grow more empathetic

Whenever I misbehaved as a child, my Puerto Rican abuela[1] blamed the Mexican in me. [...] I did not know what I was. You're American, my mother said. You're not Mexican. You're not Puerto Rican. You're American.

We lived near the border in San Diego, California. She wanted me to feel I belonged in this country – a sense she'd been repeatedly denied. [...]

"I'm a doctor and a US citizen", she told the US customs officers who threatened to slice open her car seats in search of drugs when she was returning after a trip to Tijuana with my father, an immigrant from Mexico with a green card. She wielded her citizenship like a shield, tenuous as it felt against an ever-present danger. *Puerto Ricans are US citizens,* my mother would say, with conviction. Because of my mother's body armor, I did not identify as Latina as a child, though we had piñatas[2] at our birthdays and ate arroz con gandules[3] at home.

Back then, California was a microcosm for the resurgence of white supremacy we are seeing nationally today, causing Latin American families to hide their brown or Blackness behind labels like Hispanic. In the nineties, a white backlash against the "browning" of the state manifested as bipartisan attacks on bilingual education, affirmative action, and state-funded services for people without legal immigration status. Neo-Nazi groups multiplied. The governor spoke of a Mexican "invasion." The idea that multiculturalism was a threat to civilization spread like a virus on right-wing talk radio.

[...]

It wasn't until years later that I realized American identity does not need to function like a sword hacking away at our differences, or a snake digesting them. [...]

Multiculturalism is not a threat to civilization. The only thing it threatens is extremism. As America becomes more

167

mixed, we will have a greater capacity for empathy. People with hyphenated identities are familiar with multiple ways of being; they can readily inhabit different people and diverse realities.

[...]

Americans are losing our collective sanity due to a breakdown in our willingness to communicate with one another. We are trapped in echo chambers. Corporations shape our politics, purchases, and preferences with disinformation and AI-based advertisements. Polarization is profitable, so the powerful have no incentives to unite us. The threat of domestic terrorism is escalating as people fall into post-truth rabbit holes about QAnon[4] and "white genocide." Democracy is in danger.

Maybe you're a third-generation immigrant like my niece, or a first- or second- one. Either way, you have it, too: the magic that might save us. Perhaps you were taught to reject your mestizaje[5]. But it is what allows you to imagine and bring forth a world without binaries: blurry and multitudinous, like you. You can heal a divided nation.

Perhaps in your life you've had people call you a half-breed, a wetback, a beaner. They made you feel like a mutant. They don't understand that your mixedness is your strength. You have the blood of the colonizer and of the colonized. You are the bridge that can make America sane again.

Anmerkungen:

1 abuela – grandmother

2 piñata – an object, often in the shape of an animal, that is filled with sweets; traditionally hung up at parties for children to hit it with a stick in order to break it open

3 arroz con gandulez – a Puerto Rican national dish

4 QAnon – a far-right political movement centred on conspiracy theories

5 mestizaje – ethnic mixing

Bewertungskriterien

Inhaltliche Aspekte

Einleitung:
- Begriffsklärung: mixedness
- Nennung der Autorin und der Quelle des Textauszugs
- Wiedergabe der Aufgabenstellung in eigenen Worten

Hauptteil:
- Erläuterung zur Haltung der Autorin durch Nennung der inhaltlichen Aspekte:
  - > "I did not know what I was" (Zeile 3): Identitätsfrage, Einfluss der Eltern
  - > multiculturalism and American identity (Zeile 24–38, 44–51): resurgence of white supremacy, author's understanding of multiculturalism

> dangers to democracy (Zeile 53–64): polarization due to loss of communication, profit orientation of the powerful
> the potential and power of mixedness (Zeile 72 bis Ende): the benefits of having mixed origins

- Bewertung der oben erarbeiteten Aussagen der Autorin
- eigene Argumente mit Beispielen und Erläuterungen, etwa unter Einbeziehung der Metaphern *melting pot* und *salad bowl*

Schluss
- persönliche Bewertung der Kernaussage unter Verwendung einer kurzen Zusammenfassung und eines persönlichen Fazits

Aufgabe 2: Literarischer Text

AUFGABENSTELLUNG

Write a blog entry for *Voices of Youth,* an online forum, for a young British person whose family is of Bangladeshi origin. Explain what makes up your identity and how you feel about Britishness.

Materialgrundlage

Ausgangstext: Romanauszug aus: Zadie Smith, *White Teeth,* 2000, pp. 326–327 (346 words)

White Teeth *Zadie Smith*

This is an extract from the novel "White Teeth" by Zadie Smith, which is set in contemporary London. The story focuses on three families with different cultural backgrounds whose lives become intertwined because of their children. One of the characters (Irie Jones, l.8) belongs to the second generation and has an English father and a Caribbean mother. She has fallen in love with a boy called Millat Iqbal, whose parents are from Bangladesh.

This has been the century of strangers, brown, yellow, and white. This has been the century of the great immigrant experiment. It is only this late in the day that you
5 can walk into a playground and find Isaac Leung by the fish pond, Danny Rahman in the football cage, Quang O'Rourke bouncing a basketball, and Irie Jones humming[1] a tune. Children with first and last names on a
10 direct collision course. Names that secrete[2] within them mass exodus, cramped boats and planes, cold arrivals, medical checkups. It is only this late in the day, and possibly only in Willesden[3], that you can find best
15 friends Sita and Sharon, constantly mistaken for each other because Sita is white (her mother liked the name) and Sharon is Pakistani (her mother thought it best – less trouble). Yet, despite all the mix-
20 ing up, despite the fact that we have finally slipped into each other's lives with reasonable comfort (like a man returning to his lover's bed after a midnight walk), despite all this, it is still hard to admit that there is no one more English than
25 the Indian, no one more Indian than the English. There are still young white men who are angry about that; who will roll out at closing time into the poorly lit streets with a kitchen knife wrapped in a tight fist.
30 But it makes an immigrant laugh to hear the fears of the nationalist, scared of infection, penetration, miscegenation[4], when this is small fry, peanuts, compared to what the immigrant fears – dissolution, disap-
35 pearance. Even the unflappable[5] Alsana Iqbal would regularly wake up in a puddle of her own sweat after a night visited by visions of Millat (genetically BB; where B stands for Bengaliness) marrying someone
40 called Sarah (aa where 'a' stands for Aryan), resulting in a child called Michael (Ba), who in turn marries someone called Lucy (aa), leaving Alsana with a legacy of unrecog-

45 nizable great-grandchildren (Aaaaaaa!), their Bengaliness thoroughly diluted[6], genotype[7] hidden by phenotype[8]. It is both the most irrational and natural feeling in the world.

1 **to hum:** *summen*

2 **to secrete:** to hide

3 **Willesden:** an area in North West London

4 **miscegenation:** *Vermischung ethnischer Gruppen*

5 **unflappable:** *unerschütterlich*

6 **diluted:** *verdünnt*

7 **genotype:** *genetische Veranlagung*

8 **phenotype:** *äußere Erscheinung*

TIPP Blogeintrag

Ein Blogeintrag ist meist ein informeller Text, der verschiedenste Themen behandeln kann. Im Englischunterricht wurden Sie vermutlich schon öfter gebeten, solche Beiträge für die Webseiten fiktiver oder realer Organisationen oder Foren zu schreiben und darin Ihre persönliche Meinung zu gesellschaftlich relevanten Fragen darzulegen. Struktur und Inhalte hängen von der Textvorlage ab.

Hier einige generelle Tipps für gelungene Blogeinträge:
- Wählen Sie einen interessanten Titel, der Neugier weckt.
- Ergänzen Sie Ihren Namen *(by ...)*.
- Schreiben Sie möglichst eine kreative Einleitung. Nennen Sie zum Einstieg einen realistischen Anlass für Ihren Beitrag. Beispielsweise könnten Sie ein besonderes Erlebnis oder Ereignis zum Anlass nehmen, Ihre Position zu erläutern. Ebenso ist es möglich, dass Sie Bezug auf eine interessante Lektüre nehmen (Zeitungsartikel, Buch o. Ä.).
- Beziehen Sie Ihre eigenen Erfahrungen ein. Ein Blogeintrag ist eine Form der subjektiven Meinungsäußerung.
- Achten Sie auf eine logische Argumentation. Jeder Absatz sollte mit einem *topic sentence* beginnen, damit die Lesenden Ihre Gedanken leicht nachvollziehen können.
- Schreiben Sie in einem freundlichen Ton und einer lebendigen Sprache.
- Schreiben Sie anschaulich und beachten Sie durchgängig, an welche Zielgruppe Sie sich richten.
- Enden Sie mit einer Schlussfolgerung, in der sie Ihre Erfahrungen oder Ihre Meinung zusammenfassen. Diese *conclusion* sollte die Lesenden anregen, einen Kommentar zu hinterlassen. Sie können die Leserschaft auch explizit dazu auffordern, auf Ihren Beitrag zu antworten.
- Lesen Sie Ihren Blogeintrag noch einmal durch und überprüfen Sie Rechtschreibung, Grammatik und Zeichensetzung.

Nützliche Redewendungen

Salutation

Dear readers,

Hi everyone, *(informal)*

Hey guys, *(informal)*

Introduction

Not long ago/A few days ago I saw/read/... That made me think about ...

In the news, I heard ...

For a long time I used to think that ..., but then ...

When recently I saw/ ..., I decided ...

Have you ever seen/experienced/...?

Isn't it incredible that ...?

When I saw/... for the first time, I asked myself ...

The reason I am writing this is ...

Main part

I'd like to share my experiences/thoughts with you.

I think/believe ...

Interestingly, I found out recently that ...

To my surprise it seems ...

As far as I am concerned, ...

Apart from that, ...

Therefore, .../Thus .../That is why ...

That is not all. Let us not forget that ...

That is all well and good, but ...

I think we should keep in mind that ...

I'd also like to tell you about ...

The problem here is ...

Conclusion

To sum up ...

All in all ...

It seems quite clear that ...

To conclude my opinion on this topic/issue, ...

As I previously mentioned, ...

Thanks for reading!

Lastly, I want to leave you with this question: ...

Post/Leave a comment!

Share your thoughts!

Let me know what you think!

Bewertungskriterien

Ihre Aufgabe ist es, auf der Basis Ihres Wissens über die Geschichte des Commonwealth und die britische Einwanderungspolitik einen möglichst authentisch wirkenden persönlichen Text zu verfassen. Bei der Ausgestaltung solch einer kreativen Textproduktion haben Sie ganz unterschiedliche Möglichkeiten, aber Sie müssen dabei korrektes Faktenwissen einbringen. Sie könnten folgende Aspekte zur Sprache bringen:

- The question of belonging: different cultures have been mixing in Britain; the children of immigrants feel at home there. (For instance, the person could write about his/her school, his/her circle of friends, the food and music he/she likes or certain habits that are typically British.)
- Identity: different cultures have left their mark on these young people's lives; their Britishness is different from that of people of purely British origin. Their parents often still adhere to traditions of their countries of origin. (You could use some ideas from the extract from *White Teeth* here, e.g., the person could complain about how his/her parents are too strict with him/her and forbid him/her to wear certain styles and to go to clubs or about their fear of him/her marrying a white person.)
- The writer of the blog entry might state why he/she likes this mixedness, but he/she could also give examples of the problems it causes. He/She could write about his/her parents' attitude as compared to his/her own, too.
- The writer might discuss whether British society is a salad bowl or a melting pot and what implications that has for his/her identity.

Aufgabe zu visuellen Materialien

Cartoon: *Gun control*

AUFGABENSTELLUNG

Decribe and interpret the following cartoon. Then comment on its message.

Quelle: Bill Bramhall/ Getty Images

Erwartungshorizont

Folgende Aspekte sollten berücksichtigt werden:

Topic:
Controversial discussion of gun control in the USA

Description:
– One panel showing a drawing of a machine gun
– Headline: Gun control
– Caption: lists places and institutions to which the use of such a gun is restricted: movie theaters, shopping malls, high schools, universities. The ellipsis (three dots) at the end of the list indicates that more places can be added.

Analysis:
– There is a sharp contrast between the expectations aroused by the headline and the content of the caption. While the term 'gun control' suggests a ban on firearms and the prohibition of lethal weapons, the caption reads like a sign regulating public behaviour, but tells people to use assault weapons like the one shown in the drawing only in certain places where in fact you would not expect anyone to carry a gun. In combination with the drawing, this creates a shock.

– The drawing highlights the intimidating qualities of the machine gun. Most people would feel more comfortable if the use of such guns was not restricted only to the kind of places mentioned in the caption but was completely banned.

Evaluation (background knowledge from class)
– Gun control is one of the most controversially discussed issues in the USA.
– Despite a large number of mass shootings, e. g. in places named in the caption (movie theaters, shopping malls, high schools, universities), the right to bear arms, which is laid down in the Second Amendment to the American Constitution, still remains unaffected. Conservatives especially defend this right and the National Rifle Association (NRA) is a very influential gun advocacy group.
– The combination of the martial picture of the machine gun with the cynical warning in the caption conveys the futility of attempting to modify the Second Amendment rather than abolishing it. This makes the cartoon very effective.

Aufgabe zur Sprachmittlung

Sachtext: *Gun Debate*

INFO

Sie werden sowohl im Basis- als auch im Leistungsfach im Verlauf der Qualifikationsphase eine ca. 60-minütige Sprachmittlungsklausur schreiben.

AUFGABENSTELLUNG

The article "Waffengewalt in den USA: Im Land der vielen Morde" describes the scope
of gun violence in the US and analyzes reasons for resistance to stricter gun laws. Your
class is dealing with examples of mass shootings at American schools and you are asked
to prepare a presentation in English that summarizes the reasons given in the text for
opposition to gun control. Write down what you are going to say in the presentation.

Materialgrundlage

Malte Lehming: „Waffengewalt in den USA: Im Land der vielen Morde", *Tagesspiegel*
(15.02.2023)
https://www.tagesspiegel.de/internationales/waffengewalt-in-den-usa-im-land-der-
vielen-morde-9350075.html

Waffengewalt in den USA: Im Land der vielen Morde   *Malte Lehming*

*In den USA grassiert die Waffengewalt. Doch das Recht auf Waffenbesitz einzuschränken,
ist schwierig. Denn für viele Amerikaner sind Waffen ein Teil ihrer Identität.*

Sechs Tage liegen zwischen diesen beiden Ereignissen. Vor einer Woche [...]
stand US-Präsident Joe Biden vor den Ab-
geordneten und Senatoren des Kongresses
und hielt seine Rede zur Lage der Nation. [5]
Im Kampf gegen die grassierende Waffengewalt in seinem Land forderte er ein Ver-
bot von Sturmgewehren.
[...]
Sechs Tage später [...] kamen bei einem [10]
Amoklauf in einer Universität im Bundes-
staat Michigan drei Menschen ums Leben.
Fünf weitere wurden mit schweren Verlet-
zungen ins Krankenhaus gebracht. [...]

Landesweite Proteste gegen Waffen- [15]
gewalt
Begangen wurde das Verbrechen am
Vortag des Jahrestages eines anderen Mas-
sakers [...]: Am 14. Februar 2018 hatte
ein damals 19-Jähriger an einer Schule in [20]
Parkland (Florida) mit einem legal erworbenen halbautomatischen Gewehr 14 Jugendliche und drei Erwachsene erschossen. Das
löste landesweite Proteste gegen Waffengewalt und für schärfere Waffengesetze [25]
aus.
Doch bereits drei Monate spä-
ter [...] schießt ein 17-jähriger Schüler

an der Santa Fe High School in der texanischen Stadt Santa Fe mit einem Sturmgewehr und einem Revolver seines Vaters auf Mitschüler. Er tötet acht Jugendliche und zwei Erwachsene.

Es folgen weitere tödliche Attacken an Schulen und Universitäten. [...]

Das „Gun Violence Archive" hat allein für das Jahr 2022 insgesamt 648 Massenschießereien gezählt. Bei 21 davon wurden mehr als vier Menschen getötet. 300 Millionen Schusswaffen sind in den USA im Umlauf.

Rund 40 Prozent der Amerikaner leben in einem Haushalt, in dem es ein Gewehr oder eine Pistole gibt. Etwa die Hälfte der weißen Männer besitzt eine Waffe, auf dem Land sind es mehr als in der Stadt. Doppelt so viele Republikaner wie Demokraten haben eine Schusswaffe.

Die Einwanderer setzten Waffen gegen die indigene Bevölkerung ein

Das Recht auf Waffenbesitz garantiert der zweite Zusatzartikel zur Verfassung der Vereinigten Staaten, verabschiedet am 15. Dezember 1791. [...]

Heute gilt das Recht für alle Amerikaner. Doch historisch gesehen sind öffentlich getragene Waffen ein weißes Privileg. Es ist verbunden mit Sklavenhaltern und Siedlern, dem Kampf um die Unabhängigkeit, dem Schutz von Landbewohnern vor Verbrechern und religiöser Organisationen vor staatlicher Willkür.

Im Waffenkult drückt sich ein tief sitzendes Misstrauen gegenüber dem Staat aus

Die Einwanderer setzten Waffen gegen die indigene Bevölkerung ein und um Sklavenaufstände niederzuschlagen. Britische Soldaten versuchten immer wieder, amerikanische Siedler zu entwaffnen, um die Abspaltung der Kolonien zu verhindern. Ohne Erfolg. Seitdem bedeuten eigene Waffen im kollektiven Gedächtnis vieler Amerikaner Macht, Unabhängigkeit, Selbstverteidigung, Souveränität.

Deshalb stößt jeder Versuch, ins Waffenrecht einzugreifen, meistens auf erbitterten Widerstand. Jede Maßnahme steht im Verdacht, ein erster Schritt zur Abschaffung des Rechts zu sein. Im Waffenkult drückt sich ein tief sitzendes Misstrauen gegenüber dem Staat und der Regierung im fernen Washington D.C. aus. Dieses Misstrauen geht einher mit diversen Verschwörungsmythen über Politiker, die die Freiheiten der Bürger einschränken wollen, um sie noch besser kontrollieren zu können.

Viele geschichtliche Stränge kommen im strikten Festhalten an das uneingeschränkte Waffenrecht zusammen: die Besiedelung des „Wilden Westens", der Kampf um die Unabhängigkeit, die Verteidigung der eigenen Religion gegen staatliche Einmischung. Hinzu kommt das Sicherheitsbedürfnis von Menschen, die weit verstreut auf dem Land leben. Dort heißt die Devise: „Wenn Sekunden zählen, ist die Polizei Minuten entfernt."

Zuletzt wird das Recht, eine Waffe zu tragen, auch als antitotalitäres Charakteristikum eines freiheitlichen Gemeinwesens verstanden. In kommunistischen und faschistischen Regimen wäre ein solches Recht unvorstellbar, heißt es. Mitunter wird auf den Holocaust verwiesen: Hätten die Juden in Nazi-Deutschland Waffen gehabt, hätten sie sich wehren können.

Schusswaffen als Teil der Identität: Der Preis dafür ist hoch. Nach dem letzten Massaker ist vor dem nächsten Massaker.

177

Bewertungskriterien

Formale Aspekte

- **Zielformat Präsentation:** passende Ansprache, klare Gliederung und typischer Aufbau mit Einleitung, Hauptteil und Schluss
- **Sprachregister:** gepflegtes Englisch, aber nicht zu formell, da Ihre Mitschüler/-innen die Adressat/-innen sind. Zwar schreiben Sie den Text auf, doch er sollte sich wie ein Vortrag lesen, nicht wie ein Aufsatz.
- **Einleitung:** Der Adressatenbezug (Mitschüler/-innen) muss erkennbar sein. Das Thema muss in den Kontext eingeordnet und klar umrissen werden.
- **Hauptteil:** Filtern Sie nur die Aspekte aus der Quelle heraus, die für die Aufgabenstellung relevant sind. Strukturieren Sie diese Aspekte.
- **Schluss:** Formulieren Sie ein Fazit.

Nützliche Redewendungen

Introduction

Good morning (everyone),
In the last few lessons we have talked about …
Recently we have been discussing …
My subject today is …
I was given the task to …
I have done some research and found …
I shall now discuss/explain/…

Main part

As we have seen/discussed/…
As you all know, …
You are certainly aware that …
One of the crucial points is …
Another important fact is …
Therefore/Thus/That's why/This is because …
In other words, …
That brings me to the next point.
This brings me to the key issue …

Conclusion

To sum up/summarize/conclude, …
In conclusion, …
Thank you for listening./Thank you for your attention.

Beispiellösung

Good morning,

In the last few lessons we have talked about the gun debate in the US. Most of us have been baffled by the fact that terrible mass shootings have taken place time and again, but despite large nationwide protests against armed violence, attempts at changing gun laws have usually met fierce resistance from certain groups. As we have asked ourselves in class why the right to bear arms is so important to many Americans, I have done some research and found an article by Malte Lehming in the *Tagesspiegel*. I shall now summarize the most important reasons Lehming adduces for many Americans' opposition to gun control.

As you all know, the right to bear arms is protected by the Second Amendment to the American Constitution. Nowadays all Americans have that right but in the past this used to be a privilege of white people, mainly to conquer the country and to defend themselves. The settlers used arms when they moved west fighting the indigenous tribes. Slave owners beat down slave uprisings violently. People also needed weapons to defend themselves and their religious beliefs. In colonial times, British troops often tried to disarm the settlers, but without success. Ever since those times, Americans have associated weapons with power, independence, self-defence and sovereignty.

Different historical developments have therefore influenced Americans' positive attitude towards weapons. Moreover, people living in sparsely-populated areas claim they need arms to feel safe because they can't rely on the police being fast enough to help them. Each attempt to change gun laws is met by fierce resistance because people fear that the right to bear arms will be revoked entirely. Lehming believes this shows that Americans have a deep-rooted distrust of the state as an institution and of the federal government in Washington, DC. Conspiracy theories are circulating, claiming that politicians want to infringe rights in order to be able to control citizens more efficiently.

There are also people who say that the right to bear arms is a characteristic of free societies on the basis that communist or fascist regimes do not grant their citizens such rights. Some people even claim that the Holocaust would not have happened if German Jews had had weapons.

To sum up, the right to bear arms is bound up with many American citizens' identity for reasons that reach far back into early US history. However, considering the fact that there were 648 mass shootings in 2022 alone, they are paying a very high price for their insistence on upholding this right.

Thank you for your attention.

Baden-Württemberg Abiturprüfung 2022 an den allgemeinbildenden Gymnasien – Englisch

Quelle der Aufgabenstellung

Regierungspräsidium Stuttgart[1]

Originalprüfung mit Beispiellösung

Teil I: Listening Comprehension

You will hear each recording twice. After each listening, you will have time to complete your answers.

INFO

Leider können wir Ihnen diesen Hörbeitrag aus rechtlichen Gründen nicht zur Verfügung stellen. Die Aufgabe ist hier abgedruckt, damit Ihnen die vollständige Prüfung vorliegt und Sie sich mit dem Format dieser Hörverstehensaufgabe vertraut machen können.

Task 1: Book reviews   5 BE

Preparation time: 40 seconds
You will hear the beginnings of five book reviews.
Choose from the list (A–G) which description best applies to which book review (1–5).
For each book review there is only one correct answer. There are two more descriptions than you need.

Descriptions	
A	Dealing with characters' secrets
B	Describing a character's dreams
C	Tracing a character's self-exploration
D	Inspired by very different historical events
E	Presenting the lives of prominent individuals
F	Telling the story of formerly overlooked people
G	Based on historical events and connected to current issues

Book review	1	2	3	4	5
Description					

Now listen to the recording again.

[1] Die Lösungen sind keine amtlichen Lösungen.

Task 2: Baroness Trumpington

14 BE

Preparation time: 1:30 minutes
You will hear a radio report about Lady Jean Trumpington
(born Jean Campbell-Harris, 1922–2018, a British politician).

You can listen to the report by following this link:
https://www.bbc.co.uk/sounds/play/b098bqr1

While listening, fill in the missing information. You need not write
complete sentences. Unless otherwise specified, name one aspect.

1.	Why did Lady Trumpington's departure from politics attract so much attention?	
2.	Why does the host of a TV show mention the invention of television?	
3.	Which incident made Lady Trumpington widely known?	
4.	What is said about her education?	
5.	In which two different fields of work was she active during World War II?	•_____ •_____
6.	Why did she return to Great Britain?	
7.	What did she change in her life during her time in Cambridge?	
8.	Why did she choose the title "Baroness Trumpington"?	
9.	What was special about her holding her governmental position at the end of the 1980s?	
10.	What did she do in Downing Street that helped her keep her position?	
11.	What was her duty as Baroness in Waiting?	
12.	Which interest will she continue to pursue after retiring?	

Now think of the text as a whole. Tick the correct answer (a, b or c). There is only one correct answer.

13. In the radio report, Lady Trumpington's personality is presented as being

a	charitable and caring.	☐
b	cautious and level-headed.	☐
c	self-confident and unconventional.	☐

Now listen to the recording again.

Task 3: Sea otters   6 BE

Preparation time: 1:30 minutes
You will hear a radio report about research on sea otters in Canada.

You can listen to the report by following this link:
https://www.npr.org/2020/06/11/873885445/sea-otters-can-be-money-makers-but-not-everyone-benefits

While listening, tick the correct answer (a, b or c). There is only one correct answer.

1. The research focuses on the

a	effects of sea otter populations on the local economy.	☐
b	behavioural patterns of sea otters living close to humans.	☐
c	consequences of climate change for sea otter populations.	☐

2. There was more seafood in the area after the Europeans had arrived because

a	sea otters were exterminated.	☐
b	Europeans relied mainly on farming.	☐
c	the native population was moved inland.	☐

3. The scientists have chosen Vancouver Island for their research project because

a	university facilities are readily available.	☐
b	a particular species of sea otters lives there.	☐
c	the place is suitable for comparative field studies.	☐

4. The sea otters affect the ecosystem because

a	they tend to destroy habitats of other species.	☐
b	their feeding behaviour fosters the growth of fish.	☐
c	they help to reduce the impact of invasive species.	☐

5. Ecologist Edward Gregr addresses the issue that

a	visits to the area need to be regulated.	☐
b	not everyone in the area profits in the same way.	☐
c	too many sea otters threaten the fragile ecosystem.	☐

6. Native Canadians living in isolated communities perceive the growing population of sea otters as

a	a potential threat.	☐
b	a minor nuisance.	☐
c	a welcome source of income.	☐

Now listen to the recording again.

Schriftlicher Prüfungsteil[1]

Materialgrundlage:

Emily Badger, "How 'Not in My Backyard' Became 'Not in My Neighborhood'", *New York Times,* January 3, 2018

Zugelassene Hilfsmittel:

- ein einsprachiges Wörterbuch (Englisch)
- ein zweisprachiges Wörterbuch (Englisch – Deutsch/Deutsch – Englisch)
- Nachschlagewerke zur deutschen Rechtschreibung

Bearbeitungszeit:

210 Minuten + 30 Minuten einschließlich Auswahlzeit

Hinweise:

Sie erhalten eine zweiteilige **Textaufgabe.**
Teil II: Reading Comprehension
Teil III.1: Analysis
Teil III.2: Composition
           Bearbeiten Sie **eine** der beiden Aufgaben von Teil III.2.

Neighborhood   *Emily Badger*

Der Text kann aus lizenzrechtlichen Gründen nicht abgedruckt werden.

Sie finden ihn unter dem folgenden Link:
https://www.nytimes.com/2018/01/03/upshot/zoning-housing-property-rights-nimby-us.html

Annotations:

mortgage interest deduction – Zinsermäßigung auf einen Kredit für eine Immobilie

asset – *here:* sth of financial value, like property

zoning – the practice of defining areas of land to be used for a particular purpose

home equity – hier: Immobilienbesitz

---

1 Die schriftlichen Prüfungsteile werden ab dem Abitur 2024 anders nummeriert (siehe Seite 9).

Teil II: Reading Comprehension
content 10 VP

Instructions:

- Tick the correct answer / statement or statements as indicated.
- Provide a quotation from the text to support each correct answer: the first three and the last three words of the quotation.
- If the quotation is six words or shorter, write it down in full.

0   Example: Tick the correct answer (true/false).

	true	false
People in LA have the same expectations of their neighborhood as people in San Jose.	☐	☑

In Los Angeles ... want tiny homes. |0

1   Tick the correct statement.

When people in the U.S. possess their own real estate, they feel

- ☐ eager to buy more property.
- ☐ responsible for their property.
- ☐ urged to mobilize their neighbors.
- ☐ entitled to influence their neighborhood.

quote: _____ |1

2   Tick the correct answer.

	true	false
People were provided with financial incentives to establish a sense of belonging.	☐	☐

quote: _____ |1

3   Tick the correct statement.

According to Vicki Been, the development of a neighborhood

- ☐ is linked to the voter turnout.
- ☐ is a top priority in urban regions.
- ☐ must not depend on everyone's agreement.
- ☐ presents a major concern for young families.

quote: _____ |1

4   Complete the statement in your own words.

Due to recent modifications in the tax system, owning a house

_____ | **1**

5   Complete the statement in your own words.

Trying to influence one's neighborhood was not relevant in rural areas
because

_____

and because

_____ | **1**

6   Complete the statement in your own words.

Despite a Supreme Court ruling in 1948, whites

_____

and because

_____ | **1**

7   Tick the TWO correct statements.

Zoning

☐   led to increased tensions.
☐   resulted in nuisance laws.
☐   imposed rules and restrictions.
☐   provided stability in a community.
☐   strengthened homeowners' rights.

quotation for 1st correct statement:

_____ | **1**

quotation for 2nd correct statement:

_____ | **1**

8   Complete the statement in your own words.

According to Nathan Connolly, the overall benefit of homeownership is

_____ | **1**

9 Tick the correct statement.

A desired effect of town planning is that people become

☐ passionate advocates of their rights.
☐ generous members of the neighborhood.
☐ responsible citizens willing to compromise.
☐ tolerant neighbors towards ethnic minorities.

quote: _____ |1

Teil III.1: Analysis

INFO

Im Jahr 2022 gab es für den Teil III.1 Analysis zwei Aufgabenstellungen (A und B). Die Schule wählte eine Aufgabenstellung aus, die den Schülerinnen und Schülern vorgelegt wurde.

AUFGABENSTELLUNG A

Teil III.1 A: Analysis

content 10 VP
language 15 VP

The author of the article mentions "the belief that owning a home in America today means that you effectively own a neighborhood, too."
Briefly explain the quote in the context of the article and examine to what extent Walt Kowalski in *Gran Torino* can be said to embody this idea.

AUFGABENSTELLUNG B

Teil III.1 B: Analysis

content 10 VP
language 15 VP

"Our homes have become our wealth."
Briefly explain the quote in the context of the article and examine to what extent this is true for Walt Kowalski in *Gran Torino*.

Teil III.2: Composition

AUFGABENSTELLUNG A

Teil III.2: Composition

content 10 VP
language 15 VP

Choose **ONE** of the following:

a) "Alienation is a form of living death." *(Martin Luther King Jr.)*
   Assess to what extent this quote applies to Larry Ott in *Crooked Letter, Crooked Letter*.

   OR

b) Interpret the cartoon and comment on its message.

Biden's big job

Source: Theo Moudakis, https://www.thestar.com/opinion/editorial_cartoon/2021/01/21/theo-moudakis-bidens-big-job.html; accessed October 15, 2021

total 60 VP

AUFGABENSTELLUNG B

Teil III.2: Composition

content 10 VP
language 15 VP

Choose **ONE** of the following:

a) "Alienation is a form of living death." *(Martin Luther King Jr.)*
   Assess to what extent this quote applies to Larry Ott in *Crooked Letter, Crooked Letter.*

   OR

b) Interpret the cartoon and comment on its message.

Source: Bruce MacKinnon, https://calgaryherald.com/gallery/the-heralds-latest-editorial-cartoons:
reprint of March 11, 2020; accessed October 17, 2021

Annotation: The Queen's grandson Harry and his wife Meghan have left the royal family.

total 60 VP

Beispiellösung

Teil I: Listening Comprehension
Task 1: Book reviews

Book review	1	2	3	4	5
Description	G	A	D	E	C

Task 2: Baroness Trumpington

1.	Why did Lady Trumpington's departure from politics attract so much attention?	She had been there for so long. / She retired at the age of 95. / It was hard to imagine the House of Lords without her.
2.	Why does the host of a TV show mention the invention of television?	To show Lady Trumpington's (advanced) age. / Because Lady Trumpington was born before TV was invented. / To introduce a guest in a humorous way.
3.	Which incident made Lady Trumpington widely known?	Making the V-sign. / Swearing (at a fellow peer). / Making a rude gesture.
4.	What is said about her education?	Had limited formal education. / (Fairly) typical of women's education at the time. / Has never taken an exam. / Finished school in Paris which gave her good French and German.
5.	In which two different fields of work was she active during World War II?	• Farming / agriculture / (working as a) land girl • Code breaking / (work as a) cipher clerk / intelligence / office work
6.	Why did she return to Great Britain?	Followed her (English) husband. / Because of her husband's job.
7.	What did she change in her life during her time in Cambridge?	Started her political career. / Became a councillor and then a mayor.
8.	Why did she choose the title "Baroness Trumpington"?	Name of the nearest village. / She did not like the other options (Barker / Six Mile Bottom).
9.	What was special about her holding her governmental position at the end of the 1980s?	First (ever) female Minister at Agriculture. / First (ever) woman holding that position. / Stayed in office when the Prime Minister changed.

10.	What did she do in Downing Street that helped her keep her position?	She cried. / She made the Prime Minister feel sorry for her.
11.	What was her duty as Baroness in Waiting?	To represent the Queen on formal occasions.
12.	Which interest will she continue to pursue after retiring?	Horse racing.
13.	In the radio report, Lady Trumpington's personality is presented as being …	self-confident and unconventional.

Task 3: Sea otters

1 a
2 a
3 c
4 b
5 b
6 a

Teil II: Reading Comprehension

1 When people in the U.S. possess their own real estate, they feel
entitled to influence their neighborhood.
quote: *owning a parcel … beyond its boundaries.*
OR: *homeowners have expanded … their lot lines.*

2 People were provided with financial incentives to establish a sense of belonging.
true
quote: *"One of the … in their communities,"*

3 According to Vicki Been, the development of a neighborhood
must not depend on everyone's agreement.
quote: *"Communities always need (and we can't) … veto over change."*

4 Due to recent modifications in the tax system, owning a house
might become less desirable.

5 Trying to influence one's neighborhood was not relevant in rural areas because
people lived far away from each other
and because
the value of a piece of land depended on its usability / the yield of its crop.

6 Despite a Supreme Court ruling in 1948, whites
continued to be apprehensive about non-whites / did not welcome non-whites
because
a mixed neighborhood might decrease the value of their homes.

7 Zoning
imposed rules and restrictions.
provided stability / made homeowners expect stability in their communities.
quotation for 1st correct statement: *Zoning, rather than … a certain height (… considered nuisances before.)*
quotation for 2nd correct statement: *And it helped … little over time.*

8 According to Nathan Connolly, the overall benefit of homeownership is
that it offers people financial security in (potentially) difficult times.

9 A desired effect of town planning is that people become
responsible citizens willing to compromise.
quote: *We want people … live there, too.*
OR: *We want to … the region needs.*

Teil III.1: Analysis

In den Lösungsvorschlägen für Teil III finden Sie Stichpunkte, die Sie in Ihrer Lösung berücksichtigen sollten.

Aufgabe 1a)

Explanation of the quote

- Homeowners are increasingly expecting and demanding to have a say when it comes to changes within their residential areas.
- Shaping and preserving one's neighbourhood has become important for most homeowners.
- A residential area is believed to be "ideal" or "desirable" when there is as little diversity as possible.
- The style and structure of buildings in an area are not the only aspects affected. Factors such as the types of residents and the maintenance of the neighbourhood also play a significant role.
- As a result, homeowners are primarily concerned about their neighbourhood, which can sometimes lead to the neglect or blocking of the needs of the entire community during a decision-making process.

How Walt in Gran Torino embodies this idea

In the beginning:
- Walt knows exactly what his neighbourhood should be like: exclusively white, tidy, clean and safe.
- He feels disconnected to his surroundings and perceives behaviour different from his own as a threat. Therefore he repeatedly uses racial slurs against his Hmong neighbours and makes derogatory remarks about the gangs that terrorize the neighbourhood.

Walt's development:
- He defends his idea of a safe neighbourhood by confronting the Hmong gang, even at the risk of his own safety. In doing so, he demonstrates his sense of responsibility towards his neighbourhood for he believes that it should be a place for law-abiding individuals who contribute to a peaceful community life.
- He takes into consideration the needs of the community, as he drives off the gang not for his personal benefit, but to protect Sue, Thao and their family.
- Over time, he becomes more accepting of a community that is diverse and acknowledges the Hmong's set of values.
- His desire to help his neighbours in becoming accepted residents is evident in the way he teaches Thao about his idea of a "good and safe neighbourhood" and the American ideal of hard work.

Conclusion	– Walt undergoes a transformation and embraces a new, positive belief that being good neighbours entails taking responsibility for one another and being open-minded, rather than simply sharing the same cultural or ethnic background.

Aufgabe 1b)

Explanation of the quote	– The neighbourhood in which a home is located defines its property value. – Property is expected to provide financial security. – The term "home" implies a sense of belonging and well-being. People want to live in neighbourhoods that match their preferences. Even renters now display that attitude. – Residents often fear changes because they think it might make their property worth less.
Walt in Gran Torino	– The value of Walt's house represents his success as a worker in the lower middle class at Ford car company. – The size of the house is important because it can accommodate his cars in the garage, which gives it a certain status. – Walt does not seem visibly concerned about the potential decrease in property value after the arrival of the Hmong. However, his behaviour suggests a sense of insecurity that might also be related to financial worries. – Walt holds an idealistic view of his home, feeling safe enough in his predominantly white, lower middle-class neighborhood to not put up a fence. – He takes pride in his property and shows it by taking good care of it, such as mowing the lawn, and displaying a flag. – His sense of safety is threatened by his new neighbours and the gang. He uses a gun to defend his "castle" and the porch becomes his secure vantage point. – His house is truly his home, and Walt does not consider leaving it as an option, despite suggestions from his children.
Conclusion	– Walt is more afraid of feeling culturally isolated than of the actual decrease in property value when the Hmong people arrive. – Gradually, he starts to recognize and appreciate his neighbours' set of values, which emphasize respect and care instead of materialistic ideals. – The symbolic significance of his house as a secure and sheltering place becomes evident when he bequeaths it to the church.

Teil III.2: Composition

Aufgabe 2a)

Explanation of the quote	– "Alienation" means feeling like an outsider, being distant from others and not fitting in with a specific group.
	– The phrase "living death" describes a life that feels meaningless, lacking warmth and human connection. It is like being in a zombie-like state with the lowest possible quality of life.
Larry's sense of alienation from his family, friends and community	– Within his family, Larry is rejected by his father, who sees him as lacking strength, health and masculinity.
	– Carl makes him fight with Silas, which causes alienation between the two friends.
	– Socially, Larry feels like an outsider due to his shyness and introverted nature. His love for reading sets him apart from his peers.
	– Larry has been a victim of bullying from an early age.
	– He desperately tries to fit in with his group of friends, but this only pushes him further away from them.
	– After Cindy's disappearance, the community completely rejects him.
	– He is labeled as an outsider ("scary Larry").
	– His business is shunned by others.
	– Larry finds it difficult to trust people and judge their behaviour, as seen with Wallace.
	– His only form of interaction is through his involvement with his animals (chickens).
Larry's life as a form of living death	– Larry withdraws into a reclusive life of complete solitude and passively accepts his fate as socially dead.
	– Despite his isolation, he still demonstrates human emotions by showing empathy towards his demented mother and even towards monsters, indicating that he is still "alive" in some sense, even though just barely.
	– He tries to contact Silas to share the truth.
	– The zombie mask serves as a symbol of his existence as a socially "dead" person who continues to walk among the living, still capable of feelings and communication.

Possible conclusion	– The quote applies to Larry, particularly in the beginning when his alienation is caused by his differences, leading to a lack of acceptance from the people around him.
	– As a result, he is excluded and marginalized after Cindy Walker's disappearance.
	– He leads a life that is mostly devoid of meaningful social interaction and a sense of belonging.
	– In the end, Larry reconnects with the world of the living. He reaches out to Silas, finds validation and discovers the inner strength to forgive him.

Aufgabe 2b)

Cartoon "Biden's big job" by Theo Moudakis:

- The Statue of Liberty has been cut into distinct pieces with clean breaks. The fragments are piled on top of each other.
- Democracy is facing significant jeopardy, potentially stemming from President Donald Trump's contentious domestic policies, such as immigration restrictions targeting Mexicans and Muslims, encroachments on black voting rights, and other measures.
- The attack on the Capitol can be seen as a manifestation of radical skepticism towards democratic institutions.
- The Statue of Liberty's face, the torch, and hands holding a tablet are still intact. They can be interpreted as symbols representing values like life, liberty and the pursuit of happiness, which still have the power to unite the country. This demonstrates the enduring belief in and appeal of America's core principles.
- Joe Biden is depicted in the left-hand corner, holding a small bucket of ready-mix cement and a trowel. This can be interpreted as Biden being the last person standing, capable of repairing the damage and rebuilding the country.
- The cement symbolizes the need to unite the nation, which involves making democratic processes more acceptable to a wider range of people, reaching out to Republicans, investing in infrastructure to help the unemployed or disillusioned, creating more job opportunities, and reinstating Obamacare.
- The bucket is very small and does not contain enough cement to repair the damage. The statue may remain unstable after its reconstruction and scars will remain visible. This illustrates the enduring and dramatic effects of Trump's policies.
- Biden's appearance seems small and delicate compared to the massive statue and he is not properly dressed for the task, but the thought bubble with the words "This won't be easy" portrays him as a realist.
- The cartoonist intends to express doubts about whether the task may prove too immense for Biden, implicitly raising questions about his suitability for the role of president.

Cartoon by Bruce MacKinnon:
– In the foreground of the cartoon, there is a fishbowl with the Queen, Charles, Camilla, William and Kate.
– They are separated from society and live in their own small world.
– They are always being watched by the media and society.
– The Queen is in the centre. At the time the cartoon was published, she was the current monarch.
– The space in the fishbowl is very limited. The royal family feels suffocated, which means their lives are greatly restricted in terms of how they behave, what careers they choose, and their freedom of speech.
– They are dressed in formal and conservative clothes. This might suggest that the monarchy is seen as outdated.
– They are not looking at each other and their facial expression seems grumpy, showing their disapproval of Harry and Meghan's decision to leave the royal family and their royal duties behind.
– The Queen, Charles and Camilla have turned their backs on Harry and Meghan, while Kate and William have turned sideways and are looking after the two. This may indicate that they would like to live a more independent life themselves.

Harry and Meghan:
– They are holding hands as they run away towards an unknown future.
– Meghan is looking straight ahead, showing that she has no regrets and does not feel any sense of loss.
– Harry might be looking at Meghan, focusing on their future together outside the royal fishbowl. Alternatively, he might be glancing backwards, feeling the sadness of leaving his family behind. Nevertheless, he is moving forward.
– Harry and Meghan felt disconnected due to the lack of freedom, their experiences with racism and the constant scrutiny from the media. Now they have escaped the suffocating restrictions of the fishbowl and can breathe freely again. They feel liberated and can live a life that they choose for themselves.

Stichwortverzeichnis

Quellenverzeichnis

Textquellen:

- Biden, Joseph: Inaugural Address: https://www.whitehouse.gov/briefing-room/speeches-remarks/2021/01/20/inaugural-address-by-president-joseph-r-biden-jr/ (accessed: 18 April 2023) (Seite 161)
- "Climate Change": https://www.npr.org/2022/02/28/1083580995/some-effects-of-climate-change-are-irreversible-but-theres-still-hope (accessed 18 April 2023). ©2022 National Public Radio, Inc. NPR report titled "Some effects of climate change are irreversible, but there's still hope" was originally broadcast on NPR's All Things Considered on February 28, 2022, and is used with the permission of NPR. Any unauthorized duplication is strictly prohibited. (Seite 153)
- DeGrazia, Emilio: "Our American Nightmare: Detroit", in: *Twin cities: Daily Planet,* 11. April 2013; https://www.tcdailyplanet.net/our-american-nightmare-detroit/ (last accessed: 18 April 2023) (Seite 158)
- Guerrero, Jean: "I used to be confused by my mixed identity. But mixedness will heal America": *The Guardian,* 28.10.2020; https://www.theguardian.com/commentisfree/2020/oct/28/i-used-to-be-confused-by-my-mixed-identity-but-mixedness-will-heal-america (last accessed: 18 April 2023). Copyright Guardian News & Media Ltd 2023 (Seite 167)
- Harris, Kamala: "Remarks by Vice President Kamala Harris As Delivered to the Commission on the Status of Women", March 16, 2021 (accessed 18 April 2023); https://www.whitehouse.gov/briefing-room/speeches-remarks/2021/03/16/pre-taped-remarks-by-vice-president-kamala-harris-as-delivered-to-the-commission-on-the-status-of-women/ (Seite 155)
- Lehming, Malte: „Waffengewalt in den USA: Im Land der vielen Morde", *Tagesspiegel;* https://www.tagesspiegel.de/internationales/waffengewalt-in-den-usa-im-land-der-vielen-morde-9350075.html (15.02.2023; accessed: 18 April 2023) (Seite 176)
- Smith, Zadie: *White Teeth,* London, 2000, p. 326–327 (Seite 170)
- Trump, Donald: "Inaugural Address", https://trumpwhitehouse.archives.gov/briefings-statements/the-inaugural-address/; (accessed: 18 April 2023) (Seite 160)

Bildquellen:

- Bramhall, Bill: Cartoon "Gun Control", Bill Bramhall/Getty Images (Seite 174)
- Theo Moudakis: Cartoon "Biden's big job", https://www.thestar.com/opinion/editorial_cartoon/2021/01/21/theo-moudakis-bidens-big-job.html; accessed October 15, 2021 (Seite 188)
- Bruce MacKinnon, Cartoon about the British royal family, https://calgaryherald.com/gallery/the-heralds-latest-editorial-cartoons: reprint of March 11, 2020; accessed October 17, 2021 (Seite 189)